The Films
of the Eighties

The Films
of the Eighties

DOUGLAS BRODE

A CITADEL PRESS BOOK
Published by Carol Publishing Group

Acknowledgments:
The author and publisher gratefully wish to acknowledge the assistance
of: Mercy Sandberg Wright, Nat Segaloff, Charles Bornstein, Mary
and Frank Judge, Bill Klein, the staffs of the *Syracuse Post-Standard*
and *Syracuse New times*, and our friends at Orion, Paramount,
Vestron, Warner Brothers, MGM, MGM-UA, 20th Century Fox, Walt
Disney Productions, Buena Vista-Touchstone, Lorimar, Miramax,
New Line Cinema, Universal, Island Alive Films, and DEG films.

First Carol Publishing Group Edition 1991

Copyright © 1990 by Douglas Brode

A Citadel Press Book
Published by Carol Publishing Group

Editorial Offices   Sales & Distribution Offices
600 Madison Avenue   120 Enterprise Avenue
New York, NY 10022   Secaucus, NJ 07094

In Canada: Musson Book Company
A division of General Publishing Co. Limited
Don Mills, Ontario

Citadel Press is a registered trademark of
Carol Communications, Inc.

Queries regarding rights and permissions
should be addressed to: Carol Publishing Group,
600 Madison Avenue, New York, NY 10022

Designed by A. Chistopher Simon

Manufactured in the United States of America

10 9 8 7 6 5 4 3 2

Carol Publishing Group books are available at special discounts
for bulk purchases, for sales promotions, fund raising, or
educational purposes. Special editions can also be created to
specifications. For details contact: Special Sales Department,
Carol Publishing Group, 120 Enterprise Ave., Secaucus, NJ 07094

Library of Congress Cataloging-in-Publication Data

Brode, Douglas, 1943-
        The films of the eighties / Douglas Brode
            p.   cm.
        "A Citadel Press book."
        ISBN 0-8065-1162-1 (paper) : $15.95
            1. Motion pictures--United States. 2. Motion pictures--Plots,
    themes, etc. I. Title.
    PN1993.5.U6B675   1990
    791.43'750973--dc20
                                                    90-2262
                                                    CIP

To

CHARLES BORNSTEIN

former student
current collaborator
future filmmaker
forever friend

Contents:

Introduction

Perhaps it was actress Elizabeth Ashley who summed up the decade more succinctly than anyone else: "Money," she said, "is the long hair of the Eighties." As always, there were the characters who most vividly caught the public interest at a particular point in time, signifying in exaggerated form our collective if sometimes unconscious attitude at the moment: In the Eighties, it was Donald Trump in real life, building or buying up most of Manhattan before the Japanese could get their mitts on it; in the era's most popular and representative cartoon, it was Garfield the Cat. They were the era's icons, believing that self-interest was ultimately in the best interest of the country at large, and that ultimately there was nothing the self could be as interested in as money and what it would buy. Which helps explain why, at the decade's beginning, Americans who by and large held "liberal" social attitudes (generally believing in a woman's right to an abortion, or the post-Sexual Revolution right of couples to live together in an unmarried state) overwhelmingly elected a president whose conservative agenda opposed everything they held dear. In addition to his personal charm and formidable charisma, Ronald Reagan promised everyone a tax break.

That appealed to the same instincts which, earlier in the century, had caused Coolidge and Hoover to be elected. But Reagan also offered something new: as the first movie and TV star to win the highest office, he

THE RETURN OF PATRIOTISM: Following the election of President Reagan in 1980, Hollywood quickly adopted his old-fashioned flag-waving attitudes. In *Superman II*, Christopher Reeve carries the red, white and blue ever upward; in *Rocky IV*, Stallone literally draped himself in the American flag.

AN ICON FOR THE EIGHTIES: With a former movie star as President, oftentimes relating "true" anecdotes that turned out to be sequences from Hollywood fictions, a key subject of new movies was the blurring of real and reel. In Woody Allen's *The Purple Rose of Cairo*, movie characters step down from the screen and mingle with people in the audience.

seemed the perfect symbol of an age that appreciated style over substance. His harshest critics claimed he was not being president so much as playing the role of president; one book about him was even titled *The Acting President,* with an ironic adjective. Certainly, a public which had grown disenchanted with the intellectual Jimmy Carter, in part because he was such a poor performer on the TV news and gave the appearance of being a weakling, found much to admire in Reagan, who certainly appeared every inch a strong, sincere president. In short, the public had elected a person who might have nicely played the part of the president in a movie.

In so doing, we completely broke down the barriers between actuality and the movies. Almost everyone wishes real life were more like the way life is depicted in films; by electing Reagan president, we collectively pushed reality in that direction. Indeed, part of the President's huge appeal was that he did not comprehend where the one ended and the other began. One remarkable book, *Ronald Reagan: The Movie,* documents a case in point: Reagan, always anecdotal in nature, literally cried during a televised speech as he talked of the need for a resurgence of heroism, citing a Korean War incident in which an airman sacrificed his life for his fellows. When reporters, moved by the President's profoundly touching memory, contacted the Pentagon to ask for more specific details, they were informed that the President—apparently quite sincere in his intense recollections—had been referring to a scene in the totally fictitious *The Bridges at Toko-Ri.* Earlier, others had

noted that in his 1980 campaign insistence on getting our hostages back from Iran at any cost (President Carter had been unable to achieve this), Reagan inadvertently quoted directly from John Wayne's dialogue in *The Searchers* (in which the Duke attempted to extricate Natalie Wood from the Comanches), one of Reagan's favorite films.

The term "Teflon president" quickly became associated with Reagan, as incidents which would have destroyed any other leader's credibility appeared to bounce harmlessly off him. There might have been public outcry over and critical inquiry into the 1983 death and wounding of more than 300 marines in Beirut when their headquarters was bombed by terrorists had President Reagan not swiftly thereafter ordered an invasion of Grenada, insisting the lives of some American students were at risk. Another tragedy that did not affect the public's positive opinion of their president was the 1986 explosion of the space shuttle *Challenger*, which took the lives of the seven crewmen, including one of the teachers-turned-astronauts Reagan had called upon to lead America's youth into space. Other world leaders have been destroyed by disastrous events taking place "on their watch," even if they were in no way responsible; that was not the case with Reagan.

If Ron and Nancy often appeared more like America's figurehead leaders than an actual working president and first lady, the allure of royalty caused a decade-long fascination with the youthful British couple, Prince Charles and Lady Diana. Television likewise reflected

10

REVAMPING THE WESTERN: Since the new President was a former cowboy star, who successfully campaigned in a stetson standing in front of the Alamo, it made sense that filmmakers would revive the genre. *Silverado* played like *thirtysomething* on the range; *Young Guns* featured the Brat Pack in photo opportunity poses.

this interest in royalty through shows as diverse as *Lifestyles of the Rich and Famous,* which allowed have-nots to ogle what the lucky few possessed, and the glitz-glamour soaps such as *Dallas* and *Dynasty,* in which the men amorally accumulated wealth which the women then spent on clothing and perfume. Such shows premiered on the eve of Reagan's election, then slipped in the ratings eight years later, even as he left office. Even Madonna, whose punk-funk fashions reflected the era's streetwise outlaw attitude, sang (half seriously, half in self-parody) about the joys of being a Material Girl, a superficially catchy ditty providing as fitting an anthem for the decade's womanhood as "I Am Woman" had been to the fighting feminists of the late Sixties and early Seventies.

Such commitment to causes was not now blowin' in the wind. Amazingly, even the man who penned that line in the late Sixties—Bob Dylan—suddenly "saw the light," gave up his old "save the world" attitudes, and settled into the now trendy neoconservativism, along with such other Sixties radicals as Eugene McCarthy, Dennis Hopper and Eldridge Cleaver. Communes were out, commodities were in; as the country did a right turn, the youth of the Eighties soon formed its own identity. Those Americans who lived the good life to the hilt, enjoying every imaginable consumer item and creature comfort, though sometimes failing to save a single penny for the future, were shortly dubbed yuppies—young upwardly mobile professionals. And in their amoral quest for material possessions, they rejected such previous agendas as suburban conformity (the Fifties), commitment to social issues (the Sixties), or

A NEW ERA FOR DISNEY: Sensing it was time to get in touch with the modern moviegoing audience, the Disney company tried some daring experiments. Though a fling with state-of-the-art computer animation led to the disastrous *Tron* (above), it fared far better with *Splash*, featuring some surprisingly sexy scenes.

12

solitary spiritual growth (the Seventies). On TV, they were the subject of *thirtysomething;* in the movies, *The Big Chill* and *St. Elmo's Fire.* Those were among the special films yuppies were willing to line up for; more often, they stood in line at video stores to rent the latest movies for home video consumption.

Yuppie cocooning, that was called: in part owing to the escalating potential for violence on the street, in part because of a political-cultural mind-set emphasizing individual activity over community engagement, the yuppies transformed after hours into couch potatoes, enjoying the home entertainment revolution which, through cable TV and the VCR, allowed for contemporary, uncensored entertainment in their living rooms. Suddenly, little movies that hadn't had a chance in competition with the big blockbusters were developing cult followings with the yuppie couples, who were exposed to X-rated features as never before, since it was far more acceptable to rent one from a video store than to venture into an adult movie house. So if their politics were most often traditionalist, their taste in entertainment tended toward the funky: Johnny Carson made room for David Letterman and Arsenio Hall; Bob Hope took a back seat to Jay Leno, Sam Kinnison, Howie Mandel. Network TV, attempting to lure back some of

THE WAR ON DRUGS: Taking their cue from reality, films began to deal with this serious social problem. In *Colors* (above), Robert Duvall and Sean Penn played street cops confronting the barrio "crack" scene; in *Clean and Sober*, Michael Keaton and Kathy Baker were upscale yuppies trying to kick their cocaine habits.

their dwindling viewers who had defected to home video and uncensored cable systems like HBO, relaxed many of its old restrictions to win back the yuppie audience.

The yuppies liked designer ice cream, compact discs, fax machines, home computers, cosmetic surgery, telephone answering machines, cellular phones, Trivial Pursuit, anything to eat or drink with the word "Lite" in its name, bottled water and haute pasta. Of course, the yuppies still occasionally ventured out of the house, invariably wearing a jogging outfit on the way to an automated teller machine, while listening to music through a Sony Walkman, allowing the yup to remain isolated even while at large in society. But the one place they avoided was what had been in the Seventies their home away from home: the singles bar. The Sexual Revolution had been born in the turbulence of the Sixties, then run its course during the Seventies, but in the Eighties it came crashing against frightful realities. First, the herpes scare, then the AIDS crisis. The casual-sex attitude of the Sexual Revolution quickly screeched to a halt; other aspects of that revolution, like the easy acceptance of unmarried couples living together (a scandalous situation only a quarter century earlier) had become ingrained in the culture.

BRATS IN PACKS: As the audience grew more youthful, so did the ensembles encountered onscreen. Irene Cara led members of New York's Performing Arts high school in an impromptu dance in *Fame*; Rob Lowe (standing) and fellow Brat Packers played recent Georgetown graduates in *St. Elmo's Fire*.

Even as the Cold War heated up during the early Eighties, Sylvester Stallone incarnated America's macho anti-Russian attitude by clobbering a Soviet gladiator (Dolph Lundgren) in *Rocky IV*; shortly after perestroika prevailed, Jim Belushi played an American cop learning to cope with a far more amenable Russian (Arnold Schwarzenegger) in *Red Heat*.

But the greater reality—including the possibility of all-out war—occasionally intruded through the yuppie's cocoon. Tension ran high when, in 1983, KAL civilian flight 007 crossed over into Russian airspace and, suspected of being a spy ship, was summarily shot down, with no survivors among the 269 aboard. The President presented the public with a simplistic assessment of the situation, referring to the Russians as "an evil empire," drawing his metaphor from the *Star Wars* films. Still, he drew the line at all-out confrontation. If Reagan managed to surprise those critics who believed he had a hair trigger by keeping us out of a shooting match with the Soviets, he had considerably less success in the war everyone wanted him to wage and win against drugs. The 1982 death of John Belushi had been only the tip of an iceberg which made America aware of the country's intense drug dependency. Whether it was a ghetto teenager hooked on "crack" or a white-collar yuppie snorting cocaine, the addiction situation was clearly out of control, demolishing careers and families in every sector, leading to the worst gang wars in our city streets since Prohibition, while also allowing rulers of the drug cartels in faraway places like Colombia to become terrifyingly powerful influences on the world

economy. Nancy Reagan's answer to it all—"Just Say No!"— may have been intended as a helpfully simple solution, but played as hopelessly simplistic and insensitive considering the condition of so many addicts.

Many of those were black or Hispanic; in part minorities turned to drugs as an escape from the hopelessness they felt during the Eighties, a period when the haves had more and the have-nots had less than ever before. True, a few blacks managed to acquire more money and fame than was imaginable even to most whites. The most popular TV, movie and musical performances were Bill Cosby, Eddie Murphy, Oprah Winfrey and Michael Jackson. Yet these were the exceptions, not the rule, and the President's wholesale dismantling of civil rights legislation that had been around since Lyndon Johnson's presidency, along with extensive cutbacks in educational programs for minorities, convinced many blacks the administration had turned a deaf ear to their interests; when the Klan began marching again, or when white youths chased a black man to his death in Brooklyn's Howard Beach area, there were those who firmly believed that, on some tacit, unspoken level, the permission to do so had come all the way from the top. As a result, racial tension led to increased violence in the streets.

No incident captured the public's frustration with such uncontrollable crime as sharply as the 1985 New York subway shooting of four black youths by Bernhard Goetz; his subsequent trial saw him treated as a pariah

WHY WERE WE IN VIETNAM? Following the success of Oliver Stone's *Platoon*, other filmmakers took a serious look at the war. Stanley Kubrick's *Full Metal Jacket* (right) provided a surreal image of Southeast Asia combat, shot in England; Bruce Willis portrayed a vet paying respects to fallen comrades at Washington's Vietnam Veterans Memorial in *In Country* (above).

THE KISS OF DEATH: The impact of AIDS resulted in an immediate revival of the vampire film. In *Vamp* (above), Grace Jones portrayed a singles bar performer whose one-night-stands find themselves suffering from a strange malady the morning after; a midwestern teenager (Adrian Pasdar) finds himself becoming ill after a brief romance with a pretty passerby (Jenny Wright) in *Near Dark* (top right). *Lost Boys* featured Kiefer Sutherland (center) as the leader of some unruly teens who are all suffering from an unspecified sexually-transmitted disease.

by those opposed to fighting violence with violence and a cause célèbre by others who simply felt it was time someone did something, however irrational or illegal. The siege mentality deepened further at decade's end when, in a night of "wilding," inner-city youths invaded Central Park and raped, then brutally beat, a lone female jogger, an incident which brought the plight of women to the forefront; feminist victors somehow had been transformed into feminine victims. For women, as for blacks, it often became difficult to grasp whether the liberal social agendas of past decades had become so firmly entrenched that they were now a given even in such conservative times, or whether the new conservative agendas would wipe out past progress. Thanks to decades of liberal campaigning, Sandra Day O'Connor became, in 1981, the first woman justice of the U.S. Supreme Court —ironically, one with a strong conservative bent. In 1984, Geraldine Ferraro became the first woman to run for vice president on a major party's ticket, and Vanessa Williams the first black woman to be crowned Miss America; but Ferraro lost, and Williams resigned in ignominy after *Penthouse* published nude photos of her. In 1982, the Equal Rights Amendment, intended to insure women equal status with men, was ratified by only 35 of the necessary 38 states and so did not become law of the land. Its passage at decade's beginning was to have solidified the accomplishments of the Seventies; instead, its failure was perceived by many as a repudiation of the previous decade's efforts.

SHADES OF THE SIXTIES: As the decade wore on, Fifties nostalgia was gradually replaced by an interest in the psychedelic Sixties. Lena Olin as a Czech woman enjoying newfound sexual freedom just before the Soviet troops invade in *The Unbearable Lightness of Being* (above); River Phoenix won an Oscar nomination for his role as the teenage son of former Sixties radicals in *Running On Empty.*

NEW FACES OF THE EIGHTIES: Like every decade at the movies, the 1980s produced its share of new stars. Clockwise, from top left: Kevin Costner in *Bull Durham*, Michelle Pfeiffer in *Ladyhawke*, Matt Dillon in *Tex*, Kim Basinger in *No Mercy*.

20

FEMINIST FANTASIES: The impact of the Women's Liberation Movement in the late Seventies caused comedies of the early Eighties to take a feminist perspective. Dolly Parton, Lily Tomlin and Jane Fonda were three women who banded together to oppose a sleazy male boss (Dabney Coleman, not pictured) in *Nine to Five*; Goldie Hawn—here with "daddy" Sam Wanamaker and "mommy" Barbara Barrie—was the Jewish American Princess who likewise learns all men are slime after finding herself as a WAC in *Private Benjamin*.

Simply, issues and ideas were ignored; appearance was everything. Even popular entertainment stressed style over substance. On Broadway, there were *Cats* and *Phantom of the Opera,* impressive feasts for the eyes and ears, but offering little food for thought. Understandably, celebrity—both the specific status and the abstract idea—took on a new significance in this changed cultural landscape. Issue-oriented Jane Fonda survived as a celebrity by putting her social consciousness aside and becoming the queen of home video workout tapes. Boy George, Dr. Ruth, and Vanna White drifted in and out of the public consciousness, though Pia Zadora was perhaps the era's ultimate example of the celebrity famous for being famous; if she hadn't existed, Andy Warhol would have had to invent her. But by decade's end, the tide was turning against such superficial glamour. When Pia's predecessor, Zsa Zsa Gabor, became embroiled in a minor traffic infraction that culminated with her slapping an officer, the judge at her trial sentenced Hollywood's reigning Hungarian to three days in jail—less for her original indiscretion than for turning the case into a media circus, which, under the circumstances, was the only thing a person of Zsa Zsa's temperament could do. But when the public, hyped by a heightened awareness of the case through tabloid TV, made clear it would enjoy seeing Gabor publicly executed, it became obvious the hollow celebrity—such a hallmark of the Eighties—had grown as tiresome as other aspects of the Greed decade.

Besides, there was a dark side to celebrity. In 1980, aging rock-poet John Lennon was shot down in the streets of New York by a man who claimed to be one of his biggest fans and who, by killing Lennon, in a bizarre way managed to possess him. A year later, when President Reagan was likewise wounded, there would be no conspiracy theories (à la Kennedy), as the act was performed by yet another deranged man hopeful of

YES, SIR, THAT'S MY BABY: The new, enlightened American male learned to cope with child-rearing. Michael Keaton as a "housewife" in *Mr. Mom* (right); John Travolta tries his old disco magic on a toddler in *Look Who's Talking*.

capturing celebrity status, and with it the attention of actress Jodie Foster, by imitating the actions of Travis Bickle (Robert DeNiro) in one of Foster's films, *Taxi Driver*—one more instance of real-life and the movies becoming surrealistically inseparable.

Even while being rushed to the hospital after being wounded, Reagan maintained his remarkable style, joking with the medics ("That guy ruined a really good suit!") as no other real-life president would, but as a president in the movies might have. And, by decade's end, even those who had accused Reagan of a simplistic approach to complex world politics had to eat a certain amount of crow. The President's insistence that only a get-tough attitude toward the Russians would bring them to the bargaining table on our terms certainly appeared to have worked when Soviet leader Mikhail Gorbachev extended an olive branch, melting down the Cold War, eventually allowing the Berlin Wall to be torn down as Reagan had, only a year before, publicly called for. At the time, Reagan's request seemed a *beau geste;* shortly, it was contemporary history as the wall finally cracked.

Cracking at home, though, were the values (some would say rather "lack of values") that had defined the Eighties. The era of greed could only last so long. When, on October 19, 1987, the bull market that had dominated Wall Street for the better part of the Reagan years temporarily disintegrated as the Dow plummeted more than 500 points in a single day, with $500 billion paper money disappearing, even the most devout believer in Reaganomics began to wonder if George Bush had been

right when, as a competitor for the Republican nomination in 1980, he'd referred to that agenda as "voodoo economics." Wall Street entrepreneurs Ivan Boesky and Michael Milken, heroes to the yuppies in the decade's early hours, swiftly became villains when their dirty financial dealings made the news. When Leona Helmsley, who had lived a self-styled *Dynasty* life throughout the decade, was convicted of tax evasion and sent to prison, the very public which had grown tired of watching *Dynasty* on TV cheered. The modern Marie Antoinette may have been a heroine at decade's beginning, but by it's end she had somehow transformed into a Dragon Lady to be hissed and despised.

The shifting tone went beyond finances. The women's movement won renewed support when the women of America rallied to counter the conservative challenge against abortion rights. The Iran-Contra scandal, and the role played in it by Oliver North, a self-styled James Bond who, like Reagan, could not readily tell where film fantasies left off and real life began ("He was always starring in his own movie," presidential spokesman Larry Speakes said of North), further tarnished the administration's credibility, if not Reagan's personal popularity. The downfall of TV evangelists Jim Bakker and Jimmy Swaggart, owing to sex and money scandals, abruptly ended the frightfully powerful influence of the religious right, setting mainstream Americans to wondering if perhaps their basic values had become twisted during their decade long search for a tax break.

Heard again, now, were voices in the popular arts

FACING UP TO APARTHEID: As the Eighties wore on, filmmakers began to deal with serious social subjects like the horrors of Apartheid. *Cry Freedom* (right) depicted the friendship of Black Consciousness leader Stephen Biko (Denzel Washington) and journalist Donald Woods (Kevin Kline); *A World Apart* featured Linda Mvusi (center) as Elsie, a black activist dealing with the death of a loved one at the hands of white police.

calling attention to those problems most Americans had been willing to temporarily overlook throughout the decade: Singers as diverse as Bruce Springstein and Tracy Chapman pointed to the overlooked Americans, the armies of jobless and homeless which had multiplied almost beyond belief. The fouling of a thousand miles of Alaskan shoreline by the Exxon Valdex's 11-million-gallon oil spill brought back to public consciousness the importance of the natural environment, something that had been all but forgotten in an age when the president had claimed that pollution is caused by trees. The strong candidacy of Jesse Jackson, followed by the first-time elections of blacks as mayor of New York and governor of Virginia, made clear that a commitment to minorities rights was returning. The *We Are the World* video, uniting numerous rock stars for a social cause, along with the coming together of celebrities for causes ranging from a protest of South African apartheid to finding a cure for AIDS, suggested that the most notable era of rugged individualism since the Twenties might in fact be coming to an end, that the Nineties would once more see Americans moving back together into something resembling a community.

If the Eighties was the first era in which life imitated the movies, it was yet another era wherein movies reflected life. The most significant films of the decade—those telling, memorable films—are the ones that capture, however unconsciously, indirectly, or even inadvertently, the way we lived for those ten years. The following 100 films are the ones that most effectively reflect the tenor of the times in which they were created.

BOMBS AWAY: Not every film was a success. Comic Bill Murray, well-loved as a ghost-buster, failed to attract audiences when playing a guru in a drama, *The Razor's Edge*; George Lucas and his entourage of special effects artists were unable to work up interest in *Howard the Duck*.

TEEN SEX: The realization that teenagers were having sex at ever younger ages led to some surprisingly sensitive films on the subject. In *Blue Lagoon* (left), Brooke Shields and Christopher Atkins gradually learn the joys of sex within the context of a meaningful relationship. In *Little Darlings*, Tatum O'Neal and Kristy McNichol engage in a light-hearted contest to see who can lose her virginity first, though the results are dark indeed.

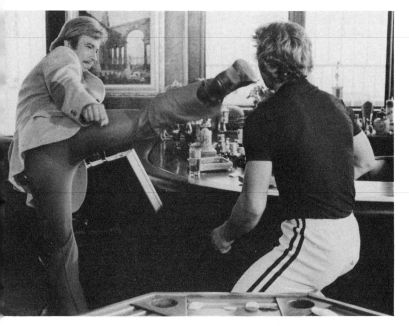

MACHO MEN: The preference for a political leader who gave the appearance of being strong, even macho, in his attitudes led Hollywood to beef up their output of action films; martial arts expert Chuck Norris kicked his way through mini-epics like *Forced Vengeance (above);* Clint Eastwood returned as Dirty Harry in *Sudden Impact*.

THE GREAT COMEDY TEAMS: In the tradition of Bud and Lou and Dean and Jerry came such pairings as: Gene Wilder and Richard Pryor in *Stir Crazy*, Dan Aykroyd and John Belushi in *The Blues Brothers*, and Arnold Schwarzenegger and Danny DeVito in *Twins*.

RETURN OF THE BLACK MOVIE HERO: In the Eighties, black characters were notably (and unforgivably) missing from the movie screen, but as the decade drew to an end, fine films once again depicted the plight of minority Americans. In *Glory* (left), a powerful study of America's all-but-forgotten black Civil War soldiers, Denzel Washington created a memorable characterization, winning himself the Best Supporting Actor Oscar in the process. *Driving Miss Daisy* (Academy Award-winning Best Picture) provided Morgan Freeman with a choice role which earned him a Best Actor Oscar nomination. (Jessica Tandy, his co-star, won Best Actress).

ORDINARY PEOPLE: The Stars pose for a publicity shot.

30

Ordinary People

A PARAMOUNT PICTURE   1980

CREDITS:

Produced by Ronald L. Schwary; directed by Robert Redford; screenplay by Alvin Sargent, based on the novel by Judith Guest; photography, John Bailey; editor, Jeff Kanew; Running time, 124 min.; Rating: R.

CAST:

Calvin (Donald Sutherland); *Beth* (Mary Tyler Moore); *Berger* (Judd Hirsch); *Conrad* (Timothy Hutton); *Swim Coach* (M. Emmet Walsh); *Jeannine* (Elizabeth McGovern); *Karen* (Dinah Manoff); *Lazenby* (Fredric Lehne); *Ray* (James B. Sikking); *Grandmother* (Meg Mundy); *Buck* (Scott Doebler).

ORDINARY PEOPLE: Following treatment at a mental hospital after his suicide attempt, Conrad (Timothy Hutton, Oscar-winning Best Supporting Actor) tries without success to communicate with his cold, classy mother; some critics felt that Ms. Moore was doing a variation on Nancy Reagan.

The first important dramatic American film of the decade, the one that early on caught the uncertain mood as the Eighties began, was *Ordinary People*. Even the title suggested this story about one family and their problems intended to reveal something universal in the unique situation depicted here. In the gradual decline and ruination of a family that initially seems to have it all, filmmaker Robert Redford created a contemporary

ORDINARY PEOPLE: At their first reunion since each left the hospital for the emotionally disturbed where they met as patients, Conrad and his only close female friend (Dinah Manoff) converse about their current struggles.

tragedy with something significant to say about the quality of life (or lack thereof) in the upcoming Reagan era, the way in which achievement of the American Dream did not guarantee happiness. ·

The key characters were certainly Reagan's Americans: the Jarrets, a family of Protestant Republicans who have known much financial success and little hardship, if also little spiritual satisfaction. Calvin, the father, is a well-paid tax lawyer, making money by managing other people's money. Money is the essence of his life, not in the sense of greed but as what he does, what he knows, the medium he works in. His wife Beth (Mary Tyler Moore) is competent and cool, a classy lady if not necessarily a warm-blooded one. Neither can understand why their handsome 18-year-old son Conrad (Timothy Hutton) has recently tried to commit suicide. It's as if he wishes he, rather than his brother Buck (Scott Doebler), had died a year and a half earlier in a Lake Michigan boating accident.

The imposing facade of their handsome home in Chicago's upper-middle-class Lake Forest suburb cannot hide the fact that something unhealthy lurks just beneath the surface of their organized, regimented lives. These are essentially the people Woody Allen attempted to analyze in his misguided and misbegotten *Interiors,* an outsider peeking into the world of WASP privilege. Judith Guest's novel more perceptively portrayed the psyches—and, in some cases, psychoses—of people who have plenty of money and no idea why they are miserable and unfulfilled. Redford brought Guest's vision to the screen without compromise, in the process winning Oscars for Best Picture, Best Supporting Actor (Hutton), and himself as Best Director. Ironically, the superstar who had never received a statuette for all his years of providing fine performances received one his first time behind the camera.

When Conrad is unable to resume his life—despite stabs at schoolwork, rejoining the swimming team, trying out for glee club—it becomes painfully obvious to the father, desperately desiring normalcy for his boy, that Conrad needs outside help. Beth can go on pretending everything is as placid as it appears; that is her pathetic way of coping, as she rushes out to overemphatically play bridge, work on her golf game, shop at Bonwit Teller or dedicate herself to any of a number of good causes for which she does charity work. But Calvin knows better, realizes something must be done and done quickly or they will lose their last son. Only when a warm, wise Jewish psychiatrist (Judd Hirsch) begins talking with Conrad does it become clear how inadequate he feels in attempting to be the son they want. The real problem is twofold: an inability on the part of all these family members to actually talk with one another about their problems or communicate about any of the demons that drive them, and an inability to express deep, heartfelt emotions within the family structure.

Though Mary Tyler Moore did not win the Best Actress Oscar she was nominated for, her performance here ranks as one of the significant achievements of actresses in the Eighties, all the more so because she had for so long been associated with lighthearted comedies in which she played giggly women whose bubbly, sometimes sincere, flippant approach to life was taken at face value. Here she revealed with flinty honesty the desperation which can exist under just such a placid exterior. Donald Sutherland, who in the Seventies had largely been associated with antiauthoritarian roles as intellectual outlaws, here handily reversed himself by perfectly playing the symbol of the Establishment, tragically trying to hold together a family falling apart for reasons they only dimly understand. Elizabeth McGovern was touching as a girl who shows Conrad he's a better person than he realizes; Dinah Manoff (daughter of actress-director Lee Grant) was likewise effective as a kindred soul at the mental ward. Hutton's anguished performance made him a star overnight, while Redford's detached approach seemed appropriate for this study of equally cool WASPs. All in all, *Ordinary People* rated as an extraordinary film.

Coal Miner's Daughter

A UNIVERSAL PICTURE   1980

COAL MINER'S DAUGHTER: Sissy Spacek won a Best Actress Oscar for her performance as Loretta Lynn, carrying the country-western singer through her girlhood relationship with miner father (Levon Helm) ...

CREDIT:

Executive producer, Bob Larson; produced by Bernard Schwartz; directed by Michael Apted; screenplay by Tom Rickman, based on the autobiography of Loretta Lynn with George Vecsey; photography, Ralf D. Bode; editor Arthur Schmidt; Running time, 125 min.; Rating: PG.

CAST:

Loretta (Sissy Spacek); *Doolittle (Mooney) Lynn* (Tommy Lee Jones); *Patsy Cline* (Beverly D'Angelo); *Ted Webb* (Levon Helm); *Clara Webb* (Phyllis Boyens); *Lee Dollarhide* (William Sanderson).

One major thrust of popular culture in the Eighties was a mainstream acceptance of country music, the

... through her first stardom at the Grand Ol' Opry, with Minnie Pearl and Ernest Tubb (playing themselves) ...

back-to-the-basics style of American song that provided the proper equivalent to Ronald Reagan's politics. Another was the advent of tabloid journalism, in which tell-all treatises (President Reagan tagged them "Kiss and Tell" books) revealed the heartbreaking secret stories of celebrities. These elements came back in the hit film *Coal Miner's Daughter,* the revealing biopic about country-western star Loretta Lynn.

The film was true to the general line of Lynn's life (in large part because she maintained control over the production), following her ascent from the small coal mining community of Butcher Holler, Kentucky (re-created for the film with stunning accuracy), all the way up the ladder of success to country-western stardom, a status which allowed her to immortalize her humble roots. No wonder, then, that Reagan was a big fan of Lynn, and she one of his most tireless campaigners. Lynn, like Reagan himself, stood as a living embodiment of the American Dream, proof it was indeed possible (if not probable) for anyone (though certainly not everyone) to rise up from the depths of financial depression and reach the top. Even the lyrics to Lynn's anthem, "I was born a coal miner's daughter," served not only as an expression of one woman's personal history, but as an inspiration for other poor Americans to emulate, an assertion that those with the humblest beginnings could achieve the loftiest heights, then look back unashamedly on their origins.

In that sense, what at first appeared to be a simple, beautifully played biography of one famous American served as an exemplary fable of how one rugged individualist was fit enough to survive the social Darwinism of twentieth-century life: *Coal Miner's Daughter* was, by implication, a political film. Certainly, though, the

... to full country-western stardom.

specifics of Lynn's unique life were played vividly on screen, thanks to an inspired (and deservedly Oscar-winning) performance by Sissy Spacek. A self-confessed ignorant country girl, Lynn had married at age 13 and by 20, was the mother of four, making her eventual achievements all the more impressive. The Loretta of the film's first half is a sweet but strong girl, loyal first to her father (Levon Helm), then her husband (Tommy Lee Jones), though always dreaming an apparently impossible dream: to sing at the Grand Ole Opry, like her idol Patsy Cline (Beverly D'Angelo, in an underappreciated performance).

There is a touch of the tragic to what follows next: Upon actually realizing that ambition, Lynn discovers—after one wonderful moment when she sings to a spellbound audience—that achieving one's dream does not, as in old movies, lead to a fade-out after which everyone involved lives happily ever. Business problems, personal problems, financial problems, marital problems, all plague Lynn when she moves into her mansion, discovering that life after success can be considerably less satisfying than what went before it. This gave the film a tough cutting edge most earlier Hollywoodized biographies, with their happily-ever-after approach, failed to acknowledge.

To squeeze so much living into a film of only a little

COAL MINER'S DAUGHTER: "I was born a coal miner's daughter ... "; though the film hardly seemed political, this was in fact a Reagan-era portrait of the American Dream coming true.

more than two hours, it was necessary to take dramatic license, "telescoping" various scenes and situations, necessitating that screenwriter Tom Rickman create certain moments for the film that didn't actually take place but that consolidated numerous real-life confrontations and thus were true to the spirit, if not the letter, of Lynn's life. The film appeared to pull punches only in its final third, softening the tough times Loretta and Mooney experienced in order to keep the film from becoming overly depressing for audiences while also protecting living people from the unpleasantnesses of too much dirty laundry in public. British director Michael Apted (*Agatha, Stardust*) conveyed the diverse settings with masterly meticulousness, even when toward the end he allowed the characterizations and their relationships to grow fuzzy. A gamble that worked, however, was allowing Spacek and D'Angelo to sing their own songs, rather than having them lip-synch to vintage recordings. Both rose to the occasion, offering renditions of the memorable country numbers that were at once true to the originals yet at the same time new, impressive interpretations of them. With *Coal Miner's Daughter*, a bygone movie genre—the inspirational biographical film—was happily revived.

Raging Bull

A UNITED ARTISTS RELEASE OF A
CHARTOFF-WINKLER
PRODUCTION   1980

CREDITS:

Produced by Irwin Winkler and Robert Chartoff; directed by Martin Scorsese; written by Paul Schrader and Mardik Martin, from the book by Jake La Motta with Joseph Carter and Peter Savage; photography, Michael Chapman; editor, Thelma Schoonmaker; Running time, 128 min.; Rating: R.

CAST:

Jake (Robert De Niro); *Vickie* (Cathy Moriarty); *Joey* (Joe Pesci); *Salvy* (Frank Vincent); *Tommy* (Nicholas Colasanto); *Lenore* (Theresa Saldana); *Patsy* (Frank Adonis); *Mario* (Mario Gallo).

Martin Scorsese's films appear to tell strikingly different stories in totally disparate styles: The gritty realism of *Mean Streets,* the stylized nostalgia of *New*

RAGING BULL: The champ: Jake La Motta (Robert De Niro), leading contender for boxing's middleweight title, raises his arms in anticipation of victory.

York, New York, the modernized Marxism of *Taxi Driver,* the oddly flat tableaus of *The Last Temptation of Christ.* Beneath the varied surfaces, however, Scorsese—like all important artists—is telling one tale (his tale) in different guises, presenting endless variations on the single theme that most haunts him. Always, his central character is unapproachable—some antisocial man harboring a remarkably romanticized misconception about the way the world works, whose personal agenda clashes so

35

La Motta (De Niro) is a street fighter turned pro, though his home life unpleasantly mirrors his approach in the ring. Everywhere he goes, Jake appears an animal, and is constantly told so by the people surrounding him. Deciding he can achieve respect only by marrying a woman out of his league, he deserts his first wife to pursue an apparently unattainable blonde goddess, Vicki (Cathy Moriarty). But the lure of the unattainable is automatically gone the moment it is possessed, so he quickly comes to loathe her for having so little class as to marry vermin like himself. Still, he fights harder than ever in the ring to win her respect, even corrupting himself by throwing a fight for the mob, never grasping that what Vicki needs is human compassion.

De Niro's performance (which won him the Best Actor Oscar) stands as the most striking achievement of his remarkable career. After training with La Motta himself for a half a year, De Niro convinced the former champ that he (De Niro) could succeed as a boxer if he ever tired of acting. To play the aging La Motta in the film's framing 1964 sequences (where he appears at the Barbizon Plaza in a mocking tribute, "An Evening with Jake La Motta," receiving fleeting pop mythologization), De Niro gained 50 pounds, becoming all but unrecognizable as the bloated ex-boxer. His performance is, by turns, dazzling, depressing, demanding—for, like the movie itself, De Niro made no concessions to his audiences or compromises calculated to win commercial success.

Scorsese, meanwhile, once more took a totally unrepresentative man and set his peculiar story against a specific period to reveal society in transition. *Raging*

RAGING BULL: The youthful Jake romances Vickie (Cathy Moriarty), an impossibly pretty blonde with a grotesque streetwise accent.

violently with the objective reality around him that he unknowingly sets into motion the mechanics of his own eventual destruction. At the final fade-out, he invariably stands alone—having achieved success in his chosen field to win the woman of his dreams but becoming so involved with the means that he's ironically demolished any hope for happiness with the end.

No wonder, then, that Scorsese and his frequent star, Robert De Niro, were attracted to the story of former middleweight boxing champ Jake La Motta, whose life plays like a Scorsese script in embryo. In *Raging Bull*,

RAGING BULL: Jake confers with his brother and manager Joey (Joe Pesci); Martin Scorsese's film, one of the handful of truly great movies made during the decade, offered a vision of the past without romanticization, and a scathing indictment of the American Dream gone sour.

RAGING BULL: Overweight and out of condition after winning and then losing boxing's Middleweight Championship, Jake takes part in an evening of self-mythologization; De Niro won a much-deserved Oscar for his performance.

Bull, like *New York, New York,* begins in the postwar boom and subsequent big economic letdown, then rambles through the politically, socially, culturally gray days of the Fifties, ending with the turbulent change in America's mood during the mid-Sixties. But unlike the more popular, amenable films of the early Reagan years, Scorsese's is antinostalgic in impact, partly explaining why this hard-pill-to-swallow was never a great commercial success, despite being the greatest single American movie since *Citizen Kane,* which it resembles (but never mimics) in both style and substance. Scorsese took wild gambles, playing the gutwrenching fight sequences against symphonic music, juxtaposing documentarylike sequences with flamboyant moments of extreme visual stylization, resulting in an aesthetic tour de force masquerading as kitchen-sink melodrama. While Ted Turner may lay awake nights fantasizing about getting his hands on a print, then gleefully colorizing *Raging Bull,* Scorsese's decision to shoot in black-and-white (a rarity in modern-day filmmaking, with a gritty realism by

cinematographer Michael Chapman) was totally organic. For as La Motta said in his autobiography: "When I think back, I feel like I'm looking at myself in an old black-and-white movie."

In retrospect, *Raging Bull* can be considered a criticism of the attitude happily espoused by Reagan, who revived the Hoover-Coolidge American Dream notion that every rugged individualist could slug his way to the top in the contemporary jungle of social Darwinism. As Scott Fitzgerald had done more than half a century earlier in *The Great Gatsby,* Scorsese artistically revealed the hollowness felt when the attained dream fails to satisfy and sours into a nightmare.

The Empire Strikes Back

A 20TH CENTURY-FOX RELEASE OF A LUCASFILM PRODUCTION   1980

CREDITS:

Executive producer, George Lucas; produced by Gary Kurtz; directed by Irvin Kershner; written by Leigh Brackett and Lawrence Kasdan, from a story by George Lucas; photography, Peter Suschitzy; editor Paul Hirsh; Running time, 124 min.; Rating: PG.

CAST:

Luke Skywalker (Mark Hamill); *Han Solo* (Harrison Ford); *Princess Leia* (Carrie Fisher); *Darth Vader* (David Prowse, voice by James Earl Jones); *C3PO* (Anthony Daniels); *Chewbacca* (Peter Mayhew); *R2-D2* (Kenny Baker); *Yoda* (Frank Oz); *Lando Calrissian* (Billy Dee Williams); *Ben Kenobi* (Alec Guinness).

The mass audience's appetite for modernized space opera of the Flash Gordon/Buck Rogers variety was whetted in 1977 when George Lucas unleashed *Star Wars* and created a phenomenon. His first sequel, *The Empire Strikes Back,* proved not only bigger but also better than the first film, offering a more elaborate set of special effects and technical wizardy but also a more fascinating story line—courtesy of Howard Hawks's favorite screenwriter, Leigh Brackett (in her last assignment, working with talented newcomer Lawrence Kasdan)—and more fully developed characterizations for the leads. Who would have guessed, for instance, the wicked Darth Vader would turn out to be innocent Luke Skywalker's father? In addition, there were fascinating

THE EMPIRE STRIKES BACK: *Star Wars* Redux: with Chewebacca (Peter Mayhew), Princess Leia (Carrie Fisher), C-3P0 (Anthony Daniels) and Han Solo (Harrison Ford) recreating their roles, the George Lucas series moved further into the popular mythology, giving President Reagan an easily accessible term to describe his new missile warning system.

science fiction flicks; as the famous opening made clear, this was not necessarily futuristic ("Long, long ago in a galaxy far, far away—") but, like all great adventures, absolutely timeless.

Like all old American films, however, it did simplify issues, giving us the kind of clear-cut good and evil that could easily be symbolized by Skywalker's white outfit and Darth Vader's corresponding black one. Not since Alan Ladd's blond Shane shot it out with Jack Palance's black-leather-clad Wilson in a muddy cowtown had any movie made the moral values so obvious. Perhaps that's part of why the public responded so strongly, as well as to the hardware and software that could be marketed as kids' toys: It was refreshing and reassuring to go back to the simplistics, identify with the good and hiss at the bad. If all that appealed to the public, it certainly went over well with the man they'd elected to the presidency. Mr. Reagan, in describing the Soviet Union, borrowed

new characters, like the lovable little old green guru Yoda and the happy addition of Lando, more than making up for the obvious lack of such a positive black character in the original. It was the unexpected success of the first *Star Wars*, though, that allowed movie brat George Lucas to come up with ever more dazzling set pieces here, including a battle on the ice between good guys and bad that borrowed liberally from the parallel scene in Sergei Eisenstein's 1938 classic *Alexander Nevsky*.

Unlike his colleague Steven Spielberg, George Lucus was always more effective as an idea man and overseer of movie projects than hands-on director, which is why the first *Star Wars* seems, in retrospect, a bit cold and clinical, the actors never giving their all. That's because Lucas's genius lay in the very concept of the series, not in the execution of individual episodes, whereas this film's director, Irvin Kershner, has always been gifted at bringing out the most richly textured performances for varied actors in such fine if sadly little-known films as *Return of a Man Called Horse* and *The Luck of Ginger Coffey*. Kershner breathed life into Lucas's ideas; from the moment John Williams's already famous theme resounded at the movie's inception, while the audience was informed by the printed crawl that we were watching chapter five of an old-time movie serial, viewers were thrilled and delighted, making this the number-one box-office champ of the year. *Empire* borrowed as liberally from old westerns and World War II films as from

THE EMPIRE STRIKES BACK: In stark silhouette, the battle between good (Luke) and evil (Vader) moved past the *Flash Gordon* adventure-fantasy level of the first film and took on epic dimension.

38

from this very film—the new movie myth; the story everyone had experienced and which could thus serve as a point of reference—when he referred to Russia as the Evil Empire; in so labeling our chief competitor in the Cold War, the movie hero turned world leader further blurred the distinction between Hollywood mythmaking and everyday reality, implying we were as innocent and pure as Luke Skywalker, or at least as roguishly heroic as Han Solo.

The president's reliance on this film did not end there. When he proposed the development of a new multi-billion dollar state-of-the-art defense system to protect us from possible missile attack, Reagan referred to it as Star Wars. When the press jokingly picked up on that, the president chastised them for ridiculing the concept by referring to it as Star Wars, though in fact he had himself initiated that title. Not all his expressions came from this one film: like cool-eyed Clint Eastwood as Dirty Harry,

THE EMPIRE STRIKES BACK: The success of the first film allowed George Lucas to expand his vision with ever more elaborate sets. Here, the carbon freezing chamber in Cloud City comes to vivid, dense life.

THE EMPIRE STRIKES BACK: Ready for action: The pro-military attitude of the early Eighties was reflected in *Empire*, as rebel soldiers prepare to fire the dish laser gun on the ice planet Hoth.

39

Reagan enjoyed facing down the TV news cameras telling his political enemies, "Make my day!" And, in time, his macho stance on international issues would come to be known as Rambo politics, though there it's difficult to tell which came first, movie or reality, making clear this was the era in which the two became inseparable.

The Long Riders

A UNITED ARTISTS RELEASE   1980

CREDITS:

Executive producers, James Keach and Stacy Keach; produced by Tim Zinnemann; directed by Walter Hill; screenplay by Billo Bryden, Steven Phillip Smith, Stacy Keach and James Keach; photography, Ric Waite; editors, David Holden and Freeman Davies; Running time, 100 min.; Rating: R.

CAST:

Cole Younger (David Carradine); *Jim Younger* (Keith Carradine); *Bob Younger* (Bob Carradine); *Jesse James* (James Keach); *Frank James* (Stacy Keach); *Ed Miller* (Dennis Quaid); *Clell Miller* (Randy Quaid); *Charlie Ford* (Christopher Guest); *Bob Ford* (Nicholas Guest); *George Arthur* (Harry Carey Jr.); *Belle Shirley* (Pamela Reed); *Sam Starr* (James Remar); *Zee* (Savannah Smith); *Rixley* (James Whitmore Jr.)

If nothing else, this film would be noteworthy for its extraordinary cast, featuring real-life actor brothers as the bandit brothers who formed the most notorious bank and train robbing gang of the post-Civil War South. Fortunately, that turned out to be more than just a clever gimmick, for in *The Long Riders,* the casting of brothers as brothers was transformed, by filmmaker Walter Hill, into the film's central theme: the idea of brotherhood—what that bond means in comparison to other bonds, including marriage and friendship. Though the approach taken in this telling of the tale was docudrama, with scrupulous attention to historical detail and a deromanticizing of the mythic Robin Hood of the Old West aura that has preposterously come to surround this company of killers, Hill nonetheless managed to infuse the story with his own values.

Previous incarnations featured either Jesse James or Cole Younger as the key character. Intriguingly, this

THE LONG RIDERS: Stick 'em up! Frank James (Stacy Keach) and brother Jesse (James Keach) hold up a train in the post-Civil War west; *The Long Riders* was the most artistically (if not commercially) successful of all the western-produced shortly after a former cowboy star became President.

focused on Frank James (Stacy Keach), allowing his younger brother Jesse (James Keach) and cousin Cole (David Carradine) to stand as the opposite moral poles, Frank uncomfortably positioned between them and, finally forced at the climax—just after the disastrous raid on Northfield, Minnesota—to choose. Jesse is a total hypocrite, masking his life of crime behind a mock existence as respectable businessman Mr. Howard, with wife and children, occasionally going away "on business"; Cole is more honest about himself, a self-confessed scruffy outlaw who feels such a chosen profession does not allow room for family, instead spending time with whores like Belle Shirley (later, Belle Starr). Frank respects Cole's stance, feels their blood kindred; still, no emotion is stronger than the brotherly bond, so Frank's brief but intense soul-searching leads to the only conclusion he can make: "Sorry, Cole, but Jesse's my brother." With any other cast, that would have been nothing more than a throwaway line of dialogue; with brothers as brothers, it emerged as the key to the movie's meaning.

Though *The Long Riders* was not the runaway hit the producers had hoped for, it was the most successful of the western films following quick on the heels of former cowboy star Ronald Reagan's election to the presidency. Perhaps it clicked because it portrayed the James and Younger boys as deranged veterans of a conflict they could not put behind them; more than one critic noticed the mood among the gang members appeared to be inspired less by nineteenth-century history than the contemporary angst of so many illadjusted Vietnam vets. That made sense, since during the Thirties Hollywood's version of the gang (led by Tyrone Power) looked suspiciously like such Depression Era rural gangsters as John Dillinger and Pretty Boy Floyd, whereas in the Fifties (with Robert Wagner as Jesse) they became juvenile delinquents, rebels without a cause. In each case, history was reinterpreted so as to be relevant in the present, and *The Long Riders* proved no exception.

What removed this film from other versions was the refusal to make Jesse a pleasant character or to deemphasize the violent, wanton killings perpetrated by the gang. The dialogue was minimalist, with character development too slight; Walter Hill originally hoped for a longer cut that would have allowed for more characterization than we see. Hill did manage, though, to include his favorite theme, the myth of Xenophon, that Greek

THE LONG RIDERS: Cole Younger (David Carradine, center) along with brothers Bob (Robert Carradine) and Jim (Keith Carradine) case a bank; whereas the James' were hypocrites who loved double lives, the Youngers made no bones about what they were: outlaws.

THE LONG RIDERS: Oh, brother! Having actor-brothers play outlaw-brothers was more than just a gimmick: (from left) David, Keith and Robert Carradine; Nicholas and Christopher Guest; Dennis and Randy Quaid; Stacy and James Keach.

41

THE LONG RIDERS: Clell Miller (Randy Quaid) joins Cole, Frank, Jesse, and Jim for the ride into Northfield, Minnesota.

warrior known for fighting his way back home from behind enemy lines. Basic to Hill's most effective movies, it was played out in such diverse settings as the modern urban jungle (*The Warriors*), the Cajun swamps of Louisiana (*Southern Comfort*), and (here) the last frontier.

Hill also transformed this into a movie about the mythmaking properties of movies, how films have created the Jesse James of our popular imagination. One old-timer encountered during a stagecoach holdup is played by Harry Carey Jr., veteran of so many classic Ford/Hawks westerns. When the gang rides into Northfield, they pass a newly invented steam engine, a symbol of the future previously employed by Phil Kaufman in his 1972 *The Great Northfield, Minnesota Raid*. When Bob Ford pulls the trigger on Jesse, the back-shooting dirty little coward comments: "I shot Jesse James!", a reference to Sam Fuller's B western. *The Long Riders* offered an accurate account of the men behind the myth, along with a sly allusion to the previous movies that created the legend here undermined.

The Elephant Man

A PARAMOUNT PICTURES RELEASE OF A BROOKSFILM PRODUCTION   1980

CREDITS:

Executive producer, Mel Brooks; produced by Jonathan Sanger; directed by David Lynch; written by Christopher Devore, Eric Bergen and David Lynch; based on *The Elephant Man and Other Reminiscences* by Sir Frederick Treves; photography, Freddie Francis; editor, Anne V. Coates; Running time, 123 min.; Rating: PG.

CAST:

John Merrick (John Hurt); *Frederick Treves* (Anthony Hopkins); *Carr Gomm* (John Gielgud); *Mrs. Kendal* (Anne Bancroft); *Bytes* (Freddie Jones); *Mothershead* (Wendy Hiller); *Night Porter* (Michael Elphick).

While most Hollywood filmmakers of the early Eighties were busily reviving and revising bygone genres like the western, the science fiction film, and the action-adventure serial, one moviemaker chose to go another route entirely. While David Lynch's *The Elephant Man* concerned a place and period of time that was ripe for nostalgia—London of the 1880s— and though he worked in a black-and-white style that harked back to the look of Forties horror films, his movie was anything but a romanticized, sentimentalized, updated pastiche of memories from past pictures. This was the work of a filmmaker who, with his cult classic *Eraserhead*, had emerged as one of the most controversial and visible avant-garde artists; his first stab at a major feature boasted everything that was best (and most disconcerting) about the alternative cinema, while also adding a grim, yet strangely beautiful, vivid, haunting narrative of the sort that had not been done since Todd Browning's bizarre *Freaks* in 1932.

Like the popular stage play that was still running when this film premiered, *The Elephant Man* took as its subject the life of John Merrick (1873–1900), a man whose appearance was so grotesque that he came to be called the Elephant Man. He was treated as a circus freak to be gawked at by the newly created blue-collar post-Industrial Revolution workers until a sympathetic doctor, Sir Frederick Treves, showed the Victorian aristocracy that beneath a hideous exterior beat a human heart. The film was not an adaption of the play, in which an actor wearing no makeup at all walked out on stage and, through his skill at suggestion, made the audience believe they were looking at Merrick. Lynch and his collaborators created an entirely new interpretation, basing their scenario on Treves's *The Elephant Man and Other Reminiscences* as well as *The Elephant Man: A Study in Human Dignity* by Ashley Montagu, thereby creating a movie that was quite clearly cinematic rather than theatrical in its approach.

Deformed at birth, Merrick was the victim of an illness called neurofibromatosis, resulting in a head twice the size of a normal human being's. Treves rescued Merrick from the carnival, attempting to normalize the man's life by providing him with a decent, quiet hospital surrounding, even introducing Merrick ultimately into London's high society. Vincent Canby best summed up

THE ELEPHANT MAN: John Hurt as the Elephant Man, a precursor of the celebrity-as-freak mentality that would pervade the Eighties.

the film's impact in *The New York Times,* hailing this as a "benign horror film, one in which 'the creature' is pursued instead of the pursuer." Lynch certainly did borrow visual techniques from the grand old monster movies, but turned such stylistic devices inside out by suggesting that society at large was the monster, whereas the monstrous creature was entirely sympathetic. So Lynch effectively held off our first shot of Merrick for as long as possible, building up audience anticipation; but by the time we finally see Merrick, he has become such an acceptable person to us that we're not at all put off by his hideous looks, and merely accept them.

The makeup by Christopher Tucker was completely convincing. The film had such an immense impact on one viewer—pop star Michael Jackson—that after screening *The Elephant Man,* he immediately set about learning the whereabouts of the real Merrick's body, purchasing the remains and attempting to at last provide Merrick with a true resting place. Though Jackson's obsession with Merrick may strike some as unlikely, it's worth noting that Merrick was in many ways the prototype of the contemporary celebrity, adored one moment and attacked the next, treated as a combination of superstar and freak, hyped into a legend-in-his-own-time by the media and then laughed at by the very same reporters. Jackson always felt himself to be treated in just such a way, while other artists also responded to the plight of the modern celebrity: two Woody Allen films from the same period, *Stardust Memories* and *Zelig,* are both meditations on the plight of a celebrity who fears

THE ELEPHANT MAN: At the London hospital, the doctor (Anthony Hopkins) attacks the night porter (Michael Elphick) who has shamelessly humiliated the disfigured patient.

even his most adoring fans do not really understand him, and that they might turn on him at any moment.

Despite being covered by an immense mask, John Hurt managed a complicated and deeply felt performance; Anthony Hopkins was equally moving as Treves. The film offered suspense when Merrick's former promoter (Freddie Jones) kidnaps him, forcing Merrick to appear on the continent, and poignancy when Traves brought the wretched Merrick back to England, where he charms everyone in a staid Victorian drawing room while sipping tea and entering into polite conversation.

THE ELEPHANT MAN: As the sympathetic doctor attempting to treat the "freak" as a human being, Anthony Hopkins (right) enlists the aid of Lesley Dunlop and Sir John Gielgud at London Hospital.

THE ELEPHANT MAN: As a West End stage star and leading London-society hostess, Anne Bancroft was woefully miscast in a role that should have gone to Maggie Smith or Vanessa Redgrave; then again, *The Elephant Man* was a Brooksfilm Production, and Bancroft was married to the boss.

The Big Red One

A UNITED ARTISTS RELEASE OF A LORIMAR PRODUCTION   1980

CREDITS:

Executive producers, Merv Adelson and Lee Rich; produced by Gene Corman; written and directed by Sam Fuller; photography, Adam Greenberg; editor, David Bretherton; Running time: 113 min.; Rating, PG.

CAST:

The Sergeant (Lee Marvin); *Griff* (Mark Hamill); *Zab* (Robert Carradine); *Vinci* (Bobby Di Cicco); *Johnson* (Kelly Ward); *Schroeder* (Siegfried Rauch); *Wailoon* (Stephane Audran); *Rensonnet* (Serge Marquand).

When Ronald Reagan reached the White House and brought with him a style of old-fashioned conservative politics that had been out of fashion for a decade and a half, it made sense that the styles of movies Reagan had once starred in—also out of favor for more than fifteen years—would suddenly stage a comeback. So the western ambled back (*Tom Horn, Bronco Billy, The Long Riders, Silverado*); but if Reagan looked like a cowboy, he talked as tough as John Wayne in an old World War II film. Concurrently, Sam Fuller, searching in vain for years to find backing for the ultimate old-fashioned Wayne war movie, finally raised enough money to make *The Big Red One*.

Though Wayne had finally succumbed to cancer in the late Seventies, Fuller—then 70—handily recast the fact-based film with Lee Marvin, an old Wayne buddy and frequent costar. Delivering his best performance since *The Dirty Dozen*, Marvin played the sergeant who, during World War One's twilight, formulates the concept of a special division, the First Infantry, identified by a red shoulder patch. The subsequent story takes place during WWII, as the sergeant finds himself flanked by a quartet of young soldiers, his Four Horsemen: Zab (Robert Carradine), a wisecracking, cigar-chewing pulp fiction writer and autobiographical stand-in for Fuller himself, serving also as the offscreen narrator of the piece; Griff (Mark Hamill), a sweet-spirited G.I. who, though essentially courageous, finds himself gripped by moments of paralyzing fear; Vinci (Bobby Di Cicco), a

THE BIG RED ONE: Lee Marvin as "The Sergeant," in Sam Fuller's well-timed resurrection of the epic World War II film; as American once again assumed a get-tough attitude, so too did American movies.

Sicilian-American with a chip on his shoulder owing to too many jokes about his relatives being aligned with the enemy; and Johnson (Kelly Ward), a homegrown WASPy American with an uncomfortable case of hemorrhoids. The film carried them through three years of rugged combat, and by its narrow focus on a small group of soldiers—totally uncomprehending of the larger scheme of the war raging around them—*The Big Red One* captured better than any film since Lewis Milestone's *A Walk in the Sun* (1946) the essence of what it meant to be a common dogface, doing a dirty job.

Though the film eventually achieved epic proportion, it did so not through any grand story (à la *The Guns of Navarone*) or an immense scale (*The Longest Day*), but rather through the careful, methodical build-up of a series of anecdotes, small moments from Fuller's memory, arranged into a vivid mosaic; sometimes humorous, more often grim, the film's power derived less from the content of any one event than the cumulative effect. This was clearly an insider's view, the cinematic equivalent of Ernie Pyle's essays combined with Bill Mauldin's sketches. Impressive too was that none of the central characters died; the most overly melodramatic ploy possible, a big death scene for one of the leads, was avoided by Fuller, who made a most atypical movie about battles (like Omaha Beach) which had over the years degenerated into cinematic cliché.

THE BIG RED ONE: The Squad, from left: Griff (Mark Hamill), Zab (Robert Carradine), Vinci (Bobby DiCiccio) and Johnson (Kelly Ward).

THE BIG RED ONE: The sergeant and his squad hit the beach and get their baptism of fire in North Africa.

Fuller made them fresh again with his insightful approach. The director of such brilliant low-budget, stylishly sleazy films as *The Naked Kiss, The Crimson Kimono,* and *Shock Corridor,* as well as equally spare Fifties war movies like *Steel Helmet* and *Fixed Bayonets,* here opted for a splashy sensibility, painting the battles in intimately intense cameos rather than large, spectacular scenes. Though that may have been due to the limits of his budget, Fuller made such restrictions work to his advantage, focusing on the faces of his five heroes, making the common man's response to the war, rather than the war itself, his actual subject.

But if this was an A film from a king of B flicks, *The Big Red One* boasted images and ideas that made clear who directed it. At one point, the camera pans past an immense stretch of bloody battlefield until it includes a large crucifix with a wooden sculpture of Christ, apparently peering down at the remains of those who failed to heed His Father's advice, Thou shalt not kill. Hardly subtle but extremely effective, as were scenes of a woman giving birth inside a tank, a devastating incident involving a starving child at a concentration camp, and the rapid crosscutting from American to German officers as each mouths the same cliché, "We don't murder; we kill our enemies." Though a highly patriotic American who had proudly served, Fuller was essentially antiwar and prohumanist, refusing to caricature the other side. He ended the film with a "signature" shot, borrowed from the beginning of his flamboyant Freudian western, *Run of the Arrow:* Here, Marvin and comrades shoot a German soldier, only to realize the war officially ended moments before. Then they attempt to revive the man and save his life. The absurdity of war has never been quite so perfectly expressed on film as in Fuller's powerful, personal vision.

Tess

A COLUMBIA PICTURES RELEASE   1980

CREDITS:

Executive producer, Pierre Grunstein; produced by Claude Berri; directed by Roman Polanski; written by Gerard Brach, John Brownjohn, and Roman Polanski from the book *Tess of the D'Urbervilles* by Thomas Hardy; photography, Geoffrey Unsworth; editor, Alastair McIntyre; Running time, 179 min.; Rating: PG.

CAST:

Tess (Nastassia Kinski); *Angel Clare* (Peter Firth); *John Durbeyfield* (John Collin); *Alec D'Urberville* (Leigh Lawson); *Parson Tringham* (Albert Simono); *Felix* (John Bett); *Reverend Mr. Clare* (David Markham); *Cuthbert* (Tom Chadbon); *Mrs. Durbeyfield* (Rosemary Martin); *Meadow Girls* (Brigid Erin Bates, Jeanne Biras).

"She lived in a world," the ads for *Tess* told the potential viewer, "that called it seduction. What she did would shatter that world forever!": A sexy sales pitch calculated to create excitement around an epic-length, handsomely old-fashioned, cautiously-paced costume film. Tess Durbeyfield/D'Urbervilles (Nastassia Kinski) was marketed as an innocent woman "wronged"—raped was the implication—by a callous, casual man (Leigh Lawson); her eventual murder of that man years later was identified as a feminist action in embryo. The only problem: none of this had anything to do with Thomas Hardy's 1891 novel or the scrupulously faithful, surprisingly controlled film Roman Polanski fashioned from it.

Throughout the story, it's clear Tess is not a naïve woman forced into her initial sexual encounter but aware of Alec's intentions, to which she gradually succumbs out of frustration, boredom and loneliness. Tess operates out of freedom of choice, and it is this exercising of free will that will doom her. If she is a victim of anything, it's the mechanism of fate that sends her off to Alec in the first place. Tess is lost that day her father, a drunken dirt farmer, learns his family dates back to William the Conqueror. His ecstatic overreaction to the news sets in motion a chain of events which, combined with Tess's own uncontrollable impulses, ultimately does her in, as she's sent packing to rich people now considered distant relatives. The irony is that the "relatives" are noveau-riche petit-bourgeois, their wealth acquired from the emerging factories; they attempted to legitimize their new status by spending a portion of their capital on a Norman title.

Hardy characterized Tess as a woman with every natural advantage—beauty, brains, strength of character—done in by a world-in-transition into which she was unhappily thrust. The representative young woman of her day, she's caught between the twisting movements of an uncertain universe—symbolized by the two complex men she finds herself involved with. There's Alec, whose fortune belongs to the future of factories and big money but whose attitudes are all of the past. And Angel Clare (Peter Firth), the gentle dairy farmer whose lifestyle represents a throwback to more pastoral times but whose radical politics hint at a collective future to

TESS: Tess (Nastassia Kinski) marries the guilt ridden Angel Clare (Peter Firth) in a poorly attended ceremony; Polanski's visuals brought Hardy's descriptions to vivid life onscreen.

TESS: Tess falls under the spell of Alec (Leigh Lawson), a suave seductor.

TESS: A feminist plea: Clutching her baby daughter, the abandoned Tess attempts to fend for herself in a world that sanctions male promiscuity but denies impulsive acts to women.

come. Each is a walking contradiction, yet they complement one another, representing past and future in dialectic ways. When we last perceive Tess, she symbolically sleeps on the ancient sacrificial altar of Stonehenge, just as the police come to arrest her for Alec's murder—a martyr of the present, doomed for the future by her connection to the past.

Hardy's world (stunningly photographed by Geoffrey Unsworth and Ghislain Cloquet) was one of the endless incongruities: newfangled threshing machines juxtaposed against solid stone mansions, a godless, money-oriented value system clashing with an ever more unworkable Victorian morality. Against this backdrop, Hardy wove his tale of a determined woman whose true

TESS: The moment of decision: Tess ponders her fate.

personality remains a mystery to each of the two men who believe they loved her. To Alec, she is a sex object; to Angel, the Virgin Mary. In his writing, Hardy struggled admirably to portray not only an emerging breed of woman but also the inability of men—the sensitive as well as the crass—to appreciate females as people. Arriving on screen at a time when women's lib, such a heated issue during the Seventies, had been pushed to a back burner of the social agenda, this story offered a vision that intelligent women of the Eighties could strongly respond to.

This is the epic Hardy told and, happily, the movie Polanski made. Hardy lavished lengthy strings of words on descriptions of rural countryside being supplanted by gray factories as a lyrical lifestyle gave way to a mechanized one. Polanski communicated the same concepts with his dazzling visual juxtapositions of just such objects. The man who, a decade earlier, twisted Shakespeare's *Macbeth* into an upscale slasher film and dark parody of the Manson murders had clearly reached a point where, despite his reputation as a violent filmmaker, he could comfortably leave the single violent act in *Tess* offscreen. Always brilliant, Polanski had not been delicate, refined and understated since his premiere picture, the 1962 Polish classic *Knife in the Water.* Having himself been accused of molesting an underage girl who may have actually participated in the "seduction," Polanski was—owing to personal experience—able to lend a poignancy to this old tale about just such a situation.

Urban Cowboy

A PARAMOUNT PICTURE   1980

CREDITS:

Executive producer, C. O. Erickson; produced by Robert Evans and Irving Azoff; directed by James Bridges; screenplay by James Bridges and Aaron Latham, from the magazine story by Latham; photography, Reynald Villalobos; editor, Dave Rawlins; Running time, 135 min.; rating: PG.

CAST:

Bud (John Travolta); *Sissy* (Debra Winger); *Wes* (Scott Glenn); *Pam* (Madolyn Smith); *Uncle Bob* (Barry Corbin); *Aunt Corene* (Brooke Alderson); *Marshall* (Cooper Huckabee); *Gilley* (Mickey Gilley).

No sooner had Ronald Reagan been elected president than the country went on a country-western kick: The kinds of clothing, food, music and dancing styles that had for decades been considered déclassé suddenly become the rage now that a former TV cowboy was occupying the White House. The type of mechanical bulls long popular in Texas honky-tonks, including Gilley's, were suddenly found all over the country, now being mounted by people who had hopped on the latest pop-culture craze, suddenly preferring chili and Lone Star beer to beluga caviar and champagne. If country-western clubs replaced disco palaces as the trendy social milieu, it made sense a film ought to address the new phenomenon in the same manner that, during the previous decade, *Saturday Night Fever* had done discos. It also seemed logical that *SNF*'s John Travolta would be brought back to star again.

Like Travolta's earlier smash, *Urban Cowboy* had its germination in a magazine article, a syndrome that would repeat itself with increasing regularity throughout the Eighties as pop-journalism joined novels and films as a primary source for movie material. As in *SNF*, much of the action took place in a bar where young people came to meet, dance and couple, allowing the filmmakers to study the mating habits of an entire generation. In particular, the story focuses on Bud (Travolta), who travels from his home in rural Texas to Houston, where he lives with his aunt and uncle and, following daily hardhat work at the refinery, heads directly for the popular Gilley's, a three-and-a-half acre honky-tonk where self-styled macho men take turns attempting to ride the mechanical bull with hopes of impressing the rhinestone cowgirls. There, Bud meets pretty Sissy (Debra Winger), with whom he is soon romantically involved and marries, settling into a trailer camp existence. But Wes (Scott Glenn), a rough-and-tumble ex-con, soon pays the young woman more attention than the immature Bud does. Shortly, the ill-conceived marriage is in danger of crumbling, as Bud takes up with a slumming socialite (Madolyn Smith) and Sissy runs off with the charismatic but dangerous Wes.

Director James Bridges (*The Paper Chase, The China Syndrome*) neatly captured the moods and tone of the rural bar scene, as well as something absolutely frightening about relationships in the Eighties, especially among those young people who were products of the Me Decade and carried its self-indulgent lifestyle into the new era. Importantly, though, the script carried its characters beyond such superficiality, for the plot charted the arc—a kind of moral growth—of both its major characters. Though Bud remains relatively inarticulate throughout, he eventually grows dissatisfied

49

URBAN COWBOY: Though Sissy (Debra Winger) and Bud are newlyweds . . .

. . . he is soon spending time with Pam (Madolyn Smith) . . .

. . . while she takes up with Wes (Scott Glenn).

with the quick-and-easy sex that girls like Pam offer, wanting to return to the marriage and work harder to make it work. Sissy likewise finds her flirtation with the nasty Wes less enjoyable than she thought she would. The movie realistically depicts the amorality of the new self-styled cowboys wearing outlandishly colorful satin outfits that old-time westerns would have scoffed at.

What kept *Urban Cowboy* from emerging as a true classic, in the same league as *Saturday Night Fever*, was the overly melodramatic script, which occasionally appeared to be parodying Forties and Fifties B westerns. If that was indeed the intention, then this approach was underplayed, because a necessary edge of irony was lacking. When Bud and Wes fight it out at the end of the movie, in the manner of a traditional cowboy movie showdown here staged in a contemporary western club, the situation seems similar to the cliché rather than a pointed satire of it. *SNF* had surprised critics by turning its mindless protagonist into a full-fledged tragic hero; *Urban Cowboy* settled instead for contrived melodrama. Its ordinary story line did not match in power its exceptional visual style.

Perhaps that's why *Urban Cowboy* was only a modest success, rather than a runaway hit like *SNF*. Also, Travolta was unable to fully recover from the disastrous *Moment by Moment*, which had teamed him, as a sensitive wimp, with Lily Tomlin in a lethargic film that emasculated his greaser image, alienating former fans. Only with 1989's *Look Who's Talking* would he recover some of this star stature. Winger, continuing her climb toward major stardom, would be a bright light throughout the decade, in hits like *Legal Eagles* and *Terms of Endearment*, until she too would eventually fall prey to bad career moves (*Betrayed*) and find her star dimming by decade's end.

The Stunt Man

A 20TH CENTURY-FOX RELEASE OF A MELVIN SIMON PRODUCTION   1980

CREDITS:

Executive producer, Melvin Simon; produced and directed by Richard Rush; written by Lawrence B. Marcus, from the novel by Paul Brodeur; photography, Mario Tosi; editors, Jack Hofstra and Caroline Ferriol; Running time, 129 min.' Rating: R.

CAST:

Eli Cross (Peter O'Toole); *Nina Franklin* (Barbara Hershey); *Cameron* (Steve Railsback); *Sam* (Allen Goorwitz); *Jake* (Alex Rocco); *Denise* (Sharon Farrell); *Raymond Bailey* (Adam Roarke); *Ace* (Philip Bruns); *Chuck Barton* (Chuck Ball); *Gabe* (John Garwood); *Henry* (Jim Hess).

With a movie star as President, delivering speeches as a President in a film might while oftentimes becoming confused as to whether past events had actually happened historically or were merely vivid, imaginative ideas from some dimly remembered film, it became more and more difficult for any of us to decipher where movies left off and reality began. Understandably, then, that became the theme of some of the decade's great films, Richard Rush's *The Stunt Man* being one of the first to provide a parable for our current politics.

On the run from the police, Vietnam vet Lucky Cameron (Steve Railsback) finds himself hitchhiking across a deserted bridge. An elegant vintage car glides by, then turns and roars directly toward him. Terrified, Lucky throws the nearest object he can find at the car's driver, then watches as the vehicle plunges into the water below. Moments later, the area is alive with people—moviemaking people—as crew members rush out of the woods and a helicopter drops cameramen and the director, Eli Cross (Peter O'Toole, in a role that revived his sagging career), down to eye-level with the awestruck fugitive. Burt, the stunt man who was driving the antique car for this World War One-era film being shot, is lost.

One of the many questions raised by *The Stunt Man* is whether Lucky's interference killed Burt: Is Lucky now a murderer as well as common criminal? Another is whether Burt is really dead, for the entire affair grows less certain as the picture progresses. That vagueness, though, was part of this film's bizarre appeal. *The Stunt Man* rated as an absolute original: It was as if the script for Burt Reynolds's *Hooper* (in which the stuntman-turned-actor played a stuntman very much like the one he had once been) were rewritten by Francois Truffaut, directed Federico Fellini, and produced by Roger Corman, an *8½* for the rural drive-in circuit. Outrageous and audacious, it struck some critics as an appealing con, cleverly but only superficially suggesting complex themes about identity and art while never going beyond a surface investigation of them. Others found it a satisfying cross between art-house item and action flick.

Eli, realizing Lucky is the fugitive the police are searching for, strikes a Faustian bargain with the youth. If Lucky will take over Burt's role as stunt man for the next three days, he can hide out with the movie people and avoid the authorities. To pull this off, everyone in the cast and crew is instructed to call Eli "Burt"; after a short while, Eli discovers he is indeed becoming Burt, for it's difficult to keep one's equilibrium while working in the wonderfully wicked world of movies, where all is illusion and nothing turns out to be quite what it seems. In a battle sequence filmed on a beach, the crowd of onlookers watches as stunt men are shot at by old biplanes, then goes into an uproar upon realizing that, by accident, all the men have actually been killed. But they haven't—it's just a remarkably well-executed stunt. Even

THE STUNT MAN: The film within the film is a nostalgic action epic, not unlike so many of the revived genre pieces being made during the Eighties.

THE STUNT MAN: A metaphor for the Eighties: As the stuntman (Steve Railsback) films a violent sequence, he suddenly finds the reel moment becoming all too real.

the people making the picture reach a point where they can't tell where film fantasy ends and everyday reality begins.

That goes beyond the special effects, to the people and their reactions. Why is Eli so concerned about Lucky's fate—is it sincere interest in him or a facile desire to get the picture finished? How altruistic is Eli's antiwar message—does he really believe in it or is he merely spouting fashionable rhetoric? Does the intense screenwriter Sam (Allen Goorwitz who, during the decade, switched back to his real name after having established himself as Allen Garfield) really live by values the others do not possess, or is that just his pose? And the unfathomable woman, movie star Nina (Barbara Hershey), who may or may not be in love with both Cross and Cameron—is she only playing a game, trying on one role after another and performing constantly, a chameleon changing colors with her surroundings?

Toward the end, *The Stunt Man* coyly appears ready to answer all those questions, then whips the carpet out from under the young hero just as he (and the film's audience) think they finally know what has been going on. Some found that unfair and deceptive of the film-makers; others saw it as their ultimate statement, the point of *The Stunt Man* being we cannot know the answers to anything, can never fully grasp where actuality ends and movie mythology begins. Watching the film—then or now—is like wandering through a fun-

. . . then takes the plunge.

house, bumping into endless mirrors that cast false reflections. *The Stunt Man* is as angering as it is irresistible, an endless series of puzzles to which there are no easy or simple solutions, as much a charming con as a genuine work of art.

Excalibur

AN ORION PICTURES RELEASE THROUGH WARNER BROS.   1981

CREDITS:

Executive producers, Edgar F. Gross and Robert A. Eisenstein; produced and directed by John Boorman; written by Rospo Pallenberg and John Boorman, adapted from Sir Thomas Malory's *Le Morte d' Arthur*; photography, Alex Thomson; editor, John Merritt; Running time, 140 min.; Rating: R.

CAST:

Arthur (Nigel Terry); *Morgana* (Helen Mirren); *Lancelot* (Nicholas Clay); *Guinevere* (Cherie Lunghi); *Perceval* (Paul Geoffrey); *Merlin* (Nicol Williamson); *Mordred* (Robert Addie); *Uther* (Gabriel Byrne); *Igrayne* (Matrine Boorman); *Gawain* (Liam Neeson); *Cornwall* (Corin Redgrave); *Uryens* (Keith Buckley)

If westerns and war films had become rarities during the Seventies, the Arthurian romance was literally gone if not forgotten by film fans. President Reagan's best friend, Robert Taylor, starred in 1953's *Knights of the Round Table*, and Cornel Wilde made *Lancelot and Guinevere* during the Kennedy administration a decade later; otherwise the tale had not been told by Hollywood filmmakers other than as a musical. Younger Americans had experienced only Monty Python's mid-Seventies spoof of the search for the Holy Grail. But if that decade had been marked by parodies of old Hollywood clichés (*Blazing Saddles, Young Frankenstein*), the Eighties was the age of serious revivals, so once more knights of old rode out on quests, though in a considerably scruffier, grimier fashion than had been possible amid the MGM gloss.

Whereas the Fifties MGM film borrowed its romantic style from Tennyson's lyrical *Idylls of the King*, filmmaker John Boorman reached back to the darker, more complex vision of Sir Thomas Malory, whose anguished collection of tales featured a tone halfway between fairy tale and nightmare. *Excalibur* traces the Arthurian legend from the dark ages before the birth of the future king through to his ascension to the throne and the

EXCALIBUR: Kissing the shining blade of Excalibur, Sir Lancelot (Nicholas Clay) swears undying allegiance to his liege lord, King Arthur (Nigel Terry); John Boorman's epic was the first serious, non-musical version of the story to play American commercial theaters in almost three decades.

EXCALIBUR: Beautiful Guinevere (Cherie Lunghi) ignores her husband/King and considers the handsome newcomer Lancelot; *Excalibur* provided a more lustful and honest, less sentimentalized version of the story than earlier filmmakers had dared present.

destruction of his magical Camelot, as well as the black period following his death. Boorman related the story in a richly detailed visualization that perfectly depicted the rugged, raunchy quality of Britain's prehistory, so the audience witnessed a legend forged in lust and lies, a romance marred by incest and adultery, and an unsentimentalized image of violence. Boorman's movie featured the look of a dream dimly remembered, a myth—part pagan, part Christian—captured on celluloid.

Essentially, he redeemed the Arthur story from the stereotypes of previous papier-maché movie styles and, in so doing, also redeemed his career. The once-promising young director (*Point Blank*, *Deliverance*) had floundered badly (*Zardoz*, *The Heretic: Exorcist II*). His *Excalibur* was a rich, dazzling film—its imagery falling somewhere between the iconography of Ingmar Bergman and the excesses of Ken Russell. Boorman took liberties with the legend—combining the sword in the stone with the sword offered by the lady in the lake to avoid audience confusion—but such changes improve rather than oversimplify the narrative line.

In terms of the costumes, Boorman struck a middle ground between romanticism and history. He took the risk of disappointing audiences by refusing to dress Merlin (Nicol Williamson) in the traditional sorcerer's cloak with star designs and a tall, pointed hat—a tenth-century imposition on the fifth-century character; how-

EXCALIBUR: Firm in the knowledge that her evil teachings have taken root, Arthur's half-sister, the enchantress Morgana (Helen Mirren, left), sends forth their incestuous-bastard son, Mordred (Robert Addie), to slay his father and claim the throne.

ever, he could not resist the temptation to bedeck knights in the opulent armor we traditionally associate with them, though such helmets and breastplates did not exist in England until several centuries later. The result is a splendid combination of authenticity and anachronism, suggesting that tradition never can and perhaps never should be entirely eliminated, even in a revisionist work.

Still, the idea of a film about Arthur receiving an R rating came as a shock to anyone raised on polite treatments like *Camelot*. When Arthur's father, Uther Pendragon, sports with another man's wife while still wearing his full suit of armor, the image provoked laughter and thought: Was the scene played straight but coming off as ridiculous, or was it meant to be tongue-in-cheek? Boorman remained coy in his refusal to offer an easy answer. The first third was filled with a sense of humor that bordered on burlesque of the genre conventions, as Merlin punctured the epic vision with his silver-tongued one-liners. But that humor evaporated as the film, depicting the lust (rather than, as in earlier films, love) between Arthur's best friend Lancelot and his wife Guenevere, turned ever bleaker.

The portrayal of Merlin was clearly influenced by Alec Guinness as Obe Won Kenobi, while the last-

EXCALIBUR: In the final hour, Sir Perceval (Paul Geoffrey, left) and Arthur do battle with Mordred and his invading army; as a Han Solo-ish Lancelot rides to the rescue, the film left Sir Thomas Malory's *Le Morte d'Arthur* behind and embraced the action-epic conventions of George Lucas' *Star Wars*.

minute return of Lancelot to help Arthur fight his illegitimate son Mordred, born of his union with his half sister Morgana, resembled Han Solo showing up to defeat the Death Star. In *Star Wars*, George Lucas had fashioned a compendium of all the elements of adventure and romance that had developed in our culture, giving them what may be their ultimate expression in cinematic art. Boorman here suggested that Lucas's film was not a dead-end apotheosis, leaving little room for a follow-up. Reaching back to the original adventure-romance, Boorman lent it a post-*Star Wars* lease on life, proving there is no tale quite like the original.

Raiders of the Lost Ark

A PARAMOUNT PICTURE OF A LUCASFILM PRODUCTION   1981

RAIDERS OF THE LOST ARK: Among the key supporting characters in the Indy series were Denholm Elliott as museum curator Marcus Brody . . .

CREDITS:

Executive producers, George Lucas and Howard Kazanjian; produced by Frank Marshall; directed by Steven Spielberg; screenplay by Lawrence Kasdan, from a story by Philip Kaufman and George Lucas; photography, Douglas Slocombe; editor, Michael Kahn; Running time, 115 min.; Rating: PG.

CAST:

Indiana Jones (Harrison Ford); *Marion* (Karen Allen); *Dietrich* (Wolf Kahler); *Brody* (Denholm Elliott); *Belloq* (Paul Freeman); *Toht* (Ronald Lacey); *Sallah* (John Rhys-Davies); *Gobler* (Anthony Higgins); *Satipo* (Alfred Molina); *Col. Musgrove* (Don Fellows).

. . . and John Rhys-Davies as Indy's comical sidekick Sallah.

If a single style emerged during the early Eighties, it was a tendency by the new wave of young (mostly film-school-educated) moviemakers then busily taking over Hollywood to revive the beloved genres which had flourished up until 1970, then all but disappeared during that uncertain, transitional decade, offering fascinating combinations of revival and parody, clichés from classic films done over with a glib contemporary sensibility. In 1981, several of the most important new filmmakers— George Lucas (*Star Wars*), Lawrence Kasdan (*Body Heat*) and Steven Spielberg (*E.T.*)—conspired to create an apotheosis of one more bygone film form, the movie serials of the Thirties and Forties.

Their stalwart hero, Indiana Jones (Harrison Ford), emerged as a man both of thought and of action, an archaeology professor who sets off on grand adventures sporting his signature brown leather flight jacket and snappy fedora. While doing the government's bidding by searching for the legendary lost ark of the covenant, he runs into Marion Ravenwood (Karen Allen), a former girlfriend now running a gin joint in Nepal. Second-cousin to a Howard Hawks heroine, she's able to trade tough talk with Indy, then either punch or kiss his face, depending on her mood at the moment. With the help of friends like the genial but unsavory Sallah (John Rhys-

Davies) and the dotty genius Brody (Denholm Elliott), he must locate the ark before the Nazis do, for he cannot allow Hitler's minions to get hold of an object reported to confer magical powers on its possessor. The film carries its hero from the Andes to Egypt, as—in true cliff-hanger fashion—Indy finds himself in a precarious do-or-die situation (dropped down into an ancient tombful of asps, or pursuing on horseback a German truck caravan) every ten to twelve minutes. Youngsters in the audience loved it because they'd never seen anything like *Raiders* before; older viewers were equally engaged as echoes were stirred of long-ago movie matinees.

An A movie that immortalized the bygone joys of B programmers, *Raiders* featured an ingenious homage to the kinds of films that had long ago been shot quickly and cheaply, on studio backlots with location footage generally lifted from more prestigious pictures. Now all those old action-adventure bits (the stalwart hero pursued by an immense rolling rock, managing to escape only to have the chase taken up by a tribe of cannibals) were shot on the grand scale that, in their minds, awestruck child-viewers had long ago believed they actually saw. Catching such serials again later in life is always a disappointment, because as grown-ups we notice all the seams. Spielberg (the movie industry's Peter Pan, somehow maintaining his sense of childlike wonder even as an adult) and company here realized on screen what an entire previous generation had created in their imaginations, devising a film that distilled the essence of all those great adventure-movie memories into a single two-hour epic, while recreating the chases, the shoot-outs and the suspense sequences with the kind

... and continuing the cliffhanger action that audiences found so appealing.

RAIDERS OF THE LOST ARK: Talented, attractive and sadly under-used by moviemakers, Karen Allen made a most admirable heroine in the first Indy adventure, reminding movie lovers of the strong willed women who had inhabited the films of Howard Hawks.

of rich detail everyone has always liked to believe was there in the originals.

Some critics carped that, as the era of Spielberg, the Eighties emerged as a period in which technical accomplishment superseded substance; that, with such meticulous attention paid to perfecting the plots of old potboilers, we'd entered a decade in which films were as stylish as they were empty. While essentially correct, they missed the point: the importance of such films as a reflection of the political tenor of these times. That the Spielberg era of popular movies coincided with the Reagan era in politics was hardly fortuitous. In electing Reagan, the public had picked a leader who still looked, acted and spoke not like a normal professional politician of either party but as a simple, forthright man of assertive deed and direct, honest thought, an old-fashioned movie fantasy-hero heading up the country, pulling the nation away from complexity and cynicism toward a brighter, more positive view of itself. Essentially, Indiana Jones was Reagan; Reagan was Indiana Jones. The subject of the films Spielberg and his colleagues created was the incredible lure of the grand old movies; in a decade when that lure had proven so intense that the public turned it into a political point of view, these movies must be seen as substantial indeed: cinematic reflections of what was going on nationwide, the purposeful blurring, blending, and confusing of contemporary reality with classic Hollywood images. No one did it better than Spielberg, and nowhere did he do it better than in *Raiders*.

Arthur

AN ORION RELEASE THROUGH WARNER BROS. 1981

CREDITS:

Executive producer, Charles H. Joffe; produced by Robert Greenhut; written and directed by Steve Gordon; photography, Fred Schuler; editor, Susan E. Morse; Running time, 96 min.; Rating: PG.

CAST:

Arthur Bach (Dudley Moore); *Linda Marolla* (Liza Minnelli); *Hobson* (John Gielgud); *Martha Bach* (Geraldine Fitzgerald); *Susan Johnson* (Jill Eikenberry); *Burt Johnson* (Stephen Elliott); *Bitterman* (Ted Ross); *Ralph Marolla* (Barney Martin); *Stanford Bach* (Thomas Barbour); *Gloria* (Anne De Salvo); *Aunt Pearl* (Justin Johnson).

In the summer of 1981, moviegoers made a surprise success out of *Arthur*, a screwball comedy of the sort Mr. Reagan had starred in when he did *Voice of the Turtle*. Neatly juggling elements from Frank Capra's *It Happened One Night* (the unlikely romance between rich and poor lovers), Gregory LaCava's *My Man Godfrey* (the butler as conscience of the rich), and Leo McCarey's *The Awful Truth* (mismatched couples planning marriage), writer turned first-time director Steve Gordon (whose career was cut short by an untimely death) provided the perfect contemporary variation on these classic comedy themes.

A fairy tale for adults, the story concerned irresponsible playboy Arthur Bach (Dudley Moore), a grown-up who looks and acts like a child. A multimillionaire playing with elaborate train sets and street prostitutes, Arthur's good life is a constant merry-go-round of desperate time-killing fun and demonstrative social drinking, until his meddling grandmother (Geraldine Fitzgerald) insists that to receive his $750 million inheritance, Arthur must wed a country-club debutante (Jill Eikenberry) with a retired-gangster father (Stephen Elliott). He'd probably do as told except that he happens across a scatterbrain named Linda Marolla (Liza Min-

ARTHUR: Arthur Bach and his love, Queens waitress—and sometimes shoplifter—Linda (Liza Minnelli).

ARTHUR: In addition to Linda, Arthur has only one totally trustworthy friend: his ever loyal butler (Sir John Gielgud, in his Oscar-winning role as Best Supporting Actor).

nelli), sometime shoplifter, sometime waitress, sometime actress. She's poor, simple, and to Arthur, utterly irresistible.

The timeworn, cliché-ridden plot was given a freshness thanks to the modern New York City settings, including a memorable opening in which Bitterman (Ted Ross), Arthur's long-suffering chauffeur, waits patiently while the drunken Arthur negotiates with an extremely up-to-date Times Square hooker. Character actress Anne De Salvo managed to make her small role into something quite striking, embodying the stereotype but reaching far beyond it. The entire supporting cast was equally superb, though the greatest kudos were reserved for Sir John Gielgud (who won a Best Supporting Actor Oscar) as the caustic butler, providing a world-weary voice of sanity above the din of social and economic accommodation.

But this was Dudley Moore's movie from start to finish. Following swiftly on his first major lead in Blake Edwards' "*10*" the diminutive Moore (previously a first-rate scene-stealer himself) managed to attain the status of unlikely superstar. Unfortunately, he then tarnished his image by appearing in some of the most embarrassing junk made during the decade: *Best Defense, Holy Moses!, Lovesick,* and *Santa Claus—The Movie.* Thus *Arthur*, which should have been the start of a memorable comedy career, remains his only gem. In it we watch the title character's "moral education"; his worldliness and naïveté are overcome when a very special person breaks through the hero's shield of humor and his shelter of high

society, forcing him to totally commit for the first time in his life. In the screenplay, filmmaker Gordon—a veteran of upscale TV comedies like *The Dick Van Dyke Show* and *Barney Miller*— managed to overcome the

Fort Apache—The Bronx

A 20TH CENTURY-FOX RELEASE   1981

CREDITS:

Executive producer, David Susskind; produced by Martin Richards and Tom Fiorello; directed by Daniel Petrie; written by Heywood Gould; photography, John Alcott; editor, Rita Roland; Running time, 125 min.; Rating: R.

CAST:

Murphy (Paul Newman); *Connolly* (Edward Asner); *Corelli* (Ken Wahl); *Morgan* (Daniel Aiello); *Isabella* (Rachel Ticotin); *Charlotte* (Pam Grier); *Jumper* (Tito Govo); *Jose* (Jaime Tirelli); *Hernando* (Miguel Pinero); *Connolly's Fiancée* (Kathleen Beller).

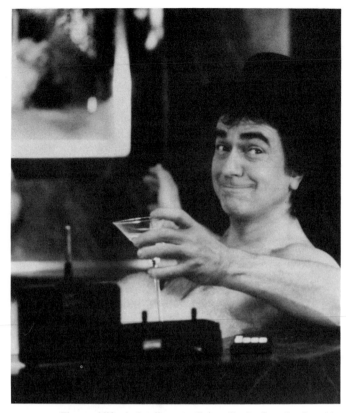

ARTHUR: The good life: Arthur lives out all the collective fantasies shared by Americans in the era of greed.

danger that Arthur would degenerate into a one-joke character, slowly but surely allowing us to see a greater emotional depth than the hysterical opening would have suggested. The film's only flaw: Jill Eikenberry's natural and immediate onscreen charm (later used to such fine effect in TV's *L.A. Law*) caused Susan to appear more sympathetic than she should; when Arthur rejects her, it seems less a moral victory for him (as it might had Morgan Fairchild been cast as a blonde bitch) than a cruel humiliation of what appears to be a nice girl.

The main difference between *Arthur* and the similar screwball comedies of the Thirties was that they had presented poverty as noble, whereas *Arthur*—true to the tenor of the Reagan era—saw it as something to be escaped from, implying no criticism of wealth. Yet at decade's end, as the shared values of the period began to pass, *Arthur* looked hopelessly dated. His casual acquaintanceship with hookers no longer seemed cute once AIDS became a mainstream fear; his constant drunkenness, taken at face value in 1981, did not appear laughable when the public became aware of the horrors of addiction. No wonder, then, that when a sudden sequel was finally thrown together in the summer of 1988, it swiftly died at the box office, a rarity in the age of sequelmania.

What a bitter irony that a movie starring Paul Newman was, on its initial release, loudly denounced as racist. More than any other American movie star, Newman over the years put his career on the line for the sake of civil rights causes. In fact, his involvement with this controversial project did not happen in spite of his social consciousness, but because of his anxieties over urban blight, the escalating crime rate and corresponding drug problem, the impact of all that on both the minority youth trapped in inner cities and the old-fashioned cops saddled with the impossible job of maintaining some semblance of order in a situation which, in the Eighties, had gone completely out of control. "It's a national problem," Newman told this author then, "and there's a South Bronx in every major city. We're hoping that by showing the conditions as they actually exist, audiences will be shocked and demand action to have those conditions improved." Instead, it sparked numerous minority rights organizations to claim the film maligned the people of the South Bronx by portraying only the criminal element, suggesting to the American mass audience that only lowlifes populated the area.

All of which raises uneasy questions about the relationship between the film experience and external reality. Like the Heywood Gould novel of the same name, *Fort Apache* was based closely on the real-life experiences of Tom Mulhearn and Pete Tessitore, two police officers who survived their assignment to the beleaguered 41st Precinct—where cops often complained of feeling like cavalrymen isolated in hostile territory (hence, the precinct's nickname)—by adopting an uncomfortably humorous approach: donning funny wigs to look less menacing, serenading the area's plentiful hookers, dancing rather than walking into apartment houses to break up family arguments. Gradually, they won begrudging acceptance as a pair of tolerable outsiders. The book and subsequent film perfectly captured *their* truth of the South Bronx, the narrow but tangible and significant reality of two white policemen—one middle-aged and Irish, one young and Italian—who, because of the profession that brought them there, come in contact with only one, unsavory, element.

The unique problem posed by film as a storytelling form is that the medium of photography blurs any distinction between objective and subjective reality. Since veteran filmmaker Daniel Petrie shot *Fort Apache* on location, this excellently acted, convincingly written, flawlessly directed movie appeared less a specific, self-contained story (as was the case with the book) than a generalized documentary on life in this area, for audiences accept what they see in such a convincing film not as an interpretation of reality, but as reality itself.

As Mulhearn (here called "Murphy"), Newman delivered what was quite possibly the best performance of his career, creating a well-rounded and fully resonant human being. Though he was passed over once again at Oscar time (and would also fail to receive the statuette for his fine work in his subsequent *Absence of Malice* and *The Verdict*), Newman eventually did win for *The Color of Money*, another excellent portrait if not quite up to his

FORT APACHE—THE BRONX: The precinct commander (Edward Asner) clashes with his independently minded officer, Murphy.

FORT APACHE—THE BRONX: Offscreen, Edward Asner, Ken Wahl and Paul Newman got along far better than do their characters in the film.

FORT APACHE—THE BRONX: Paul Newman as the compassionate street cop who becomes involved with a nurse (Rachel Ticotin), herself a prisoner of the tough turf.

61

finely textured work here. Also turning in first-rate performances were newcomer Ken Wahl (later to gain fame as TV's *Wiseguy*) as his streetwise young partner, Rachel Ticotin as a drug-addicted Puerto Rican nurse who becomes Newman's lover, and Ed Asner as the by-the-book captain who takes control of the precinct and—through his unswerving attitudes—turns an already aggravated situation into a full-scale state of siege.

Certainly, there was no attempt to whitewash or glorify the actions of the police in general. If anything, the movie suggested that the honest, sincere cops—like those played by Newman and Wahl—were clearly in the minority. Naturally, they are the film's heroes (though certainly not unblemished ones) whom we watch being overwhelmed by the forces of incompetence on one side and by arrogance on the other. To attack a film that attempted and achieved such a vision seems about as sensible as criticizing Upton Sinclair's *The Jungle* for failing to show the nicer side of turn-of-the-century Chicago, and concentrating instead on the horrors of the meat-packing industry.

Fort Apache, The Bronx was muckraking at its best: so ambiguous in its resolution and grimly honest despite its guarded optimism that it's difficult to comprehend how anyone—however heightened their social sensitivity—could fail to see this as anything but a harsh criticism of the neglect visited upon inner cities during the Reagan era.

The Four Seasons

A UNIVERSAL PICTURES RELEASE OF A MARTIN BREGMAN PRODUCTION   1981

CREDITS:

Executive producer, Louis A. Stoller; produced by Martin Bregman; written and directed by Alan Alda; photography, Victor J. Kemper; editor, Michael Economou; Running time, 107 min.; Rating: PG.

CAST:

Jack Burroughs (Alan Alda); *Kate Burroughs* (Carol Burnett); *Nick Callan* (Len Cariou); *Ann Callan* (Sandy Dennis); *Claudia Zimmer* (Rita Moreno); *Danny Zimmer* (Jack Weston); *Ginny Newley* (Bess Armstrong); *Beth* (Elizabeth Alda); *Lisa* (Beatrice Alda); *Room Clerk* (Robert Hitt); *Doc* (Loren James).

Even as the term "yuppie" was becoming a basic of Eighties vernacular, Alan Alda focused on their slightly elder counterparts in this lighthearted but serious-minded comedy drama about people who experience emptiness despite affluence. There were seven altogether, though we seldom saw more than six at any one time, and for good reason. Three married couples, longtime friends, enjoy spending seasonal vacations together, though they now have next to nothing in common. Then one of the guys (Len Cariou) wrecks everything, dumping his wife (Sandy Dennis) of some 20 years to marry an airline stewardess (Bess Armstrong) he's been sleeping with, and nothing can ever again be quite the same.

The two remaining wives (Carol Burnett, Rita Moreno) eye the blonde intruder's dazzling shape, wishing she weren't so damn nice so at least they could enjoy the luxury of hating her; the two ostensibly faithful husbands (Alda, Jack Weston) secretly lust after their friend's new bed partner, concealing their jealousy from their spouses—and themselves—by hypocritically criticizing him. All the while, the ever-changing but always attractive settings—an Ivy League campus town, a rented yacht, an isolated ski cabin—provide a deceptively tranquil series of contexts for the deep-rooted turbulence of the protagonists.

With *The Four Seasons*, Alda at last emerged as what he'd been striving toward for nearly a decade: the total filmmaker. TV's *M*A*S*H* star did not desert his series, but stole time to play the lead in *Same Time, Next Year*, then wrote a vehicle for himself (*The Seduction of Joe Tynan*), thereby demonstrating a major ambition tempered by admirable restraint. Perhaps that's why *The Four Seasons* (and to a lesser extent his *Sweet Liberty* later in the decade) succeeded. A more egotistical, less talented filmmaker might have used such a plot device to cast himself as the only truly sensitive character in the story; to save for himself all the best lines; to make himself out as the most attractive male in the group, turning other characters into caricatures. That's not the way Alda played it. He is not the sexy one who ends up with the beautiful young wife and is not unique among the group in feeling mild amusement about his friend's fantasy-come-true (though he does affect this attitude) but is as deeply, unconsciously disturbed by the young woman's presence as everyone else—perhaps more so.

Alda's character is conceived as the level-headed member of the group. Alda the filmmaker had the other people in his cast play to that role until the last scene, when they suddenly admit they've been responding to his self-image rather than their own conceptions of him—in effect, the entire relationship has been a sham, a convenience of civilized interplay, a game people play.

THE FOUR SEASONS: Alan Alda as Jack, who initially seems the most compassionate and sympathetic of the ensemble, though he will be seen in a very different light by picture's end.

Alda's refusal to stereotype went beyond characters. Even his title device of changing seasons in response to the Vivaldi score on the soundtrack was employed in original ways. The mellow scene in which the original six enjoy their final hours together would stereotypically take place in autumn; rather, it's set off by an effectively incongruous springtime scene. Instead of a facile symbol for the death of old feelings, the winter setting provided a unique backdrop for the rebirth of their friendships. The yippies of the Sixties had transformed into the yuppies of the Eighties; *The Four Seasons* strikingly chronicled their mid-life crises.

THE FOUR SEASONS: Old friends adjust to a new young element: from left, Jack Weston, Alan Alda, Carol Burnett, Rita Moreno, Bess Armstrong and Len Cariou.

Just as he twists all our assumptions about his own focal character, so does Alda effectively deflate our expectations about Armstrong. At first appearance as "the other woman," she seems a variation on the conventional role of blonde bimbo. But rather than the butt of jokes, Armstrong's Ginny establishes herself as a human being with feelings as complex as everyone else's. Initial expectations have been reversed: If Alda's character has come to look self-important and silly, Armstrong's now appears deep and sensitive.

The others all fit neatly enough into various types, but were coaxed to give those types extra dimension. Sandy Dennis, as the deserted wife, never employed her neurotic mannerisms more satisfyingly, neither the feminist cliché of the wrongfully abandoned wife nor the chauvinist's stereotype of an obnoxious shrew. Cariou is at once a heel and a highly agreeable fellow. Pudgy Weston and ethnic Moreno make a marvelous mismatch, while Burnett—a close friend and longtime TV comrade of Alda's—seemed the perfect choice to play his wife.

THE FOUR SEASONS: Watching their old friend sport with a pretty young girl makes waves in the seemingly solid marriage of Jack and Kate (Carol Burnett).

THE FOUR SEASONS: The friends enjoy a ski trip; writer-director Alda gave this glossy, upbeat film some surprisingly dark shadings and intriguing textures.

Body Heat

A LADD COMPANY RELEASE THROUGH
WARNER BROS.   1981

CREDITS:

Produced by Fred T. Gallo; written and directed by Lawrence Kasdan; photography, Richard H. Kline; editor, Carol Littleton; Running time, 113 min.; Rating: R.

CAST:

Ned Racine (William Hurt); *Matty Walker* (Kathleen Turner); *Edmund Walker* (Richard Crenna); *Peter Lowenstein* (Ted Danson); *Oscar Grace* (J. A. Preston); *Teddy Lewis* (Mickey Rourke); *Mary Ann* (Kim Zimmer); *Stella* (Jean Hallaren); *Roz Kraft* (Lonna Saunders).

Film noir had been pretty much neglected since the Fifties; indeed, Ronald Reagan's last film—Don Siegel's 1964 version of *The Killers*—struck movie lovers as a fond farewell to the kind of postwar Mean Street melodramas kicked off by Robert Siodmak's 1946 ver-

sion of the Hemingway story: jaded knights took on impressive big city enemies, the good guys and bad drawn in subtle shades of gray, distinguishable from one another largely by the codes of conduct that the anti-heroes precariously clung to; deliciously duplicitous women, sultry, sophisticated, and dressed to kill, drawn in bold, brash strokes led the men willingly to their dooms. The Seventies, that era of feminist cinematic fantasies about decent, indomitable women under the influence and sensitive men searching to find themselves, hardly lent itself to the dark, slashing style of *noir*. But the Reagan era seemed ripe for a *noir* comeback, and Lawrence Kasdan's *Body Heat* was the film.

Fashioned as an homage to the greatest of *noir* writers, James M. Cain—and borrowing heavily from his best novels, *Double Indemnity* and *The Postman Always Rings Twice,* for plot elements—*Body Heat* took place in a never-never land. Though the story was apparently set in the present, there was something vaguely 1940-ish about the milieu and métier of every-thing onscreen, from William Hurt's hat to the affluent Florida homes cooled by old-fashioned fans rather than modern air conditioning. If politically and socially we had opted for a retrofuture, then *Body Heat* visually represented our contemporary collective consciousness by mixing and matching the Forties and the Eighties until the two blurred into a single strange vision.

Ned Racine (William Hurt), a shady lawyer, shuffles from one sleazy case to the next. One evening, he pauses on a boardwalk, listening to a dance band playing nostalgic music from the Forties. The song isn't "You stepped out of a dream...," but it might just as well be, for a remarkably beautiful woman, Matty Walker (Kathleen Turner), leaves the concert and brushes by Ned. It's as if she's stepped out of the past; shortly, Ned's life will begin to resemble past pictures about weak men drawn into dangerous and deadly liaisons by similar double-dealing dames. For her, sex is like a drug; shortly after he becomes hooked on Matty ("You're not too smart," she confides to him in the film's most oft-quoted line, "I like that in a man!"), she has him plotting to kill her disagreeable husband (Richard Crenna), employing a gungy hood (Mickey Rourke) while scrutinized by his friend, a tap-dancing D.A. (Ted Danson).

At about the same time *Body Heat* was released, Bob Rafelson directed a painstaking period-piece version of *Postman*, with Jack Nicholson and Jessica Lange. Sur-prisingly, that major undertaking fizzled, while steamy *Body Heat*—at first seeming a minor-league entry—scored heavily with critics and audiences. What both films had in common was an ability to update the sexuality of the old Cain stories, presenting graphically what previously could only be suggested on screen.

64

BODY HEAT: In the grand tradition of *film noir*, amoral Ned Racine (William Hurt) meets an irresistible shady lady, Matty Walker (Kathleen Turner) . . .

. . . and quickly becomes embroiled first in romance, then a plot to kill her husband.

(When Hurt and Turner, then virtual newcomers, presented an Oscar in the spring of 1982, it was ironically for "Best Film Scoring," as their *Body Heat* sex scenes had stretched the limits of the R rating.) Rafelson, striving for a precise recreation of the past, missed the forest for the trees, whereas Kasdan wisely chose to suggest and imply the Forties feel through an attention to tone, making for a less labored film that perfectly caught the true spirit of its time and past time. It also introduced a bevy of young stars who would make their presences felt throughout the Eighties. More important, it presented Kasdan as a significant filmmaker for his era; throughout the decade, he would simultaneously revive and restructure for the Reagan era the kinds of films Reagan once starred in, ranging from sophisticated screwball (*Continental Divide*) to the epic western (*Silverado*).

True to the times in which the film was made, the characters were motivated mostly by greed of the basest order. Indeed, if anything makes the calculating Ned Racine sympathetic enough to be a movie hero, it's the fact that he and he alone is able to put lust above avarice. That may not be much of a distinction, but at least he's a slave of passion, a twisted romantic doing the dirty

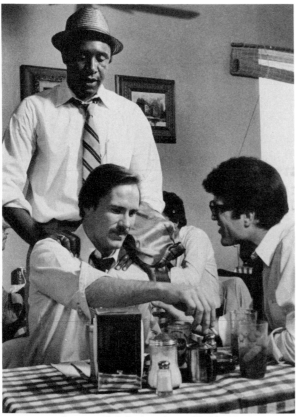

BODY HEAT: Attorney Ned Racine chats with his friend, the tap-dancing D.A. (Ted Danson) while Detective Oscar Grace (J. A. Preston) looks on.

BODY HEAT: Like Barbara Stanwyck, Lisabeth Scott, and so many other leading ladies in the classic *noirs* of the late Forties, Kathleen Turner played Matty as deliciously duplicitous: a respectable lady by daytime, a provocative manipulator at night.

deeds for the sake of a woman he loves (and, to a degree, hates) desperately, rather than for the accumulation of property and wealth at the root of everyone else's actions. The style and plot may be from the past; the implied social comment was aimed squarely at the present.

Atlantic City
A PARAMOUNT PICTURES RELEASE   1981

CREDITS:

Produced by Denis Heroux and Gabriel Boustani; directed by Louis Malle; written by John Guare; photography, Richard Ciuplea; editor, Suzanne Baron; Running time, 104 min.; Rating: R.

CAST:

Lou (Burt Lancaster); *Sally* (Susan Sarandon); *Grace* (Kate Reid); *Chrissie* (Hollis McLaren); *Dave* (Robert Joy); *Joe* (Michel Piccoli); *Himself* (Robert Goulet); *Alfie* (Al Waxman); *Buddy* (Sean Sullivan); *Vinnie* (Angus MacInnes); *Waiter* (Wallace Shawn); *Felix* (Moses Znaimer).

Most of the Reagan-inspired nostalgic films were simple, superficial, and sentimental in their treatment of the collective mythologized past and our 1980s need to reclaim it. One of the memorable exceptions was *Atlantic City*, a brilliant film set in such a subtle key, told in such a straightforward, uncluttered style, that its understated eloquence was mistaken for admirable but unremarkable craftsmanship. But in the integrity with which filmmaker Louis Malle told playwright John (*House of Blue Leaves*) Guare's essentially two-character drama, as well as the degree of depth with which he studied their psyches and the sociological phenomenom around them, he came up with a film that grows with each subsequent viewing, rating in retrospect as one of the unheralded gems of the Eighties. Understandably, the most perceptive movie made about America as a place and system of values was a Canadian-French co-production, for the Hollywood studios were not at this time inclined toward such soul searching and honest revelation.

The movie is set shortly after the legalization of gambling in the resort town of the title. That causes a state of transition and turmoil, as the grand old buildings near the boardwalk are ruthlessly ripped down to make

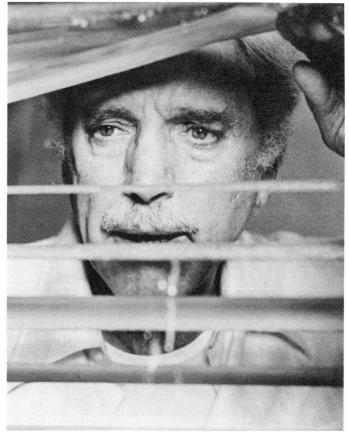

ATLANTIC CITY: Susan Sarandon as Sally, the tragic woman who bathes in lemon juice every night to wash away the smell of fish while dreaming of a far more romantic life-style.

ATLANTIC CITY: Burt Lancaster as the equally deluded Lou, once a small-time hoodlum who now believes he was a great gangland figure in the old days, and spends his time as a voyeur, peeking at Sally across the way.

ATLANTIC CITY: As a bizarre web of circumstances draw Lou and Sally together, each momentarily allows the other to live out his/her dream of a better life.

ATLANTIC CITY: Susan Sarandon and Burt Lancaster relax on the set; though the film was seen by far too few people to win the Oscars, there were no better screen performances by an actress or actor throughout the Eighties.

room for expensive chintzy casinos, the area inhabited by old-timers from the glorious past and new people arriving to make a fast buck. The man who represents the past is Lou (Burt Lancaster), who a half century earlier was in league with key organized crime figures. They may have been a sleazy bunch, but now that Lou is the last survivor, they've become, at least in his mind, legendary personages of a passing dream. Even today, Lou dresses nattily, for while his suits are worn, they are always neatly pressed. But Lou's present life has little to offer. The only work he can get is running numbers in the inner city; afterward he returns to Grace (Kate Reid), a bedridden harridan Lou gently cares for. No matter what Grace looks and sounds like now, for he prefers to remember how and why he fell in love: Grace came to Atlantic City to compete in a Betty Grable lookalike contest. As with so many other heroes of Eighties movies, Lou fell in love with what appeared to be a vision from the movies come suddenly to life. Indeed, fantasy is basic to Lou, who likes to tell everyone he's a former mob hit man, when he was only a glorified messenger boy. He's told his lie so often he himself believes it. Meanwhile, the apartment house where he lives—just off the boardwalk he loves—is marked for demolition. Representing the present is Sally (Susan Sarandon), who spends her nights shucking clams in a restaurant, then returns to her shabby apartment where she methodically washes away the smell with lemons (with Lou watching like a Peeping Tom from across the way) before running off to study for a career as a casino employee. If to Lou Atlantic City represents a shell of a more glorious past that may never have existed, to Sally it's the skeleton of a fabulous future that will never happen. She too has unrealistic fantasies, planning on someday being the first female croupier in Monte Carlo.

Lou and Sally meet owing to the arrival of Chrissie (Hollis McLaren), Sally's anachronistically hippie-ish sister; like everyone else in the film, she is out of time. Chrissie shows up at Sally's apartment accompanied by Dave (Robert Joy), technically Sally's husband, though he has run off with Chrissie and gotten her pregnant. He's carrying a load of cocaine which he stole from the mob in Philadelphia, is naïve enough to think he can simply sell it to mobsters operating near the boardwalk. Sally darts back and forth between the sophistication of the skills she's learning and the sleaziness of her surroundings. When Philadephia mobsters show up, only Lou can protect Sally, as the sad old voyeur fleetingly becomes the young woman's protector and lover. She will betray him, at the very end, for she is the modern self-interested character, so greed wins out over loyalty; he will accept that, for she has already allowed him to redeem himself and, for one moment, enjoy the romantic

incarnation of having his favorite fantasy—the movie in his mind—momentarily become real. For she has allowed him to briefly be (rather than merely pretend to be) the heroic tough guy-lover, the *film noir* fantasy man he's always imagined himself as. Though Lancaster and Sarandon were nominated for Oscars, neither won, in large part because the film had not been a moneymaker. Critically speaking, though, there were no finer performances delivered during the Eighties than the ones they offered here.

The Road Warrior

A WARNER BROS. RELEASE OF A KENNEDY MILLER ENTERTAINMENT PRODUCTION   1981

CREDITS

Produced by Bryon Kennedy; directed by George Miller; written by Terry Hayes, Dean Semler, and George Miller; photography, Dean Semler; editors, David Stilvern, Tim Wellburn and Michael Chirgwin; Running Time, 94 min.; Rating: Not rated on initial American release.

CAST:

Max Rodeatansky (Mel Gibson); *Gyro Captain* (Bruce Spence); *Wez* (Vernon Welles); *Feral Kid* (Emily Minty); *Warrior Woman* (Virginia Hey); *Big Rebecca* (Moira Claux); *Pappagallo* (Mike Preston); *Humungous* (Kjell Nilsson).

Explaining why the Australian film industry mushroomed in the late Seventies and early Eighties is as difficult as explaining why movies flourished in the depression-scarred Italy of the post-World War II era. There is, simply, no formula: Social forces and economic factors have much to do with it, but then again so does flat-out luck, the right people happening to be around at the right moment, instinctively sensing how to make the right films. Yet even as other countries once renowned for their movie output experienced a decline, the Australians—previously known for koalas and kangaroos—caused the world to take note of not only the quality but also the diversity of their output. Their films ran the gamut from feminist politics (*The Getting of Wisdom*) to antiwar melodrama (*Gallipoli*) to subtle psychological shocker (*Picnic at Hanging Rock*) to

ROAD WARRIOR: The Humungous (Kjell Nilsson) is about to unleash his best warrior Wez (Vernon Wells), as the marauding horde prepares an all-out attack on the Wasteland's oil refinery compound.

ROAD WARRIOR: An exercise in modern mythmaking: Max (Mel Gibson) and his trusted companion Dog wander through a barren and lawless land destroyed by warring industrial nations.

courtroom melodrama (*Breaker Morant*). Then, with *Mad Max*, the Aussies added another dimension to their ever-expanding range by proving they could turn out an adventure fantasy with as much action and angst as those cult classics produced by Roger Corman for American-International during the late Fifties and early Sixties.

Technically speaking, the film's actual title was *Mad Max 2, The Road Warrior*, a sequel of sorts to 1979's relatively inexpensive but genuinely exciting *Mad Max*, turned out as an offbeat experiment that paid off in more ways than one. It earned more than $100 million in box-office receipts and received widespread critical acclaim,

ROAD WARRIOR: Max joins forces with the small band of survivors of an eventual World War to defend an oil refinery under seige from the punkers who plunder the land for gasoline.

ROAD WARRIOR: Wez fights for the control of the precious oil.

including the Jury Prize of the Australian Film Institute and listing as one of *Time* magazine's 10 top films of the year. *Mad Max* introduced American-born, Australian-bred actor Mel Gibson as an angry avenger of the post-Apocalypse future, stalking the scum who rule the roads, exacting a violent vengeance for their savagery. A marvel of sorts, *Max* proved a surefire shoot-'em-up could be fashioned from a plentiful imagination and a shoestring budget. But *The Road Warrior* presented more than a second helping of the same, stretching beyond the first film's limited ambitions, offering audiences a central character who was to the Eighties what Clint Eastwood's "Man With No Name" and Tom Laughlin's "Billy Jack" had been to the Sixties and Seventies—a hero for the times, larger than life and existential in origin.

Though *The Road Warrior* was set in some unidentified future period, a voice-over narration from an age beyond even that introduces Max: the man with no past or future; the survivor with no interest beyond his own immediate safety yet finding himself drawn into a commitment to the questionable society around him; the tight-lipped, always ingenious adventurer. In place of Clint Eastwood's serape, floppy hat and mule, Mel Gibson wore a battered black leather jacket and leg brace, carried a V-8 Interceptor. Like John Wayne in *Hondo*, he was accompanied by a mangy dog, at once fiercely independent from and yet loyal to its master. Like Toshiro Mifune in *Yojimbo*, Gibson wanders alone into a scarred landscape where two fierce groups mo-

mentarily halt their battle to try and decimate him instead. Max is as closely related to the American cowboy as to the Japanese samurai, yet a totally unique variation on the theme they were earlier incarnations of: a new, valid, different example of what C. J. Jung delineated as one of those recurring heroes who unaccountably pop up in the mythologies of different cultures, the reluctant champion of an unworthy society.

Here, that society is a gasoline compound where scattered survivors of a ruined world cluster together to defend their last stashes of "black fuel." Across the wasted horizon roars a mechanized Mongol horde, bikers spotting punk hairdos. The sensibility in *The Road Warriors* is at once futuristic and feudal, the style nonstop action. This is an epic of blood lust, but as in the best of the old American B features, it rates as exploitation raised to the level of an art form. Though there were probably fewer than 50 lines of dialogue in the film, most of them less than earthshattering ("Max, I had you wrong," the beautiful Amazon warrior-woman admits, "and I'm sorry!"), this still amounted to a casebook study of editing for total effectiveness, as well as consummate pictorial composition.

More than that, the film boasted the presence of Mel Gibson. Squint-eyed, cynical, strangely remote and totally charismatic, he created a character not beyond hope of conversion to the cause of saving the very same characters who were once ready to kill him. Max was more than just a case of solid acting. He represents an exercise in modern mythmaking.

Reds

A PARAMOUNT PICTURE   1981

CREDITS:

Produced and directed by Warren Beatty; written by Warren Beatty and Trevor Griffiths; photography, Vittorio Storaro; editors, Dede Allen and Craig McKay; Running time, 196 min.; Rating: PG.

CAST:

John Reed (Warren Beatty); *Louise Bryant* (Diane Keaton); *Max Eastman* (Edward Herrmann); *Grigory Zinoviev* (Jerzy Kosinski); *Eugene O'Neill* (Jack Nicholson); *Louis Fraina* (Paul Sorvino); *Emma Goldman* (Maureen Stapleton); *Paul Trullinger* (Nicolas Coster); *Mrs. Partlow* (Bessie Love); *Van Wherry* (Gene Hackman); *Big Bill Haywood* (Dolph Sweet); *Speaker at Liberal Club* (M. Emmet Walsh).

That a movie called *Reds* could be released at a time when the nation's leading red-baiter of the past quarter century had just reached the White House seems, at first, inconceivable. On closer scrutiny, however, *Reds* was not a celebration of radicalism in Russia but a criticism of it and, by implication, a study of how the idealism of America's own late-1960s radicals had been crushed by their experiences with contemporary realpolitic.

Reds told the story of Jack Reed, real-life journalist turned activist who, as a highly born Harvard grad, became a Greenwich Village socialist during the mid-1910s. As a writer, Reed proved a lesser talent than such coffee-klatsch colleagues as Emma Goldman (Maureen Stapleton, winning the Oscar for Best Supporting Actress) and Eugene O'Neill (Jack Nicholson), yet Reed earned his footnote in history by following Trotsky's advice, ceasing to be an observer of the Russian Revolution, while covering it as a journalist, instead becoming the most important American participant in that world-shattering event. Along the way, he found time to marry Louise Bryant, a neurotic dropout from the bourgoise lifestyle who metamorphized—partly through Reed's influence, partly in spite of it—into one of the most remarkable women of her time.

At its heart, *Reds* was the story of these star-crossed lovers. Some cynics complained Jack and Louise were not nearly as attractive and appealing as Warren Beatty and Diane Keaton made them appear, their actual story never quite such a soap opera. In particular, critics sneered at one shot of Louise, crawling on skis across a

REDS: Though *Reds* sounded like an ill-timed project for the conservative Eighties, it in fact did not aggrandize the Russian Revolution but chronicled the gradual disenchantment of John Reid (Warren Beatty) with Communism.

REDS: After a long separation, the lovers John (Warren Beatty) and Louise (Diane Keaton) are reunited, as a history lesson is inflated into a Hollywood romance.

blizzard landscape to rejoin her lover, claiming it passed beyond pathos into sentimental cliché. In fact, though, *Reds* illustrated the conflict between commitment to a personal love as compared to commitment to a political philosophy, making that dichotomy the film's center. To convey the complex period, ancient witnesses were interviewed, their nobly wrinkled faces set against stark black backgrounds: What an open, articulate Adela Rogers St. John explains, a stiff, ceremonious George Jessel quickly contradicts. This 3¼-hour film broke down into two self-contained acts: in the first, *Reds* shares its hero's naïve acceptance of the Russian Revolution at face value, as the sights and sounds of 1917's *Ten Days That Shook the World* (the title of Reed's eventual book on the subject) build into a panorama of excitement and majesty. In the second, the sweetness of a seemingly successful social reform movement turns sour as corrupt and lazy bureaucrats take over, creating a tyranny every bit as bad as the czar's. Reed, the archetypal romantic, is destroyed when his dream turns to ashes; Bryant, the eternal realist, survives. (Another view of Reed's life was offered around the same time in an Italian epic starring Franco Nero.)

Warren Beatty devoted five years of his life to the project, and won the Academy Award as Best Director; he would make only one other movie during the decade, the infamous *Ishtar.* While it's possible to nibble around the edges, finding minor flaws, Reds was a cinematic

REDS: Jack Nicholson as Eugene O'Neill, the cynical writer who interferes with the loving relationship of John and Louise.

Jack Reed watched in disbelief as his vision of a people's republic turned into a nightmare of repressive dictatorship; Warren Beatty watched in similar disbelief as the seemingly liberated love children became neo-conformists. Both were shattered by what they saw. The difference: Reed lost the will to live, whereas Beatty was moved to fashion a great motion picture. Still, in telling Reed's story, he also told us his own.

REDS: Re-interpreting the past for the present, Diane Keaton played Louise as a modern Eighties post-feminist woman in embryo, insisting on equality but walking through blizzards to be reunited with her man.

feast with many satisfying courses: romantic comedy, heart-wrenching melodrama, costume picture, large-scale spectacle, history lesson, parable for the present. The conflict between Reed and O'Neill over Bryant featured an extra edge of emotion owing to the real-life contest between the two actors for the attentions of the actress. Disguised as a period piece, *Reds* offered a commentary on more recent and immediate developments. The transition period of the late 1910s and early Twenties served as an objective correlative for the late Sixties and early Seventies. Both eras were marked by unpopular wars that caused young people to consider social revolution. Like the 1917 storming of Russia's Winter Palace, symbol of that country's Establishment, the Sixties featured an equally stirring scene at the Democratic Convention in Chicago. Both movements began small, then spread to the mainstream; for one marvelous moment, each seemed ready to change popular values and lifestyles forever, ushering in eras of honesty and freedom. Then the bottom fell out: In the Twenties, the American Communist party broke into bitterly feuding factions, each struggling to amass power and become the New Establishment; the same thing happened with Students for a Democratic Society.

Chariots of Fire

A WARNER BROS. RELEASE OF AN ENIGMA PRODUCTION   1981

CREDITS:

Executive producer, Dodi Fayeed; produced by David Puttnam; directed by Hugh Hudson; written by Colin Welland; photography, David Watkin; editor, Terry Rawlings; Running time, 123 min.; rating: PG.

CAST:

Harold Abrahams (Ben Cross); *Eric Liddell* (Ian Charleson); *Lord Andrew Lindsay* (Nigel Havers); *Aubrey Montague* (Nicholas Farrell); *Sam Mussabini* (Ian Holm); *Master of Trinity* (Sir John Gielgud); *Master of Caius* (Lindsay Anderson); *Jennie* (Cheryl Campbell); *Sybil* (Alice Krige); *Lord Cadogan* (Patrick Magee); *Lord Birkenhead* (Nigel Davenport); *Jason Scholz* (Brad Davis); *Charles Paddock* (Dennis Christopher).

The return to clear-cut, traditional values—and a nostalgia for the bygone period in which they flourished—so basic to Ronald Reagan's presidency was also essential to Prime Minister Margaret Thatcher's vision for England; perhaps that parallel sensibility is why the British import *Chariots of Fire* became such an unexpected success here, as this quiet, slowly-paced film was quite the rage even winning an Oscar for Best Picture of the Year.

The story, based on an actual incident, concerned members of England's 1924 Olympic track team, focusing on two star runners: Harold Abrahams (Ben Cross), a Jew who feels the Olympics offer the perfect opportunity to prove he's the equal of the bluebloods, and Eric Liddell (Ian Charleson), a Scot with a profound religious orientation who runs as a means of serving God. They hail from two different worlds: Abrahams from the

CHARIOTS OF FIRE: The famed Vangelis theme song automatically comes to mind at the sight of the British runners exercising on an early-morning beach in the film's opening (and best) sequence.

exciting, glamorous demimonde of Cambridge University and its adjacent nightspots, Liddell from a quiet, provincial town. They come together first as competitors in a British match, then as teammates trying to win for England's honor as well as for each man's personal motivations.

One sensed immediately from the low-key approach that all concerned wanted to tell the tale as simply and honestly as possible. The filmmakers achieved that—yet what they achieved is at odds with what a sports film, at its most enjoyable, can do for an audience. At the final Olympic matches, the viewer experiences no edge-of-the-seat tension, much less a desire to jump up and applaud or shout. It's one thing for a film to speak softly, quite another if it whispers almost inaudibly.

Chariots lacked a true sense of drama for either of its protagonists. It was also impossible to get involved with Abrahams as a case study in anti-Semitism, for though we were told his reason for running, we never witnesed him experience bigotry firsthand. Indeed, Cambridge classmates like Lord Andrew Lindsay (Nigel Havers) accept him into their elite company; when they attend a posh London show, the prettiest showgirl (Alice Krige) falls for Abrahams. If we guessed this would lead to a scene in which he is crushed—she will drop him upon learning he is a Jew—we are in for a surprise, since the only problem she has is understanding why he makes such a big thing about it. The audience could well share her problem: We see a man talk endlessly about the

horrors of anti-Semitism without ever watching him actually suffer its bite.

As for Liddell, his story might have become intensely dramatic as a man who runs for God's glory and realizes his big race has been scheduled for Sunday, a devout man's sabbath. When he insists he can't run, and no less a personage than the Prince of Wales is brought in to talk sense to the lad, the movie seemed ready to sharpen its dramatic focus. But just as things were getting tense and interesting, Lord Andrew offers to change his match with Liddell's, thereby solving all the problems. Once again, the movie's potential for powerhouse drama was diffused. And while the film ran more than two hours, we actually learned precious little about either of the main characters. Their problems were conveyed in the first scenes, then repeated endlessly without being developed in any depth. In fact, the most fascinating character on view turned out to be Lord Andrew, the bridge between the two leads; his fresh-faced demeanor and cheeky humor suggested a man we'd enjoy getting to know more than the duo singled out for us.

To be fair, first-time director Hugh Hudson's *Chariots of Fire* was a beautifully photographed movie, with fine performances all around. For nostalgists, it was a treasure trove: cinematographer David Watkins handsomely, lovingly captured the richly detailed costume designs and period settings, while the unique, resonant, unforgettable, Oscar-winning Vangelis theme—performed as the team ran, in slow motion, across a beach

74

CHARIOTS OF FIRE: The past was lovingly recreated in images of stately drawing rooms . . .

. . . and breathtaking exterior shots.

CHARIOTS OF FIRE: The moment of truth.

at early morning—became an immediate classic. Why, then, did this attractive but relatively minor film win the Academy Award, only to be all but forgotten shortly thereafter? In part, because it captured and conveyed the Reagan-Thatcher notion that complex problems could be solved in simple ways, while also vividly recreating the world that both Reagan and Thatcher (and the countries that supported them) blithely looked back to. Also, there was the fact that Warner Brothers, which released the film, proved extremely effective that year in persuading its many employees who were members of the academy to vote for their nominated film out of company loyalty.

Tootsie

A COLUMBIA RELEASE OF A MIRAGE/ PUNCH PRODUCTION   1982

CREDITS

Executive producer, Charles Evans; produced by Sydney Pollack and Dick Richards; directed by Sydney Pollack; written by Don McGuire, Larry Gelbart and Murray Schisgal, from a story by McGuire and Gelbart; photography, Owen Roizman; editors, Fredric Steinkamp, William Steinkamp; Running time, 100 min.; Rating: PG.

CAST:

Michael Dorsey/Dorothy Michaels (Dustin Hoffman); *Julie* (Jessica Lange); *Sandy* (Teri Garr); *Ron* (Dabney Coleman);

Les (Charles Durning); *Jeff* (Bill Murray); *George Fields* (Sydney Pollack); *John Van Horn* (George Gaynes); *April* (Geena Davis); *Rita* (Doris Belack); *Jacqui* (Ellen Foley).

During a decade when every imaginable movie genre from the Forties was being revived and updated, it only made sense that the cross-dressing comedy would likewise be brushed off and offered to modern audiences. Ever since Cary Grant first put on a dress for director Howard Hawks in *I Was a Male War Bride* (1949), moviegoers have roared at the sight of male sex symbols in drag, a situation which reached its artistic apex ten years later with Billy Wilder's dazzling, bittersweet *Some Like It Hot*, in which Jack Lemmon and Tony Curtis awkwardly pursued Marilyn Monroe's "Sugar" while pretending to be fellow members of her all-girl band. The announcement that Dustin Hoffman would star for Sydney Pollack in a modern version of just such a comedy left little doubt that audiences would shortly be enjoying a similar charming romp done in a contemporary style. They were not to be disappointed, though the key to *Tootsie's* critical as well as commercial success was that it offered that and much, much more.

For Hoffman, *Tootsie* was the film he'd always wanted to make about the life of an out-of-work actor, a status he suffered firsthand before his breakthrough with *The Graduate* in 1967. His Michael Dorsey is just such a person: an actor who cannot get roles because he's too short or too tall, too young or too old, too this or too that. Worse still, his harried agent, George (director Sydney Pollack), admits that Michael is considered difficult to work with, so nobody wants him for that reason. His playwright roommate, Jeff (Bill Murray), has problems of his own, as he can't get anyone in Manhattan to produce one of his works, while Michael's friend, fellow actor, and occasional girlfriend, Sandy (Teri Garr), is a wimpish woman who can't understand why Michael always forgets their dates, never realizing it's her whiny personality that causes him to act as he does.

Then Michael has an inspiration: When a plum woman's role comes up on a soap opera, he slips into a dress, auditions for it, and gets the part. Soon, "Dorothy" is dealing with a sleazy producer (Dabney Coleman) while falling in love with his gorgeous, talented costar (Jessica Lange), who senses Dorothy is someone she can become very close to, even as Michael/Dorothy struggles to control his romantic urges for the woman who considers him/her a close friend. When he forgets himself and actually tries to kiss Julie, she screams, suddenly believing her gal-pal is a lesbian.

In the broadest sense, *Tootsie* does fall into the category of drag comedy. But from the very beginning, all involved were dedicated to doing something other than having Hoffman schlepp around in a dress, Milton Berle style. The film, which immediately became the all-time most successful comedy at the box office (a record which was to be broken by *Ghostbusters*, featuring Hoffman's *Tootsie* costar Bill Murray, a scant two years later), offered plenty of laughs, to be sure. More important, though, was the fact that this always remained realistic, comedy on the edge of drama, allowing us to feel deeply for Michael/Dorothy and his awkward situation on a level beyond the entertaining gag that had characterized the earlier comedy classics by Hawks and Wilder.

TOOTSIE: A mixing of symbols: This posed publicity still for *Tootsie* caught the strange mood of America in the early Eighties, the American flag symbolizing the sudden return to patriotic fervor, the cross-dressing of Dustin Hoffman capturing the (brief-lived) tolerance for sexual deviation in the post-feminist, pre-AIDS period.

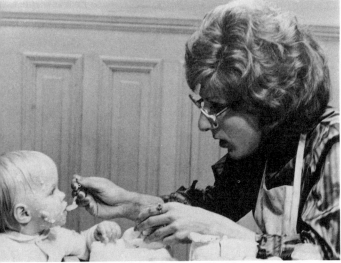

TOOTSIE: Before Michael Keaton as *Mr. Mom* or the wildly popular *Three Men and a Baby*, Michael Dorsey/Dolores Michaels was the first of the 1980s males to get in touch with his feminine side by relating to a child.

Ultimately, *Tootsie* is a film that characterizes the attitude of the upscale American male, struggling toward some sort of enlightenment during the early days of the decade. Having suffered through, and learned something from, the intense feminism of the Seventies, men generally and genuinely wanted to try and get in touch with the feminine side of themselves in order to relate to the modern woman, who expected just such a sensitivity. Understandably, then, there is a point in *Tootsie* where the gags become as "educational" as they are "entertaining": Michael learns to understand how women think and feel owing to his entrapment in a dress. When a crude male makes a vulgar pass or attempts to put his hands on Dorothy's derriere, there's a sense of outrage at the action which will stay with Michael (and the men in the audience who associate with Hoffman's hero) long after he's back in normal male attire. When he feeds Julie's baby, Michael comes to appreciate the joys of motherhood, so when his cross-dressing situation is finished, he's grown as a person.

TOOTSIE: Still very much a man, Michael attempts to break through to the woman he loves (Jessica Lange), despite her anger over his ruse; Lange won a Best Supporting Actress Oscar for her role.

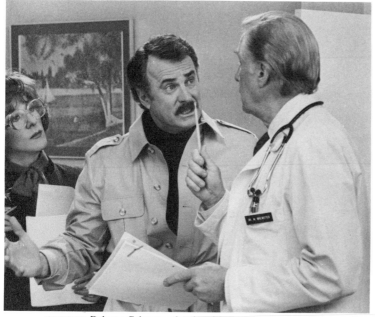

TOOTSIE: Dabney Coleman, the decade's premiere screen villain, as Ron Carlysle, the pompous producer of the daytime drama, and George Gaynes as the show's lecherous "Dr. Medford Brewster."

This was, sadly, an attitude that would all but disappear during the decade's second half, when the awareness of AIDS and the increase of violence toward women would make the sensitivity of films like *Tootsie* and its companion piece, *Victor/Victoria*, all but obsolete.

Victor/Victoria

AN MGM-UA RELEASE 1982

CREDITS:

Produced by Blake Edwards and Tony Adams; written and directed by Blake Edwards; photography, Dick Bush; editor, Ralph E. Winters; Running time, 133 min.; Rating: PG.

CAST:

Victor/Victoria (Julie Andrews); *King* (James Garner); *Toddy* (Robert Preston); *Norma* (Lesley Ann Warren); *Squashy* (Alex Karras); *Cassell* (John Rhys-Davies); *Waiter* (Graham Stark); *Labisse* (Peter Arne).

Just when it appeared as if Blake Edwards had given up all his early, lofty hopes of becoming an important comic auteur of the Frank Capra/Preston Sturges/Billy Wilder order, instead settling into the profitable business of turning out a formula *Pink Panther* picture every two years, he belied that notion by delivering two of his most ambitious movies in rapid succession: *"10"*, an appealing portrait of early middle-age/upper-middle-class angst, and *S.O.B.*, a nasty, self-serving attack on Hollywood. His next, *Victor/Victoria*, stands as Edwards' masterpiece to date, a period picture with bite, a romantic fairy tale for adults with something serious to say about changing sexual roles in the early Eighties.

Julie Andrews (Mrs. Edwards in real life) plays a down-and-out Paris chanteuse, circa 1934, who along with her homosexual pal Toddy (Robert Preston) cooks up a wild scheme calculated to make her a star. Dressing in male garb, she passes herself off as a female impersonator—a woman pretending to be a man pretending to be a woman. Which works well enough until a handsome American gangster, King (James Garner), wanders into the club and, catching her in mid-act, falls in love. Only at the performance's end does she reveal (falsely, of course) she's a man, leaving King to nervously question his own sexual identity: If he's as macho as he thought, how could he possibly have been attracted to a man?

The first half of the film follows his attempts—played out with good-natured comedy skirting the edge of painful desperation—to prove Victor/Victoria actually is a woman, thereby justifying his attraction. Writer-director Edwards takes this clever comedic plot device and turns it into something much more: a means for wreaking havoc on the notion of sharply defined sexual roles. In so doing, he revamped this old tale (based on a 1933 German "lost masterpiece" by Rheinhold Schuenzel, *Viktor und Viktoria*) into something that, by implication, was completely contemporary, an indirect comment on post-Sexual Revolution attitudes about men and women in America. Other appealing films of the early Eighties likewise tackled this serious theme in a comical way—*Tootsie, Mr. Mom*—but few compared to *Victor/Victoria* in impact. Edwards did not make cross-dressing something to laugh at, but rather with. At a time when an amazing number of high-minded movies openly tackled the once-taboo subject of homosexuality in the context of Hollywood pictures, mostly making it the subject for sanitized and mundane melodramas (*Making Love, Personal Best*), Edwards effectively deflated people's preconceptions through humor.

The funniest moments were also the most telling, as when Victoria and Toddy, platonically sharing a bed, admit to each other their desires to become involved with King. Garner, a traditional movie star, was a perfect choice to represent the macho male, owing to the types of parts he has played over the years; then his character here undergoes a significant transformation. At mid-movie, when Garner finally kisses Andrews for

VICTOR/VICTORIA: Julie Andrews as the down-on-her-luck singer who discovers a strange means of making a success in the theater world; filmmaker Blake Edwards gave this opening sequence a fitting fairytale quality.

VICTOR/VICTORIA: Victor/Victoria (Andrews) finds fame and fortune as a "female impersonator," though she's in fact doing an impersonation of that; the lavish song and dance numbers were throwbacks to the golden days of the movie musical.

VICTOR/VICTORIA: "I don't care if you're a man or a woman—I love you!" Such a line from King (James Garner) characterized the enlightened post-Sexual Revolution early Eighties, but would have been quite impossible in the AIDS-hysteria later in the decade.

the first time, he openly, sincerely admits: "I don't care whether you're a man or a woman—I love you." That may sound innocuous enough, but it represented the attitude of the early Eighties, when Gay Lib made remarkable inroads toward mainstream acceptance; then the growing scope of the AIDS epidemic at mid-decade caused an immediate resurgence of homophobia, render-ing such thinking, such dialogue, such movies a thing of the past.

This may have been a wild, knockabout farce, with zippy gags and plenty of sexy slapstick humor, set against lavishly staged production numbers (music by Henry Mancini, of course, this being a Blake Edwards movie) and delightful dancing, but it was always enter-tainment with a bite, humor that transcends laughter. Once Edwards happily bedded his two leads with half a movie still to go, he then took off on a variety of topics—contemporary problems presented within the innocuous setting of a costume film. Victoria and King

79

argue heatedly over whose career should take a backseat to the relationship, as the lady finds herself enjoying the rights and freedoms denied to women of her time, but allowed to her only so long as she maintains her masquerade. By picture's end, Edwards developed a theme that linked the film to classic screen comedy, when we realize everybody on view is playing a role, whether it is the gangster who parades as an honest businessman or the strong, silent bodyguard (Alex Karras) who has spent a lifetime denying his own gay instincts. The character of Victor/Victoria—who at first seems perverse compared to all the "normal" people in the movie—is not, we realize, the exception to the rest of the world but only the extreme, exaggerated example of society at large.

E.T.—The Extra-Terrestrial

A UNIVERSAL PICTURES RELEASE OF AN AMBLIN ENTERTAINMENT PRODUCTION   1982

CREDITS

Produced by Steven Spielberg and Kathleen Kennedy; directed by Steven Spielberg; written by Melissa Mathison; photography, Allen Daviau; editor, Carol Littleton; Running time, 115 min.; Rating: PG.

CAST:

Mary (Dee Wallace); *Elliott* (Henry Thomas); *Keys* (Peter Coyote); *Michael* (Robert MacNaughton); *Gertie* (Drew Barrymore); *Greg* (K. C. Martel); *Steve* (Sean Frye); *Tyler* (C. Thomas Howell); *Pretty Girl* (Erika Elaniak); *Schoolboy* (David O'Dell).

A director of machines, not people: that's how the critical establishment has tried to write off Steven Spielberg. From the battling vehicles in his made-for-TV cult hit *Duel* to the endless lines of cars in his first theatrical feature, *Sugarland Express*, the rubber shark in *Jaws*, the flying saucers in *Close Encounters of the Third Kind* or the endless gimmickry of *Raiders of the Lost Ark*, Spielberg turned out a succession of crowd-pleasing box-office bonanzas. Nonetheless, the huge success of almost all his vehicles elicited cynicism from more sophisticated quarters—changes that Spielberg was nothing more than a maker of "pinball machine movies," films able to light up in neon colors, make all sorts of marvelous noises, provide plenty of fun for the mass audience and do everything but (*1941* and the later *Always* excepted) tilt. How about people, though? Spielberg sometimes seemed less an explorer of the human condition than a charter of complicated computer responses.

Understandably, that was an impression he wanted to change, and *E.T.* was an attempt to do just that, enhancing his image as a creator of memorable screen people while retaining just enough of his special-effects wizardry to satisfy his built-in following. The gamble was risky if worthwhile. *E.T.* told the story of a pint-sized creature from another world who finds himself stranded on earth when his frightened fellow travelers are forced to abandon him or risk being captured themselves. E.T. hides out in the garage of a typical American family of the early Eighties: Mary (Dee Wallace), single working mother; Michael (Robert MacNaughton), a pressured teenager; Elliott and Gertie (Henry Thomas and Drew Barrymore), two little children. In a series of comic misadventures, E.T. joins the family disguised as a stuffed toy, soon adding the very ingredient that's been missing in the household: a strong center capable of holding all the free-floating people together in a pattern that orders their lives.

The children come to understand each other better thanks to their varied individual responses to E.T., as well as their growing abilities (with the minicreature serving as a catalyst) to accept each other's different

ways of reacting, just as the mother is shaken into an awareness of her children following a growing realization that one of the ornaments in the kids' playroom is alive, if not altogether well. The little boy (Henry Thomas), who proves most open to the lovable creature, is named Elliott, a key to what the movie is actually all about. *Variety* in its review of *E.T.*, neatly psyched out the film's intentions, claiming "*E.T.* may be the best Disney film Disney never made." in fact, screenwriter Melissa Mathison wrote *E.T.* with the notion that it would sell at Disney, though that studio passed on it, to its doubtless everlasting regret. Such a decision seems unconscionable today, but it must be remembered that this was the period when Disney was attempting to update its product

and fortunes with such films as *Splash, Never Cry Wolf* and *Tron*; in fact, *E.T.* was precisely the sort of story Disney (wrongly) believed the public would no longer buy. Elliott was the dragon who communicated with a lost little boy in that studio's *Pete's Dragon*. Like that film, this one concerned an isolated child who forges a friendship with an alien whom he, in his loneliness, relates to. Like that earlier youngster, this little-boy-lost of *E.T.* at last forces his entire community to "see" the creature once visible exclusively to him.

The important connection, though, was not to a particular Disney film but to the entire Disney canon. That sense of wonder and awe at the universe's magnitude, coupled with a positive mind-set in spite of much

81

E.T. THE EXTRA-TERRESTRIAL: The team of searchers pursue E.T. after the small creature has been inadvertently left behind on earth . . .

. . . and little Elliott watches as they approach his home.

evidence to the contrary, is part of what Spielberg shares with Disney; a wondrous ability to dazzle audiences with the plausible impossible, achieved through special-effects magic, is another important part of it. Like Disney, Spielberg is an optimistic filmmaker, especially effective at creating the bittersweet "up-cry," in which an audience is manipulated into sobbing but feels good about it afterward. The parting of Elliott and Henry, when the little creature finally goes home, is as heart-breakingly happy a moment as when Snow White must leave the Seven Dwarfs for her prince. Like the visionary Disney, Spielberg is a meticulous craftsman, fascinated by the technical aspects of filmmaking and eager to create innovations in that area. All of which helps explain why Spielberg's ability to touch a common chord represents the most impressive talent of this type to emerge since the golden days of the Disney studio.

An Officer and a Gentleman

A PARAMOUNT PICTURES RELEASE OF A LORIMAR PRODUCTION   1982

CREDITS:

Produced by Martin Elfand; directed by Taylor Hackford; written by Douglas Day Stewart; photography, Donald Thorin; editor, Peter Zinner; Running time, 125 min.; Rating: R.

CAST:

Zack Mayo (Richard Gere); *Paula Pokrifki* (Debra Winger); *Sgt. Emil Foley* (Louis Gossett, Jr.); *Sid Worley* (David Keith); *Lynette Pomeroy* (Lisa Blount); *Byron Mayo* (Robert Loggia); *Casey* (Lisa Eilbacher); *Emiliano Serra* (Tony Plana); *Perryman* (Harold Sylvester).

AN OFFICER AND A GENTLEMAN: Richard Gere sweeps Debra Winger off her feet. Filmmakers responded to the Reagan presidency and the new era of American pop culture it ushered in by providing updatings of the kinds of films Reagan had once starred in; *Officer* was an old-fashioned fairy-tale view of male-female relations, as well as a return to pro-military views, given a state-of-the-art look.

During the golden age of Hollywood, movies like *An Officer and a Gentleman* were more plentiful in theatres than "Smoking in Balcony Only" signs. An outwardly flippant, inwardly anguished young serviceman tries to hustle his way through Officer's Candidate School. An outwardly gruff, inwardly sensitive sergeant sees the great potential lurking beneath that obnoxious attitude, deciding to make or break the brash youth by turning on the pressure. An outwardly superficial, inwardly decent girl snuggles up to the hero, attracted at first by the status he'll someday achieve, gradually realizing she's actually in love. An outwardly easygoing, inwardly confused best friend helps the protagonist through his rougher moments only to discover he can't cope with his own mounting problems.

Movies like that don't get made anymore or, at least, that's what people thought throughout the Seventies. But the macho men of the military and women who want a marriage more than a career were suddenly "in" again; like so many other film formulas that seemed gone forever, this was ripe for revival in the Reagan era, if only some clever filmmakers could dress it up for modern audiences by adding graphic sex and rough language. *An Officer and a Gentleman* was that film, at once predictable and contrived, custom-made for an

audience which clearly hungered for trendily packaged traditional entertainment. *Officer* was tossed onto the movie marketplace with little promotional fanfare or advance advertising, but the public found it anyway, making a hit out of the movie while setting Richard Gere and Debra Winger on their way to major stardom. (The Gere role reportedly had been written with John Denver in mind.) What people saw in the film was an effective dramatic statement of what most Americans obviously wanted to believe in once again: that the American Dream works, that men from the lowliest station in life can struggle within the system to better themselves and go to the top, that women stuck in third-rate factory jobs could marry the man of their dreams if they only live a life of decent values.

In the Forties, such decent values would have included chastity, but that old-fashioned this film definitely was not. In fact, the sexual bouts between Zack (Gere) and Paula (Winger) were among the most vivid ever presented in a mainstream movie; though she quickly moved on to more ambitious roles, Gere never com-

AN OFFICER AND A GENTLEMAN: "Don't eyeball me, mister!" Louis Gossett, Jr. (Oscar winner as Best Supporting Actor) as the tough D.I. who makes Officer's Candidate School a living hell for the young man from the streets.

AN OFFICER AND A GENTLEMAN: Though the storyline was old-fashioned formula, the sex scenes were modern and graphic.

pletely moved from hunk star to serious actor, especially after his appearance in the lame-brained *Breathless* the following year. *Officer* remains his most memorable hit, effortlessly addressing itself to the collective hopes of its audience by presenting old movie myths of professional success and personal romance in a *nouveau-realistic* setting, making the fantasy appear absolutely attainable.

Screenwriter Stewart (himself a Navy Officer's Candidate School survivor) and director Hackford fashioned a film which made audiences feel good about themselves and their country despite, during the course of the story, several brutal beatings and a strangulation suicide. The movie implied that while the world may oftentimes be an

AN OFFICER AND A GENTLEMAN: The American Dream was aggrandised in images of the working class girl marrying up thanks to her luck and pluck, a Horatio Alger story by way of a paperback romance novel.

84

ugly and unpleasant place, there still exists in it the potential for personal accomplishment, the possibility of eventual happiness and, therefore, ample reason for continued optimism. Since most Americans want to believe in that, they understandably elected Reagan president and made this movie a hit.

An Officer and a Gentleman featured a sly restatement of traditional American values; if it appeared hip on the surface, willing to stretch the boundaries of language and eroticism, it was rock conservative underneath: pro-military, pro the American system, pro old-fashioned relationships. Though ultimately nothing more than a shallow pastiche of earlier potboiler plots, it presented its tired (if less-than-true) blue-collar fairy tale-for-adults in such a vivid and convincing manner that viewers could hardly help but respond on cue, standing up to cheer for a frog-turned-prince who showed up at just the right moment (the last possible moment) to carry Cinderella off the factory floor amid cheers and huzzahs.

One of the movie's modernizations was to have the knowing drill sergeant played by a black actor (although color was not a script consideration). Louis Gossett, Jr., took ordinary lines ("Don't eyeball me, mister!") and made them sound inspired, winning a Best Supporting Actor Oscar in the process. Alternately fire and ice, he continually exploded in a movie that otherwise proceeded with quiet self-assuredness. Its phenomenal success despite the familiarity of the story line only proved American audiences had not outgrown the appeal of filmgoing as ritual experience.

Difner

Diner

A METRO-GOLDWYN-MAYER RELEASE OF
A JERRY WEINTRAUB
PRODUCTION   1982

CREDITS:

Executive producer, Mark Johnson; produced by Jerry Weintraub; written and directed by Barry Levinson; photography, Peter Sova; editor, Stu Linder; Running time, 110 min.; Rating: R.

CAST:

Eddie (Steve Guttenberg); *Shrevie* (Daniel Stern); *Boogie* (Mickey Rourke); *Fenwick* (Kevin Bacon); *Billy* (Timothy Daly); *Beth* (Ellen Barkin); *Modell* (Paul Reiser); *Barbara*

DINER: In the tradition of *Mean Streets* and *American Graffiti* is Barry Levinson's coming-of-age tale; (standing, from left): Mickey Rourke, Steve Guttenberg; (sitting, from left): Daniel Stern, Kevin Bacon and Timothy Daly, all save one being downscale guys caught in an upscale moment.

(Kathryn Dowling); *Bagel* (Michael Tucker); *Mrs. Simmons* (Jessica James); *Diane* (Kelle Kipp).

Diner was to the early Eighties what *American Graffiti* had been to the early Seventies: the film which captured and distilled for its audience an earlier way of life, or at least a nostalgic, romanticized vision of the way we liked to believe we were. In that sense, it was not only a remarkably well-crafted work of entertainment, marking the impressive directing debut of screenwriter Barry Levinson, but also as a coming-of-age film about five young men, as well as definitive motion picture of the Reagan era which implied, through its story, the very ideology that was prevalent in contemporary politics: an overriding desire to return to the simpler, bygone days of 1959, that last happy point in the Eisenhower era before America unknowingly hopped onto the wild social and cultural roller coaster ride of the turbulent Sixties.

But whereas George Lucas had overly sentimentalized the California scene of the early Sixties in *Graffiti*, Levinson supplied a grittier, more honest vision with a rough realistic edge. Though his film was shot in color, Levinson encouraged his director of photography, Peter Sova, to seep away any bright hues, making for a bleak

DINER: At the diner, four of the guys relax, gab and enjoy french fries dunked in brown gravy.

DINER: Ellen Barkin as Beth, the neglected wife who tries to get the attention of husband Shrevie (Stern).

portrait of his (Levinson's) native Baltimore. Even the diner that lends the film its title is a far cry from Mel's malt shop in Lucas's film; instead of a trendy-tacky neon-lit hot spot where surfer girls congregate, Levinson's diner was a drab place where guys could meet for greasy french fries and brown gravy after their disappointing Friday night dates. However, Levinson did provide a counterpart to Suzanne Somers's dream girl, continuously driving by Richard Dreyfuss in her car and appearing so near and yet so far, in a key moment when several of Levinson's guys leave the gray downtown surroundings and venture into the suburbs, where they spy an upper-middle-class girl, seemingly carefree and beyond their petty problems as she spends her afternoon horseback riding. It is a lifestyle they are allowed to peek in on only momentarily, before they return to their working-class world, slightly embittered after glimpsing a sacrosanct and exclusive demimonde which is actual but, for them, apparently unattainable. If they could only follow the girl home, and note her lifestyle was probably as hollow as anything seen in *Ordinary People*, they might have an easier time readjusting to their dingy but relatively happy homes.

When first glimpsed, the boys are two years out of high school and still adjusting to real life. Shrevie (Daniel Stern), overly anxious to sleep with a woman every night, was the first to marry but now is depressed at having a wife (Ellen Barkin) he can't talk to. Eddie (Steve Guttenberg) is about to marry but won't unless his bride-to-be (unseen throughout the film) passes a sports test (with an emphasis on his favorite team, the Baltimore Colts) he's designed. Fenwick (Kevin Bacon) is the standout rich kid among the group, though the cynical sneer on his privileged face suggests he's actually less happy with his lot in life than are his blue-collar pals. Boogie (Mickey Rourke), though hardly the best looking among them, is the Don Juan of the group, thanks to his suave moves, seducing women by creating an elaborate fantasy life in which he pretends to be a law student, though he's in fact an underpaid beautician. Billy (Timothy Daly), the one member of the group who has gone on to college, has a pregnant girlfriend, yet he can't coax the liberated woman into marrying him.

Most of the actors were all but unknown at the time of the film's release: each quickly became a permanent fixture in films and television thanks to this superb showcase for their talents. Levinson displayed the qualities which would make his future writing so charmingly unique: When, for instance, the boys argue heatedly over whether Frank Sinatra or Johnny Mathis is the better pop singer, it's a prelude to the scene in Levinson's later *Tin Men* when the aluminum salesmen in the very same diner heatedly debate the merits of TV's *Bonanza*. Like that subsequent film, this one also shows off Levinson's great gift for vividly recreating and authentically depicting those working-class worlds that he knows so well. As one of the key filmmakers of the decade, Levinson would falter only once, when he moved out of his range of vision and mounted *The Natural*, a pompous, pretentious version of Bernard Malamud's mythological baseball tale. *Diner* was a little movie that proved to be a big hit, and as such was partly responsible for saving the movie business from the over-elaborate Big Event pictures or slapdash slob comedies then threatening to overrun theatres.

Gandhi

A COLUMBIA PICTURES RELEASE   1982

CREDITS:

Executive producer, Michael Stanley-Evans; produced and directed by Richard Attenborough; written by John Briley; photography, Billy Williams and Ronnie Taylor; editor, John Bloom; Running time, 188 min.; Rating: PG.

CAST:

Mahatma Gandhi (Ben Kingsley); *Margaret Bourke-White* (Candice Bergen); *General Dyer* (Edward Fox); *Lord Irwin* (John Gielgud); *Judge Broomfield* (Trevor Howard); *Viceroy* (John Millers); *Walker* (Martin Sheen); *Kasturba Gandhi* (Rohini Hattangady); *Charlie Andrews* (Ian Charleson); *General Smuts* (Athol Fugard); *Patel* (Saeed Jaffrey).

GANDHI: Ben Kingsley as Mohandas K. Gandhi, the role that won an Academy Award for this stage actor little known outside of his native Great Britain.

GANDHI: Martin Sheen as "Walker," a composite of several real-life journalists who at various times covered Gandhi and the changing face of India.

GANDHI: Famed photojournalist Margaret Bourke-White (Candice Bergen) is touched by the benign leader.

GANDHI: Sir Richard Attenborough (far left) directing Ben Kingsley in a sequence of Gandhi; for the actor-turned-director, bringing this tale to the screen was the fulfillment of a ten year dream.

In 1963, director David Lean and screenwriter Robert Bolt presided over the release of *Lawrence of Arabia*, immediately dubbed the first "thinking man's epic." Shortly, the two were approached by an Indian civil servant who hoped to interest them in doing a similar study of the soft-spoken modern apostle of nonviolence, Mohandas K. Gandhi (1869-1948), likewise beginning with the great man's death, then flashing back to observe his life through the eyes of a composite American journalist who would create the film's point of view. Lean and Bolt turned down the project as lacking the necessary excitement and vitality, but another English filmmaker, actor-turned-director Richard Attenborough, got wind of it, then read the Louis Fisher biography and secured the rights, eventually spending two decades convincing potential backers to make a movie about a man—and a message—that had become very dear to him.

A key problem was finding the right actor, someone who could take Gandhi through 56 of his 79 years, showing the man's metamorphosis from a brash but self-satisfied lawyer in South Africa into his country's crusader for self-rule as well as the 20th century's greatest spokesman for nonviolence. Attenborough found that man in Ben Kingsley, a British actor who is part Indian and was a respected performer with Britain's Royal Shakespeare Company. The big-name supporting cast of English heavyweights and Indian actors also included American stars Candice Bergen, as photographer Margaret Bourke-White, and Martin Sheen, as the fictional reporter who frames the film. Included in the movie are such landmark events as the 1919 massacre at Amritsar, an incident in which British General Dyer (Edward Fox) gave his troops the order to fire on Indian women and children attending a peaceful meeting, and the Chauri Chauraa riots, in which nearly two dozen policemen were murdered by pro-Gandhi demonstrators, an incident which resulted in Gandhi's entering the period of total fast that changed the course of history.

Such scenes were stirring, and the powerful theme (a rarity in movies during the early Eighties) was basic to the film's receiving the Academy Award as Best Picture. But when Attenborough touchingly, tearfully accepted his award, he acknowledged that it was more for the real Gandhi and what he had stood for than for Attenborough and the film he made. In truth, Sir Richard was not merely being humble, for this admirable movie—though sweeping and spectacular—was also more simplistic than such a long movie ought to be. The film tactfully sidestepped a number of fascinating if problematic aspects of Gandhi's life, including his cool relationships with his own sons, something that might have been effectively contrasted to his warm and loving relationship to the entire outside world. Audiences did not see the Gandhi who, to put his own vow of abstinence to the extreme test, regularly slept beside attractive young girls. Were such material included, the portrait would have been richer, more complex, if a bit less sympathetic and saintlike.

Despite that disappointing dramatic aspect, the film was a visual marvel, containing some of the most magnificent images of India ever captured on film. The photography, directed by Billy Williams and Ronnie Taylor, captured impressions of the land and the people, as well as the Indian way of life, that oftentimes threatened to dwarf the memorable man who served as the story's centerpiece. Still, Kingsley created an image of dignity and doggedness in a cause that impressed the motion picture academy enough to award him the Best Actor Oscar. But the film, though surprisingly popular at the time, has not worn well over the years, attested to by the fact that it is never in any great demand on home video or cable television. Watching *Gandhi* is more a dutiful experience than a delightful one; other than in the large-scale action sequences, *Gandhi* appears formal and lifeless, a sincere movie though seldom a deeply involving one. And while Kingsley most convincingly played the various stages of Gandhi's development, the screenplay by John Briley never allowed the audience to feel they had slipped inside the man's mind and were able to understand him in depth. Considering the extremely long running time, that was a flaw which could not be overlooked. Gandhi seemed very much like one of those films about Jesus—*Kings of Kings, The Greatest Story Ever Told*—which approach their subject with such great reverence, trepidation even, that any kind of exciting drama is all but impossible. For all his qualities, Gandhi was a man, not a god, and this film would be more satisfying if it had recognized his human failings as well as his numerous good qualities.

Eating Raoul

A 20TH CENTURY-FOX PRESENTATION OF A QUARTET FILM   1982

CREDITS:

Produced by Anne Kimmel; directed by Paul Bartel; written by Richard Blackburn and Paul Bartel; photography, Gary Thieltges; editor, Alan Toomayan; Running time, 87 min.; Rating: R.

CAST:

Mary Bland (Mary Woronov); *Paul Bland* (Paul Bartel); *Raoul* (Robert Beltran); *Mr. Leech* (Buck Henry); *Mr. Kray* (Richard Paul); *Doris the Dominatrix* (Susan Saiger); *Sex Shop Owner* (John Paragon); *Party Guests/Assorted Victims* (Dan Barrows, Ralph Brannen, Edie McClurg, Darcy Pullam, Ed Begley, Jr., Hamilton Camp, Billy Curtis).

Every decade has its cult films, those offbeat little items which generate initially small, intensely loyal followings of fans who watch the film over and over again until they know the dialogue so well they can call it out before the actors do. In the Seventies, the representative cult film was *The Rocky Horror Picture Show*, a first in big cities, then around the country, cinemaddicts enjoyed dressing in costumes corresponding to the film's freaky characters and, vampirelike, attending "Midnight Madness" screenings. The first cult film of the Eighties was *Eating Raoul*, a wickedly funny, low-budget, independently produced feature picked by by 20th Century-Fox's International Classics division and consciously marketed to create the kind of following that had spontaneously formed around *Rocky Horror* and to a lesser extent Brian DePalma's *Phantom of the Paradise*. Though less successful theatrically, *Eating Raoul* rated as the first cult movie hit of an emerging Eighties

EATING RAOUL: The Blands (Paul Bartel and Mary Woronov) are awakened by a mysterious intruder; *Rocky Horror Picture Show*, move over!

phenomenom, becoming a home video rental and late-night cable staple.

Writer-director Paul Bartel played the part of Paul Bland, with veteran B movie villainess Mary Woronov cast as his loving, devoted wife Mary. Now early middle-aged and upper middle-class, they are the kind of people who, in the late Sixties, sneered at the idealistic hippies and, during the Seventies, were proud to be out of synch with the Sexual Revolution, thoroughly enjoying their creature comforts while scoffing at the developing Me Decade trends of spiritual soul-searching, physical-exertion body building, and open experimentation with the joys of sex. Couch potatoes before the term existed, Paul and Mary enjoy quiet, sexless evenings together, sipping white wine while exchanging low-key pleasantries.

The Eighties are incredibly appropriate for the Blands: a bland decade, with its emphasis on money, greed and accumulation, the entire country inches closer to the style Paul and Mary have lived for a long time. But if they're amazed to discover they are no longer far removed from the the emerging mainstream sensibility, are what everybody suddenly want to be, they're still not completely happy. For all around them, there's the aftereffect of the Sexual Revolution; people still partying and partaking of vulgar physical pleasure. The Blands, of course, consider themselves superior to such animalistic impulses, looking down their noses at the mindless fellow inhabitants of their L.A. apartment house, ultimately believing the world would be a better place if all such libertines were eliminated. Meanwhile, they go about their lives of self-delusion: the slightly prissy Paul, a salesman at a liquor store, dreams of being a wine-tasting connoisseur, while the repressed-nymphomaniac Mary, a hospital dietician, would like to open a gourmet restaurant somewhere in the quiet countryside, where she'll serve their pièce de résistance, "The Bland Enchilada."

Their lives change when a drunken intruder, who mistakenly wanders into their apartment from a sex party down the hall, tries to rape Mary. Though she seems ripe to respond, Paul shows up and disposes of the man with one of the iron skillets he ordinarily employs for his culinary feats. The body is tossed into the trash compactor, after the Blands have helped themselves to the man's money, as they are low on funds. This gives the greedy but resourceful Blands an idea: They will take out classified ads in the weekly papers, luring would-be swingers to their apartment. When the sex maniacs arrive, they will be victimized just like the initial intruder. Paul and Mary will have the money they need to finance their upscale lifestyle, feeling no moral compunctions or guilt about what they do since these are "horrible, sex-crazed perverts nobody will miss anyway." The avaricious representative couple of the Eighties will finance their lifestyle by killing off the remnants of the Sexual Revolution Seventies; in the age of AIDS, casual sex will lead to death. An entire coterie of swingers is destroyed by a single well-placed electric light bulb thrown into their hot tub: things go well until an ambitious Chicano, Raoul (Robert Beltran), tries to cut himself in on the deal—and on Mary's body. As the title implies, there's only one surefire way to eliminate him.

This dark comedy about cannibalism—in which sex, death and food become inseparable—was directed in a purposefully low-key style, then photographed in a correspondingly flat technique to make the movie's sensibility as appropriately, disarmingly bland as the Blands themselves. With its image of smug, complacent, superior yuppies killing off the last of the sexual libertines from the previous decade, *Eating Raoul* rated as a dark comedy allegory for the Eighties.

The Year of Living Dangerously

AN MGM/UA RELEASE OF A McELROY & McELROY PRODUCTION   1983

CREDITS:

Produced by James McElroy; directed by Peter Weir; written by David Williamson, C. J. Koch, and Peter Weir; photography, Russell Boyd; editor, Bill Anderson; Running time, 115 min.; Rating: R.

CAST:

Guy Hamilton (Mel Gibson); *Jill Bryant* (Sigourney Weaver); *Billy Kwan* (Linda Hunt); *Pete Curtis* (Michael Murphy); *Colonel Henderson* (Bill Kerr); *Wally O'Sullivan* (Noel Ferrier); *Kumar* (Bembol Roco); *Hortono* (Domingo Landicho); *Tiger Lily* (Kuh Ledesma).

The early Eighties are not remembered as a time of thoughtfully reflective films, so *The Year of Living Dangerously*, an Australian import, proved a happy surprise, vividly recreating the political powderkeg of Indonesia in 1965, just before the fall of Sukarno, and employing that as the backdrop for a memorable romance much in the style of *Casablanca*.

Mel Gibson, then establishing himself as one of the key stars of the decade, left his rugged *Mad Max/Road Warrior* image behind to play soft-spoken Guy Hamilton, an Aussie radio commentator who first views his new assignment as nothing more than a golden opportunity for personal advancement. As such, he perceives the suffering of the Indonesian people as a strong subject for his regular broadcasts. Then his life is plunged into emotional confusion and intellectual doubt when he meets the fascinating, mysterious Jill Bryant (Sigourney Weaver), a sophisticated but shady lady

THE YEAR OF LIVING DANGEROUSLY: As Jill Bryant, British Embassy attache and shady lady, Sigourney Weaver played a mysterious, sophisticated lady, making clear that her macho woman role in *Alien* was but one of the many parts she could play; to the left is Bill Kerr as Col. Henderson.

working in some undisclosed position at the British embassy.

Guy immediately falls madly in love, at the same time striking up a bizarre friendship with Billy Kwan, a half-caste dwarf. This male role was played by actress Linda Hunt, in a remarkable performance that deservedly won her an Oscar—though the motion picture academy was reportedly at first unsure whether she should be nominated for Best Supporting Actress or Actor. Billy, grasping just how blasé Guy is about the world around him, undertakes the job of supplying Guy with a moral education, forcing him to actually see (rather than merely look at) the intense suffering around him, to realize that if you only observe the ugliness and inequities in the world (such detachment being basic to Guy's profession), then you actually contribute to it. Billy forces Guy to make the kinds of hard choices that shortly cause him to transform from a watcher to a doer, becoming directly involved in all that's happening.

Peter Weir, who had already guided Gibson through the impressive antiwar film *Gallipoli*, subtly approached this story. Even his large-scale sequences (riots in the

THE YEAR OF LIVING DANGEROUSLY: Recent history intrudes on the romantic couple, as Guy Hamilton (Mel Gibson) covers the Indonesian civil war of 1965 and finds himself confronting a military roadblock.

streets, romantic encounters between hero and heroine, and one supporting character's fatal act of self-sacrifice) were downplayed, adding to the understated sense of realism. This film adaptation of C. J. Koch's well-regarded novel did not leap out from the screen and devastate an audience, as was the case with Roland Joffe's *The Killing Fields*, but rather quietly touched the viewer, then proved haunting and memorable afterward.

THE YEAR OF LIVING DANGEROUSLY: Guy and Billy Kwan (Linda Hunt, with camera) find themselves surrounded by political demonstrators and attempt to capture the moment for the media.

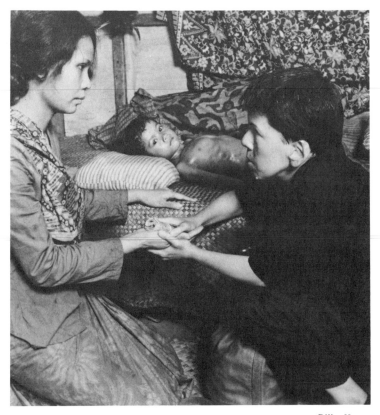

THE YEAR OF LIVING DANGEROUSLY: Billy Kwan confronts Ibu (Norma Uatuhan) over the impending death of her infant son.

THE YEAR OF LIVING DANGEROUSLY: Linda Hunt as Billy Kwan, the first time an Oscar was ever awarded for a performer playing a member of the opposite sex.

There was an illusion maintained throughout *The Year of Living Dangerously* that the characters were merely going about their business in a random way, happening to bump into one another by accident or quirk of fate. Which means that the filmmakers conveyed the quality of real life, while in fact carefully creating a plot that moved toward its logical conclusion with the inexorability of a Greek tragedy. Not since Costa-Gavras's 1970 film *Z* had any one movie balanced its politics and personal drama so perfectly. Like that film, *Year* could be viewed as a slick, exciting romantic thriller; like it too, this film conveyed (without undue didacticism) a precise recreation of a particular time and place, sharing with us the director's anger and anguish over political power at its most raw and unfair levels, while radicalizing an audience that had been immediately hooked by the film's entertainment values.

As such, *Year* demonstrated yet another dimension of the Australian film industry. It also further propelled Mel Gibson toward an impressive superstar status. Had he made the wrong movies after *The Road Warrior*, Gibson might have shortly been perceived as an Australian Sylvester Stallone, gliding from one macho movie to the next. Instead, he found diverse roles—the shy man here, the innocent Mr. Christian in the revisionist version of *Mutiny on the Bounty* and the crazed, suicidal cop of *Lethal Weapon*—proving himself a solid actor as well as a magnetic star. Perfectly cast opposite him was Sigourney Weaver, a striking beauty best remembered as Bill Murray's amorous interest in *Ghostbusters* and the survivor of space creature attacks in both *Alien* features. As the fascinating, oblique woman here, the devious corporate climber in *Working Girl* and the dedicated protector of simians in *Gorillas in the Mist*, Weaver would firmly establish herself as a key character actress, lovely leading lady, and impressive comedienne, one of the decade's busiest and best performers.

Never Cry Wolf

A BUENA VISTA RELEASE OF A WALT DISNEY PRODUCTION   1983

CREDITS:

Executive producer, Ron Miller; produced by Lewis Allen, Jack Couffer and Joseph Strick; directed by Carroll Ballard; written by Curtis Hanson, Sam Hamm and Richard Kletter, based on the book by Farley Mowat; photography, Hiro Narita; editors, Peter Parasheles and Michael Chandler; Running time, 105 min., Rating: PG.

CAST:

Tyler (Charles Martin Smith); *Rosie* (Brian Dennehy); *Ootek* (Zachary Ittimangnaq); *Mike* (Samson Jorah); *Drunk* (Hugh Webster); *Woman* (Marth Ittimangnaq); *Hunters* (Tom Dahlgren, Walker Stuart).

Throughout man's history, few creatures have been more universally maligned than the wolf. A figure of terror that's haunted humans since our earliest civilized experience, the wolf still terrorizes small children as the creature that menaces Little Red Riding Hood, then works it way into our adolescent fantasies as the werewolf. In our century, no filmmaker has done more to augment that perception than Walt Disney. In his 1930s short *The Three Little Pigs*, the Big Bad Wolf not only pursued those charming porkers but emerged as a symbol for The Great Depression. Intriguingly enough, the Disney Studio of the mid-Eighties offered moviegoers their first revisionist image in a film suggesting the wolf might not be so bad, after all; it was also the first of the new wave of Disney films.

Never Cry Wolf was based on the true story of Canadian Farley Mowat (here called Tyler, and played by Charles Martin Smith), awarded a government grant to study wolves in the Arctic circle, amassing proof that timber wolves are the prime reason why the great caribou herds are fast disappearing. His mission, then, was "scientific" in the worst sense. Rather than objectively observing in order to arrive at a logical conclusion, Mowat started with the conclusion, selectively accumulating evidence supporting it. By doing this, he would provide the government with what it wanted, a rationale to move in and kill off the wolves. In time, though, Mowat came to understand the wolves do not feed on caribou (surprisingly nonexistent in this area anyway) but rather on the mice that would threaten to overrun the place if the wolves were not around to keep the number down. Far from being the scourge of the Far North, the wolves are in fact a useful, even necessary element of nature's balance. Which put Mowat in the awkward position of making a moral choice. In doing that, he was transformed spiritually and intellectually.

This was a movie about escaping prejudices, whether they be about wolves or anything else. But there was a greater liberation going on, which had to do not with the specifics of wolves but the wider notion of the North itself as a representation of nature. Initially, we see Mowat as unfit, with little chance of survival during the

NEVER CRY WOLF: A young biologist (Charles Martin Smith) is stranded after being air-dropped into the Arctic wilderness to begin a perilous study of wolves; the Disney company revived what was best about its old "True Life Adventures" and added a contemporary attitude on ecology.

NEVER CRY WOLF: The boisterous bush pilot (Brian Dennehy) agrees to fly the young scientist into an isolated region where he's to study wolves—but learns about himself.

bleak. The theme here is survival of the fittest, not only in the sense of natural selection, but also in terms of what the movie ultimately targeted as the most dangerous animal of all: man. A gregarious fast-talking pilot (Brian Dennehy), who seems good company early on, appears after Mowat's transformation a force of evil, menacing the hard-edged natural beauty with get-rich-quick schemes for exploiting the land. Even one of the Eskimos, at first so removed from the white man's avarice, willingly sells out the land of his fathers and the law of his ancestors for a shot at worldly success.

harsh winter. But he learns, partially from the Eskimos who befriend him and partially on his own, how to survive. The man we first meet is soul-sick, without a sense of self-worth. In learning to appreciate nature, he learns to like himself.

For a Disney film, *Never Cry Wolf* was surprisingly

NEVER CRY WOLF: A crate of light bulbs has incongruously been included in the supplies; Charles Martin Smith's characterization was based on the real-life experiences of Farley Mowat, making this one more Eighties film that blurred the distinction between drama and documentary.

Director Carroll Ballard shot and edited this film in much the same style as his most famous work, the lyrical 1979 *Black Stallion*. At times, Ballard's tendency to begin almost every sequence with a disconcerting close-up, then gradually open the image up to allow us a sense of place, seemed more unnerving than could be justified. It was a minor flaw in what was, overall, a highly satisfying film, one which announced that the Disney product was about to take a sharp turn away from predictability through a single remarkable image: when a starving Mowat survives by eating a mouse sandwich (their little feet stick out, all in a row, between the slices of bread), the vision derives much of its meaning from the fact this film was produced by Mickey's studio. The photography of the wolves and other natural phenomena was on a level not seen since the great Disney "True Life Adventures" of a quarter-century earlier. Likewise, the theme of man's endangering nature was presaged by *Bambi*. In evidence was the old Disney genius for storytelling: enchanting children with the animal characters while holding their parents' interest through sheer technical virtuosity. Still, this was a departure, for the film—considered a mite too "intense" for younger audiences—received a PG rating (mild for any other studio, but a breakthrough for the ordinarily G-rated Disney product). With *Never Cry Wolf*, Disney retained the essence of their traditional vision while beginning to make movies more in tune with the times.

Risky Business

A GEFFEN COMPANY RELEASE THROUGH WARNER BROS.   1983

CREDITS:

Produced by Jon Avnet and Steve Tisch; written and directed by Paul Brickman; photography, Reynold Villalobos and Bruce Surtees; editor, Richard Chew; Running time, 98 min.; Rating: R.

CAST:

Joel Goodsen (Tom Cruise); *Lana* (Rebecca De Mornay); *Miles* (Curtis Armstrong); *Barry* (Bronson Pinchot); *Glenn* (Raphael Sbarge); *Guido* (Joe Pantoliano); *Joel's Father* (Nicholas Pryor); *Joel's Mother* (Janet Carroll); *Vicki* (Shera Danese); *Rutherford* (Richard Masur).

There was no way to guess on its initial release that *Risky Business* would be anything more than another youth-exploitation flick like *The Last American Virgin* or *Private Lessons*, those sleazy items about typically Eighties teenagers and their first sexual encounters. But from the first frame of this remarkable movie, audiences were aware of being in the presence of something very special: A film that immediately rose above its genre in the way that, nearly 30 years earlier, *Rebel Without a Cause* stood head and shoulders above the routine 1950s juvenile-delinquent flicks its plot vaguely resembled. What *Rebel* was to the Fifties, *The Graduate* to the Sixties, and *Saturday Night Fever* to the Seventies, *Risky Business* was to the Eighties, the film that most perfectly caught the temper of its times from the point of view of youth adjusting to the adult world.

For Joel Goodsen (Cruise), an affluent but sex-starved teen growing up in Chicago's chic suburbs, making money is everything. If Dustin Hoffman's Benjamin Braddock represented an entire generation of idealistic young people when he refused to take an adult friend's advice to get into "plastics," that's precisely the kind of advice Joel is eager for. A child of the Eighties, he and his high school friends Miles, Barry, and Glenn hang around together at a McDonald's munching on fries while casually discussing which college's business

RISKY BUSINESS: Rebecca De Mornay and Tom Cruise in the publicity pose that pre-sold the picture.

RISKY BUSINESS: Joel and his new "business partner" Lana take a memorable ride on the Chicago el; though viewers remember it as one of the most intensely erotic movie sequences from the Eighties, the scene is surprisingly suggestive rather than graphic.

RISKY BUSINESS: Joel finds himself managing Lana and her friend (Shera Danese) after they move into his parents' suburban home and quickly turn it into a brothel.

RISKY BUSINESS: Tom Cruise as Joel: a star-making performance.

school is likely to land them the highest paying jobs when they graduate in four years. Joel wants to get into Harvard, not because of the quality of education there but only because he's positive a degree from America's premiere school translates into megabucks.

Then, Joel's parents take off on a vacation, leaving him alone to study for the college boards. Joel amuses himself in the evenings by dancing around the house in just T-shirt and shorts, grabbing a candlestick and pretending it's a microphone as he rocks and rolls (Cruise and Brickman improvised the classic moment, not in the script, while shooting) until he grows bored. Joel then calls a hooker out-service he finds listed in the classified ads. Vicki, the black girl who answers Joel's call, is a bit much for him; realizing how inexperienced he is, she sends over Lana (Rebecca De Mornay), a knowledgeable whore who nevertheless has the appearance of an angel.

Joel's little adventure is fine fun, until Lana refuses to leave the morning after, and he's forced to go to high school while a hooker waltzes around his parents' house all day. When he finally gets her to leave, she takes along Joel's mother's beloved crystal egg; when he pursues her to retrieve it, Joel is shortly locked in in conflict with Lana's killer pimp, Guido. Eventually, Lana and her friends move into Joel's house, which he operates as a brothel for his upscale buddies. When a college recruiter (Richard Masur) shows up, he's so taken with Joel's entrepreneurship that he immediately accepts the lad into the Harvard business school.

Paul Brickman, who had written the razor-sharp screenplay for Jonathan Demme's sadly neglected *Citizen's Band*, made a formidable directing debut here. Among the memorable comedy scenes was one in which Joel's father's Porsche drifts downhill toward the lake, while Joel makes ever more desperate (and doomed) efforts to save it. Another striking sequence has Joel and Lana making love in a subway; it remains one of the most intensely erotic sequences in American movies, despite the impressive fact that it's suggestive rather than graphic, actually devoid of any nudity at all, though almost everyone recalls seeing Cruise and De Mornay completely nude. Simply, the greatest sex scenes are the ones viewers *think* they see rather than actually *do* see.

Cruise was immediately catapulted to stardom with his performance, which unsparingly satirized the greed of Joel (and the Reagan-era youth in general) while still making him sympathetic enough that an audience cared about Joel and what would eventually happen when his parents arrived home. His arc from wide-eyed innocent to smirking pseudosophisticate, thoroughly corrupted and happy to be a winner by playing dirty, remains a striking achievement for so young an actor, though it was only a prelude to the even greater things he would shortly do and the major star he was to become in the Eighties. While Brickman's film was happily devoid of polemics, it did suggest that in the Eighties, everyone was in some way or another a whore, the only difference between Joel and Lana being her honesty about her profession. That cynical assessment was presented most stylishly in *Risky Business*.

WarGames

AN MGM/UA RELEASE   1983

CREDITS:

Produced by Harold Schneider; directed by John Badham; written by Lawrence Lasker and Walter F. Parkes; photography, William A. Fraker; editor, Tom Rolf; Running time, 113 min.; Rating: PG.

CAST:

David (Matthew Broderick); *Jennifer* (Ally Sheedy); *McKittrick* (Dabney Coleman); *Falken* (John Wood); *General Berringer* (Barry Corbin); *Pat Healy* (Juanin Clay); *Cabot* (Kent Williams); *Watson* (Dennis Lipscomb); *Conley* (Joe Dorsey); *Richter* (Irving Metzman).

WarGames, in the tradition of *Dr. Strangelove* and *Fail-Safe*, was a doomsday thriller that seduced an audience with highly involving suspense, then delivered a powerful message about the dangers of our Cold War mentality. What made *WarGames* such a satisfying (and commercially successful) exercise in the genre was the

WARGAMES: David Lightman (Matthew Broderick), a Seattle high school student with a home computer, demonstrates his abilities to enter their school's system and alter information regarding grades, to his girlfriend Jennifer (Ally Sheedy).

WARGAMES: Tensions run high at NORAD control when the countdown for a nuclear attack cannot be thwarted, once David has inadvertently set the mechanics of World War Three into motion while playing computer games.

way in which it neatly updated that concept for the age of Pac-Man and the arrogant, amoral youth of the Eighties that had little on its mind other than computer games. Matthew Broderick, one of the more talented among the new generation of actors, here found a role which allowed him to reach full movie star status. Filmmaker John Badham did not (thankfully) pander to the youthful audience as so many of his colleagues already had, instead providing a heavy cautionary fable about a world in which computers were allowed to control national security though dangerously mismanaged by semicompetent bureaucrats, as well as a morality play in which a smug teenager gradually grows as a human being.

David Lightman (Broderick) is a bright Seattle high school student, accused of an "attitude problem" only by those teachers who aren't smart enough to satisfy his keen intellect. At home, David fools around with video games and computer technology, showing his girlfriend Jennifer (Ally Sheedy) how he can use his equipment to enter the school's computer systems and "adjust" his grades any way he wants. Discovering ways to invade the computer banks of faraway toy companies, he's begun to peek at the new video games before they are made public. One day, he finds himself matching wits with a difficult unknown system he inadvertently calls up on his computer screen. Trying to access the system's code to play the elaborate games he finds there, David little suspects he's in fact entering WOPR (War Operations Plan Response), the Air Force's secret computer system located at the North American Aerospace Command hidden in the Cheyenne Mountains of Colorado. Pricking this system into playing games with him, David inadvertently sets into motion World War Three.

The superb supporting cast included Barry Corbin as an eager general ready to roll up his sleeves and start shooting, Dabney Coleman as the computer scientist who believes David is a clever Communist agent safely operating out of a suburban home, and British stage actor John Wood as the reclusive eccentric who originally programmed the computer called "Whopper," creating a complex link between it and the bombers, missiles, and submarines ready to put into action a retaliatory strike at the computer's request. He must be located and contacted within hours, for WOPR has been (much like H.A.L. in *2001: A Space Odyssey*) programmed to single-mindedly carry out its operation against the Soviet Union without humans being able to intervene and stop it.

Like so many Hitchcock heroes (Robert Donat in *The 39 Steps*, Cary Grant in *North by Northwest*), David must set out on a time-limited journey, in the process abandoning his glib attitude, becoming committed to a decent cause. Likewise resembling a Hitchcock hero,

he's pursued by the local police and federal men who mistakenly believe him to be an enemy agent. To be sure, the plot sometimes became contrived, though in fact, on close examination, that's also true of the Hitchcock classics. This was, ultimately, a work of popular entertainment, though hardly a diversion calculated to take our minds off current problems.

Indeed, it did the opposite, focusing public attention on such matters. *The New York Times* went so far as to follow up Vincent Canby's review with an article by Richard Halloran called "Could It Ever Happen?" And while government spokesmen in Washington asserted this was only a fantasy film with a far-out nightmare scenario, the public recalled that only a year earlier, several bright students in Manhattan used their school's computer to scramble the banking system in Canada for several days, while other state-of-the-art pranksters had entered the computers at a major hospital complex, rearranging the records of various patients there. Just as the evidence of computer viruses and the danger they could do began hitting the headlines, anxiety about possible nuclear confrontation had escalated since the election of Reagan, with his macho approach to world politics. Critic Peter Rainer perfectly tagged the film: "Pac-Man delivers Armageddon." Despite official assurances it could never happen, the public was not so readily assuaged.

WARGAMES: Dabney Coleman as McKittrick, director of computer control at the NORAD headquarters.

FLASHDANCE: A post-feminist fairy-tale for the Eighties: Alex (Jennifer Beals) is a blue collar worker by day (and an equal to the men around her), but transforms into an exotic dancer (though never revealing "all") for those same men each night.

FLASHDANCE: Nicky (Michael Nouri, left) learns from a friend (Don Brockett) that the gorgeous dancer he's watching actually works for him during the day.

FLASHDANCE: Dealing with the modern woman: Nicky must be careful to support Alex without taking over her life, though he finds that flowers are as irresistible to women of today as ever.

Flashdance

A PARAMOUNT PICTURES RELEASE OF A POLYGRAM PICTURES PRODUCTION   1983

CREDITS:

Executive producers, Peter Guber and Jon Peters; produced by Don Simpson and Jerry Bruckheimer; directed by Adrian Lyne; written by Tom Hedley and Joe Eszterhas from a story by Hedley; photography, Don Peterman; editors, Bud Smith, Walt Mulconery; Running time, 96 min.; Rating: R.

CAST:

Alex Owens (Jennifer Beals); *Nicky Hurley* (Michael Nouri); *Katie Hurley* (Belinda Bauer); *Hanna Long* (Lila Skala); *Frank Szabo* (Phil Bruns); *Cecil* (Malcolm Danare); *Secretary* (Lucy Lee Flippin); *Richie* (Kyle T. Heffner); *Rosemary Szabo* (Micole Mercurio); *Junior Jean* (Sunny Johnson); *Tina Tech* (Cynthia Rhodes).

Rocky for women: that's the way most critics dismissed *Flashdance*, drubbing it as a simplistic fairy tale, an old-fashioned fantasy film given an effective if ultimately false realistic edge by enough rough language and overt sexuality to win it an R rating, as well as on-location shooting in the blue-collar sections of Pittsburgh. And, of course, they were essentially right, for this was a formula film featuring a timeworn plot, though brought to the screen with such energy and excitement that any such synopsis fails to do justice to the film's mass appeal.

Flashdance is a postfeminist fable. The heroine, Alex, has long since been accepted as an equal by male workers at a Pittsburgh steel plant, where she's a welder. Unlike the radical woman of the Seventies, she's not uncomfortable with the sex-goddess side of herself, at night moonlighting as an erotic dancer, becoming a temptress to the very guys who work alongside her during the morning shift. Though the club where Alex dances is a blue-collar dive, we're asked to believe that it features expensive dance routines, with remarkable costumes and lavish set designs of the sort one might see at a Vegas show or the Folies Bergère in France. Incredibly enough, Alex and the other girls tease slightly without ever revealing all (Janet Maslin of *The New York Times* tagged the choreography by Jeffrey Hornaday "a combination of new wave sadomasochism and calisthenic pornography," with a touch of street-smart break dancing thrown in for good measure), hardly the kind of stuff two-fisted blue-collar beer drinkers go for, quite preposterous to anyone who's ever seen how far a stripper must go in today's sleazy working-class pubs.

Reviewers who laughed at the ludicruousness of this failed to take into account that in so many revered movie musicals of the Thirties, sequences begin with a choreographed number supposedly taking place on a Broadway stage, which then magically expands to the greater limits of a Hollywood soundstage; to be appreciated, *Flashdance* had to be perceived as a modernized musical. Likewise, Alex's immense loft-apartment would realistically be beyond the means of such a girl. *Flashdance* could be dismissed as a a fairy tale, to be sure; considering its widespread appeal, it made more sense to appreciate it as a fairy tale, study the clever and charming way in which it took collective fantasies of our culture and convincingly presented them in a contemporary manner.

Every fairy tale must feature a Prince Charming: here, Nicky (Michael Nouri), the incredibly rich, impossibly handsome, extraordinarily enlightened boss who falls for Alex. Modern enough to accept her ambitions for a career, old-fashioned enough to want to marry her, he's the Eighties' ideal man. *Flashdance* illustrated and embodied the postfeminist myth that anything is possible for today's woman, however humble her origins. Alex wants to study ballet, and wins a place at the prestigious school after a whirlwind audition combining elements of a Jane Fonda workout with the kink of Paris's Crazy Horse Saloon; having wowed the admissions board, she then walks out onto the streets where she joins hands with (for an eventual marriage to) Nicky, whom she's temporarily turned her back on owing to his masculine desire to intervene with the admissions board on her behalf, whereas Alex wants to do it all herself. The movie does not suggest everyone in America will succeed: Alex's friends who hope to make it as a stand-up comic and ice-skater fail miserably. Even Alex has moments of self-doubt, as when she initially enters the Carnegie building to audition and, comparing her trendily-torn jeans, grease-stained work boots, and scruffy fatigue jacket to the elegant leotards and toe-shoes of other hopefuls, runs away in tears. But she has the luck and pluck to return, that magical something which makes her the rare rugged individualist who survives the social Darwinist odds against her and rises to the top. If the evidence of numerous people failing was hardly encouraging to audiences, the image of Alex succeeding was certainly inspirational: an idealized though convincing portrait of the one in a million for whom the American Dream does come true.

The final image, then, insists that if in ancient fairy tales the poor girl can marry a prince, then in the modern American Dream version the working-class girl can likewise marry her boss, and also have a highly creative career. Like the Hollywood musicals of yore, this ultramodern but implicitly traditionalist film made the impossibly perfect seem absolutely attainable.

FLASHDANCE: "And they lived happily ever after . . . "; at least in fairytales, and old-fashioned movie plots given an ultra-modern look.

Trading Places

A PARAMOUNT PICTURES RELEASE 1983

CREDITS:

Executive producer, George Folsey, Jr.; produced by Aaron Russo; directed by John Landis; written by Timothy Harris and Herschel Weingrod; photography, Robert Paynter; editor, Malcolm Campbell; Running time, 116 m.; Rating: R.

TRADING PLACES: Billy Ray Valentine (Eddie Murphy) finds himself transformed from a street person hassled by Philadelphia police ...

... to a pampered yuppie served by a butler (Denholm Elliott) in his very own townhouse.

TRADING PLACES: Mortimer (Don Ameche) and Randolph (Ralph Bellamy) Duke manipulate the innocent Billy Ray to their own ends; what was initially accepted as an enjoyable escapist comedy was in fact an early indictment of the Eighties greed mentality.

CAST:

Billy Ray Valentine (Eddie Murphy); *Louis Winthrope III* (Dan Aykroyd); *Coleman* (Denholm Elliott); *Randolph Duke* (Ralph Bellamy); *Mortimer Duke* (Don Ameche); *Ophelia* (Jamie Lee Curtis); *Penelope Witherspoon* (Kristin Holby); *Attendant* (Robert Earl Jones); *Harry* (Nicholas Guest); *Corrupt Cop* (Frank Oz); *Pawnbroker* (Bo Diddley); *Baggage Handlers* (Al Franken, Tom Davis); *Harvey* (James Belushi).

Only three years into the Eighties, it was clear that the current policy of benign neglect had already created a gap in the economic structure far in excess of anything in recent history: thanks to the new tax breaks, the haves had more than ever before, while owing to the extensive cutbacks in aid to the poor, the have-nots had absolutely nothing. While it was once again chic to be rich, and the middle-American yuppie culture strove for that status, there were more and more street people, the homeless who did not have any opportunity—other than some miracle—to rise above their station, the American Dream having been systematically removed from the realm of their possibilities. So even as the great comedies of the past (Frank Capra's in the Thirties, Preston Sturges's in the Forties, Billy Wilder's in the Fifties) seduced the public into laughing at then-current problems, so did John Landis create classic topical comedy out of our decidedly unfunny reality.

A thought-provoking film, with a lighthearted bent, *Trading Places* featured characters representing the extremes of the new situation. Louis Winthrope III (Dan Aykroyd) is the penultimate preppie, complete with WASP bloodline, a social set of friends sporting names like Tod and Muffy, and an important position with the age-old, highly respected, thoroughly corrupt Philadelphia money-management firm of Duke and Duke. Billy Ray Valentine (Eddie Murphy) is the consummate street hustler, a jive-talking, freewheeling con man who will try anything short of violence to turn a fast buck. Louis and Billy Ray would never meet but for an accident. When they bump into each other outside the exclusive Heritage Club where Louis is exiting after an afternoon drink while Billy Ray pathetically panhandles outside, Billy Ray politely attempts to hand Louis the attaché case he's dropped, while Louis—closer to a black face than ever before in his life—recoils in horror, certain he's being mugged.

The relationship would go no further were *Trading Places* anything but an updating of the old screwball comedies. Since it is just that, the elderly Duke Brothers (veteran actors Ralph Bellamy and Don Ameche) are seen engaging in their running lifelong argument about heredity and environment as through the window they

TRADING PLACES: Hustler Ophelia (Jamie Lee Curtis) helps Billy Ray and defrocked yuppie Louis Winthorpe III (Dan Aykroyd) plot revenge on the two conniving brothers.

gents, rather than the cruel caricatures they might have been, Landis gave the film a double cutting edge. Even as we watch their nasty little game, we tend to laugh along with them, until that powerful moment in a men's room when we (along with Billy Ray) are forced to confront the enormity of their evil. Landis made his comedy as timely as possible, constantly associating the Dukes with President Reagan through an autographed photo of him kept, whenever possible, in the frame with the Dukes, implying that the brothers' attitudes were extensions of current political philosophy. Though *Trading Places* featured a near-fantasy narrative line, it took a hard and honest look at some unpleasant realities of the Eighties.

The Right Stuff

A LADD COMPANY RELEASE THROUGH WARNER BROS.   1983

CREDITS:

Executive producer, James D. Brubaker; produced by Irwin Winkler and Robert Chartoff; written and directed by Philip Kaufman; based on the book by Tom Wolfe; photography, Caleb Deschianel; editors Glenn Farr, Lisa Fruchtman, Stephen A. Rotter, and Douglas Stewart; Running Time, 191 min.; Rating: PG.

CAST:

Chuck Yeager (Sam Shepard); *Glennis Yeager* (Barbara Hershey); *Alan Shepard* (Scott Glenn); *John Glenn* (Ed Harris); *Gordon Cooper* (Dennis Quaid); *Gus Grissom* (Fred Ward); *Pancho Barnes* (Kim Stanley); *Betty Grissom* (Veronica Cartwright); *Trudy Cooper* (Pamela Reed); *Deke Slayton* (Scott Paulin); *Scott Carpenter* (Charles Frank); *Wally Schirra* (Lance Henrikson); *Lyndon Johnson* (Donald Moffat); *Sally Rand* (Peggy Davis); *Government Recruiters* (Jeff Goldblum, Harry Shearer); *Louise Shepard* (Kathy Baker); *Eric Sevareid* (Himself).

notice this incident. Like gods on Mount Olympus who kill us for their sport, the brothers decide to manipulate the ultimate experiment, proving once and for all whether nature or nurture determines a man's position in life. They will force the unwilling Louis and the unwitting Billy Ray to trade places. If Billy Ray rises to the top in business once given this opportunity, while Louis is forced into a life of crime to survive, then environment is the key factor; if Billy Ray can't make it in the commodities market and Louis somehow emerges with his dignity intact, then genes and blood will triumph.

Here viewers encountered the contrivance that made *Trading Places* difficult for some to accept: the implausible (indeed, perhaps impossible) notion that the Dukes, no matter how large a fortune or how far-reaching their power, could manipulate lives so easily. We are given the impression that the entire Philadelphia police force and judicial system would not hesitate to cooperate with their whimsical if perverse game, and we could not comprehend why a character as sympathetic as Winthrope's butler (delectably played by the estimable Denholm Elliot doing a Gielgud turn straight out of *Arthur*) would cooperate with so cruel a joke. Anyone who objected to this lack of logic was both right and wrong: right that it all was unlikely, wrong in that—considering the conventions of comedy—we need not worry about logic.

Landis avoided the more obvious and raucous sight gags of his earlier *Animal House*, fashioning a moral fable. By portraying the Duke brothers as attractive old

At first, *The Right Stuff* sounded all wrong for a theatrical release: a study of the post-WWII conquest of space, from the earliest experiments to the first great successes of Project Mercury, with large ensemble cast, epic scope, and a running time of well over three hours, it sounded far more appropriate for a TV miniseries than a theatrical feature. But filmmaker Philip Kaufman knew precisely what he was doing. Forsaking the detached docudrama approach appropriate for TV but somewhat ineffectual for movies, opting instead for a freewheeling blend of comedy, drama, and social commentary adding up to an unlikely but highly appealing "movie-movie" (it might have been subtitled "The Magnificent Seven on the Moon"), *The Right Stuff* was clearly a work of popular entertainment rather than an educational film, blowing up actual events into movie mythology.

THE RIGHT STUFF: The seven Mercury astronauts in space suits and full gear march down the hall to imminent glory.

True to the spirit if not the letter of Tom Wolfe's book, the film translated the author's verbalized reflections into visual statements. Framing the story of the original astronauts is their predecessor daredevil test pilot Chuck Yeager, portrayed by playwright-actor Sam Shepard as a Gary Cooper-type hero, a twentieth-century cowboy wandering the Muroc Desert, testing his manhood on experimental planes rather than the horses of an earlier era. The first man to break the sound barrier, he is nonetheless not asked to be an astronaut, as the government wants only clean-cut, college-educated types; The men are picked only in part for their abilities, as Wolfe saw it, more for the way in which they will represent the country's future when photographed for *Life*.

In addition to being trained for the tasks they will eventually perform in space, the men are also exploited by the government and media, which together work at presenting these people to the public so as to make all Americans feel good about themselves; the space program is co-opted by public relations, while lost along the way is the purity of Yeager's quest, performed without thought of social responsibility or potential profit but only for the thrill of personal accomplishment. Even as *Life* portrays, to a public hungry for heroes during those first dark, confusing days of the Cold War, the seven as simple, straightforward men of action, we see their insecurities and idiosyncrasies, all of which made them human—fallible and fascinating—in a way carefully kept from the public, while these astronauts are packaged and sold to America as the best and the brightest. In the film's finale, the astronauts are lavishly entertained by Vice President Lyndon Johnson (wickedly caricatured by Donald Moffat) at a grotesque Texas barbeque, where down-home cooking is consumed even as fan dancer Sally Rand performs, while—through brilliant crosscutting—Yeager, alone and all but forgotten, sets yet another speed record (practically dying in the process) in the NF-104; implicit is the notion that true heroes are overlooked in favor of consciously created hero figures, all but wrapped, for public consumption, in plastic.

Kaufman's extremely long though never tiresome film combined brilliant special effects, raucous humor, and romantic melodrama into a spectacular entertainment underscored by an interpretation of what the U.S. space program actually meant, as compared to what the public was told at the time it should mean to them. Though on the surface it appeared to offer a satisfying Reagan era helping of patriotic fare, *The Right Stuff* was so sharply satirical and unrelentingly critical of our government's deeper motives that it never attained the box-office success that had been hoped for. One fascinating issue raised by the film was whether it would help or hurt the concurrent presidential campaign of Senator John Glenn,

THE RIGHT STUFF: Sam Shepard as Chuck Yaeger, predecessor of the astronauts, and his beloved Glennis (Barbara Hershey) stand in the burned ruins of Pancho's Fly Inn, remarking on the end of an era in pioneer aviation.

THE RIGHT STUFF The John Glenn ticker tape parade in New York City after his triumphant return; Ed Harris as Glenn, Mary Jo Deschanel as his wife Annie, and Donald Moffat as Vice President L.B. Johnson.

portrayed in the film (by Ed Harris) as a fussy, self-important, but ultimately courageous man. If the film was a huge success, would that propel Glenn to the Democratic nomination? Likewise, if Glenn was doing well in the polls, would that stir further interest in the film? Was, in fact, the studio wrong in releasing the movie on the eve of the primaries, exploiting and confusing the situation? A fascinating question, to be sure, though one that would temporarily be set aside. As the movie did only disappointing business and Glenn's campaign crumbled, the issue—the ultimate 1980s example of reality and film becoming confused—seemed a moot point.

THE RIGHT STUFF: John Glenn (Ed Harris) and Scott Carpenter (Charles Frank) go through intensive physical tests for being chosen for the space program.

The Big Chill

A COLUMBIA PICTURES RELEASE   1983

CREDITS:

Executive producers, Marcia Nasatir and Lawrence Kasdan; produced by Michael Shamberg; directed by Lawrence Kasdan; written by Barbara Benedek and Lawrence Kasdan; photography, John Bailey, editor, Carol Littleton; Running time, 103 min.; Rating: R.

CAST:

Sam (Tom Berenger); *Sarah* (Glenn Close); *Michael* (Jeff Goldblum); *Nick* (William Hurt); *Harold* (Kevin Kline); *Meg*

THE BIG CHILL: The film's ensemble company, from left: JoBeth Williams, Jeff Goldblum, Mary Kay Place, Tom Berenger, William Hurt, Meg Tilly, Glenn Close and Kevin Kline.

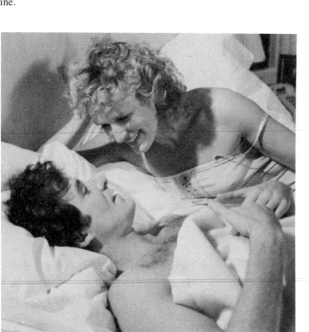

THE BIG CHILL: Kevin Kline and Glenn Close, as yippies turned yuppies, host a gathering of their college friends for a long, memorable weekend.

(Mary Kay Place); *Chloe* (Meg Tilly); *Karen* (JoBeth Williams); *Richard* (Don Galloway); *Alex* (Kevin Costner).

In 1980's *Return of the Secaucus Seven*, independent filmmaker John Sayles offered a study of Sixties radicals who met, once again, in the early Eighties, discovering how each had sold out on his or her idealistic dreams of a decade earlier. Though Sayles is a darling of the critics, and while his $60,000 film attracted an enthusiastic if limited art house following, it never broke through to become a mainstream hit. Then, three years later, Lawrence Kasdan—emerging as one of the new decade's leading writer-directors—fashioned a similar tale, only done with a Neil Simon slickness of upscale sitcom style, an assortment of hot new stars and old Hollywood gloss, creating a polished product that became, for an entire generation, the movie they related to as members of the Lost Generation of the Twenties had to Ernest Hemingway's novel *The Sun Also Rises*. *The Big Chill* was, in the minds of thirtysomething moviegoers, not just *a* story, but *their* story.

In the opening, the brilliant physicist and onetime student radical Alex—glimpsed in fleeting fragments—commits suicide, causing a number of his former schoolmates from the University of Michigan to come together again at the funeral. The eulogy admits that despite his great mind, Alex hadn't done much since graduation, too pure for the jaded world around him. Afterward, the survivors feel a need to be together, so they all head for the lovely lakeside South Carolina home of Harold (Kevin Kline), who has become wealthy by marketing running shoes to the new yuppies, and his wife Sarah (Glenn Close), a doctor who was, before moving in with Harold, Alex's girlfriend. Karen (JoBeth Williams), a still-gorgeous housewife and mother of two, is delighted when her decent, dull husband (Don Galloway) leaves the happy/unhappy reunion. This allows her to pick up a longtime flirtation with Sam (Tom Berenger), who once hoped to be the next Brando, settling instead for a lucrative starring role in a superficial but successful TV detective series; though in love with Sam, Karen refused

THE BIG CHILL: Early in the morning, two old friends (William Hurt and Kevin Kline) joke and reminisce about their student activist days—and the close friend who recently committed suicide; Kevin Costner, who was to play the suicide victim in a flashback, was cut out of the film at the last moment.

THE BIG CHILL: Meg Tilly, memorable as the understated but perceptive young girl who sees through all the mental games played by her elders.

marriage to an actor because she wanted a solid life and good provider. Nick (William Hurt), sexually incapacitated during the Vietnam War (his name suggests the hero of Hemingway's "In Our Time" stories, his situation that of Jake Barnes in *The Sun Also Rises*), now deals drugs and snorts cocaine. Meg (Mary Kay Place), who idealistically/naïvely left college to be a crusading lawyer for the poor and minorities, grew disillusioned and now works for high-paying corporations. Silently considering the interactions is Alex's young lover, Chloe (Meg Tilly), a spacey but surprisingly perceptive girl, while observing them all is Michael (Jeff Goldblum), onetime radical journalist who wrote stories that shook up the system and now makes a living selling fluff articles about celebrities to *People*. During the weekend of personal intermingling, difficult soul-searching and bittersweet nostalgia, Michael realizes that in the fates of his friends, there might be a major magazine story about an entire generation, and how their values of the hippie era were, during the ten years following, dashed against the rocks of reality.

"The Big Chill" of the title was never clearly articulated by any of the characters, rather communicated by the story's implications: this was about the first death to claim a member among a small circle of friends, and the way such an event forces each one of that group into an awareness of his or her diminishing youth and eventual mortality, as well as to honestly look at the way in which he's copped out on his greatest dreams. Under Kasdan's knowing direction, the ensemble cast convincingly suggested they were indeed longtime friends; memorable moments like a makeshift spaghetti dinner and impromptu dance session, all set to the beat of funky Motown music of the late Sixties, convinced the movie's upscale, early middle-aged audience that this was the film which spoke directly to and for them. The characters, commercially successful in their fields, all ultimately confessed they felt like sellouts, wondered how anti-Establishment yippies like themselves had gradually transformed into middle-class yuppies. Some critics complained Kasdan's approach was engaging but superficial, never exploring the characters in enough depth. Whatever truth there was to that, *The Big Chill* unquestionably "worked"—sending a chill through the millions of moviegoers who could relate firsthand to the compromises of these characters, likewise sensing that, despite their own current prosperity, the great times had ended in 1969.

TERMS OF ENDEARMENT: Debra Winger and Oscar winner Shirley MacLaine as the daughter and mother in a complex, strange, believable story of their 30 year relationship.

TERMS OF ENDEARMENT: Starting over: The unfaithful husband (Jeff Daniels) promises Winger he'll be faithful this time around as he and his family move into a new college community. Troy Bishop, Megan Morris and Huckleberry Fox are the children.

Terms of Endearment

A PARAMOUNT PICTURES
RELEASE   1983

CREDITS:

Produced, written and directed by James L. Brooks; based on the novel by Larry McMurtry; photography, Andrej Barthowiak; editor, Richard Marks; Running time, 132 min.; Rating: R.

CAST:

Aurora Greenway (Shirley MacLaine); *Emma Greenway Horton* (Debra Winger); *Garrett Breedlove* (Jack Nicholson); *Flap Horton* (Jeff Daniels); *Vernon* (Danny DeVito); *Sam* (John Lithgow); *Janet* (Kate Charleson); *Patsy* (Lisa Hart Carroll); *Emma's Sons* (Huckleberry Fox, Troy Bishop).

When *Terms of Endearment* won a well-deserved Oscar for Best Picture of the Year, it made clear that James L. Brooks had emerged as the most admirable creator of intelligent, adult-oriented films during a decade when Spielberg-style special effects were the order of the era. A disarming film that begins as sweet-spirited situation comedy and ends as full-blown domestic tragedy, *Terms* took the viewer on an unexpected but powerful change of tone at mid-movie managing to make that all-but-impossible transition work beautifully. In the process, it established Debra Winger as a major young star and won Shirley MacLaine her long overdue Academy Award as Best Actress. Jack Nicholson, the performer who seemingly could do no wrong, also won an Oscar—this time as Best Supporting Actor—continuing his longtime insistence on not being pigeonholed as either a top-billed star or a character player as he gleefully danced back and forth between the two delectable possibilities.

An intriguing portrait of a mother-daughter relationship surviving the postfeminist traumas, *Terms* focused on Aurora Greenway (MacLaine), a Boston-bred, Houston-based matron, and her independently minded daughter Emma (Winger), carrying them through a thirty-year period of highs and lows, as the well-intentioned but utterly exhausting Aurora attempts to manage her daughter's life, something Emma is ever less willing to let her mother get away with. Their greatest conflict is that Emma has married Flap Horton (Jeff Daniels), a likable loser Aurora has never approved of. Emma shares his nearly itinerant life as they travel around the country from junior college to junior college, Flap always managing to find some new job as an English teacher without earning tenure anywhere. Aurora is concerned that Flap will never be able to support her daughter in the manner to which she's become accustomed to living; Emma is more upset that her husband cannot remain faithful.

An old-fashioned woman's picture at heart, but one accurately reflecting the temper of our times, *Terms* studied the sweet but doomed affair between Emma and a gentle Iowa banker (John Lithgow), then turned into a tearjerker when it suddenly became obvious that Emma suffered from cancer. This revelation—the kind of devastating news that can hit anyone in real life at the most unexpected moment—seemed at first inappropriate, considering the upscale sitcom quality that had been quietly, carefully established by Brooks, a veteran TV writer/producer of such classic fare as *The Mary Tyler Moore Show* and *TAXI*. Things like cancer may occur randomly in real life, but they don't in a work of art that we implicitly believe will continue in the style we've adjusted to. So the tendency was to guess this was but a temporary aberration, that Emma would soon get a bill of good health and we'd shortly be watching as she continued her lighthearted relationships with mother and husband.

Instead, she became progressively sicker, eventually succumbing to the disease. Despite that, the film never degenerated into a maudlin wallow, on the order of the "Disease of the Week" TV movies chronicling some character's heartfelt and horrifying death. Gradually darkening the film's tone, though still managing to keep it entertaining, thanks to Aurora's nervous love affair with her jaunty neighbor, a former astronaut (Nicholson), Brooks came up with a totally unique film. In summation, the story may sound routine, but anyone who has ever seen it knows it does not play that way: from first moment to last, this is clearly a classic.

The difference between a typical TV movie on such a subject and what we see here is the fine distinction between base sentimentality and brilliant sensitivity. This was not merely a mother-daughter relationship comedy, a disastrous affair tale, a young-woman-dying-of-cancer melodrama or any other easy-to-pigeonhole potboiler, though it contained elements of all those and other story lines. Brooks did not simply take a single thesis and then embellish it into a full-length feature; instead, he employed Larry McMurtry's fine novel as a starting point and created an ensemble portrait of various people who engage in unlikely but completely believable relationships with one another. For that reason, it's quite impossible to outguess the film while watching it for the first time, to predict whether Emma will live or die. That rarity of rarities, *Terms of Endearment* was a Hollywood movie that managed to catch and convey the divergent patterns of life itself.

TERMS OF ENDEARMENT: Women dealing with women dealing with men: the daughter ignores her husband to talk to her Mom . . .

. . . while Mom ignores her lover (Jack Nicholson), the astronaut next door, to converse with daughter.

109

COUNTRY: Jessica Lange as Jewell Ivy.

Country, together with *Places in the Heart* and *The River*, all released the same year, constituted a unique genre of Eighties movies, the cinematic equivalent of Farm Aid, that media event staged by country performers to draw the nation's attention to the plight of our breadbasket. Each movie dealt with a Midwestern family held together by a strong woman (Jessica Lange, Sally Field and Sissy Spacek) beleaguered by crises major and minor in her day-to-day work by and an unfeeling government which has failed to support the country's heartland industry. Whether done as period-piece (*Places*) or contemporary (*Country*), the farm films captured the anguish of America's single family farmers, who supplied the nation with food even as their escalating costs of production began to exceed any possibility of even modest profits. Actress/activist Lange brought her celebrity clout to this worthy cause, begging Washington for financial help. Putting her money where her mouth was, Lange coproduced *Country*.

Country

A TOUCHTONE FILM RELEASED THROUGH BUENA VISTA   1984

CREDITS:

Produced by William D. Wittliff and Jessica Lange; directed by Richard Pearce; written by William D. Wittliff; photography, David M. Walsh; editor, Bill Yahraus; Running time, 109 min.; Rating: PG.

CAST:

Jewell Ivy (Jessica Lange); *Gil Ivy* (Sam Shepard); *Otis* (Wilford Brimley); *Tom McMullen* (Matt Clark); *Marlene Ivy* (Therese Graham); *Carlisle Ivy* (Levi L. Knebel); *Arlon Brewer* (Jim Haynie); *Louise* (Sandra Seacat); *Fordyce* (Alex Harvey).

COUNTRY: Jewell comforts her son, Carlisle (Levi L. Knebel), when the family is faced with the loss of their farm.

COUNTRY: Jewell and her husband Gil (Sam Shepard) enjoy themselves at the town dance, before heading back to their failing farm, mounting bills, and terminal debt; as in all the "farm films," it is the woman, not the man, who sees the family through.

Places in the Heart had opened first, to generally rave reviews (one critic tagged it "The *Terms of Endearment* of 1984"), and so did best at the box office, despite its overly sentimental approach. *The River*, opening third, struck the public as anticlimactic (Hadn't they already seen this movie?) and archly melodramatic. By far the most honest of the farm films was the one that received the least attention. *Country*, criminally undervalued on its initial release, rates as an American masterpiece in *The Grapes of Wrath* genre.

At once tough-talking and tender-hearted, *Country* vividly illustrated the angst of simple (but, significantly, nonromanticized) people at the mercy of natural disasters and federal bureaucracy, somehow surviving both with that quiet dignity which has always been the hallmark of true Middle America. Set in contemporary Iowa, *Country* avoided the serious mistakes which severely limited the impact of *Places*. There, writer-director Robert Benton never decided whether he was making a large ensemble film about a cross section of people or a more intimate, intricate portrait of a single family. From its first moment to its last, *Country* revealed an effective narrow focus, the battle for survival waged by Jewell Ivy (Lange) and her brood: a borderline alcoholic husband (Sam Shepard), a confused teenage son (Levi L. Knebel), a pleasantly precocious daughter (Therese Graham) and a sometimes gentle, occasionally gruff grandpa (Wilford Brimley, who quickly became typecast in such roles).

As in *Places*, the people here weather a sudden tornado but appear less likely to withstand a man-made

COUNTRY: Following a devastating tornado, the Ivy family counts its blessings at still being alive.

outrage of fortune called foreclosure. As in *Places*, the father figure quickly dissipates, allowing the woman (formidably played by Lange) to prove, as novelist Ellen Glasgow once phrased it, her vein of iron. As in *Places*, the people derive their endless reservoir of strength from continued contact with the land. But whereas *Places* waxed gushy, *Country* remained gritty and grim. Nowhere, thankfully, did audiences note in director Richard Pearce's approach the prissy pictorialism which, in *Places*, made the Great Depression look like a lark to be lovingly recalled; not once, just as thankfully, did audiences ever get the impression that farmers have no daily routines, only immense traumas to be resolved in the most dramatic manner possible, as in *The River*. The almost saccharine spirit of the former and the uncomfortably shrill tone of the latter here gave way to a stark vision, boasting accurate images of weather-beaten barns and the lined faces of people who have prematurely aged owing to daily duels with the elements and the accountants.

Comparing *Places* and *Country* is like contrasting paintings by Norman Rockwell with those of Andrew Wyeth. The former offers us an agreeably romanticized image of ourselves as a people; the latter forces us to look hard at our true selves, without illusions. One marvelous touch in the knowing script by William D. Wittliff was having Lange constantly serving huge dinners of fried chicken to her family, even as they talked about fear of foreclosure. Some misguided critics actually complained that, for a family facing financial disaster, the Ivys were eating high off the hog. In fact, it's impossible to work even a day on a farm without eating well, so the filmmakers were to be commended for not taking the easy, obvious approach of having the characters look half-starved, playing to audience preconceptions. To call *Country* the best of the farm films is to unfairly understate the case. Though all but unseen, it remains one of the great ones of the Eighties.

The Killing Fields

A WARNER BROS RELEASE OF AN
ENIGMA PRODUCTION   1984

CREDITS:

Produced by David Puttnam; directed by Roland Joffe; written by Bruce Robinson, based on *The Death and Life of Dith Pran* by Sydney Schanberg; photography, Chris Menges; editor, Jim Clark; Running time, 141 min.; Rating: R.

CAST:

Sydney Schanberg (Sam Waterston); *Dith Pran* (Haing S. Ngor); *Al Rockoff* (John Malkovich); *Jon Swain* (Julian Sands); *Military Attaché* (Craig T. Nelson); *U.S. Consul* (Spalding Gray); *Dr. Macentire* (Bill Parterson); *Dr. Sundesval* (Athol Fugard); *Pran's Wife* (Katherine Krapum Chey).

Despite the title, images of killing were not what audiences took away from *The Killing Fields*. Certainly, there were brutal moments in this fact-based film, necessarily since it concerned the occupation of Cambodia by the Khmer Rouge after the withdrawal of American military forces, and the atrocities visited upon the gentle people of that country during what emerged as an unpublicized holocaust. Based on eyewitness reports, including those of then-*New York Times* journalist Sydney Schanberg (recipient of the Pulitzer Prize for his coverage and soberly, splendidly played in the film by Sam Waterston), the visual depictions of brutality rang true. Yet, in retrospect, the depiction of violence, however intense and convincing, recedes somewhat in the memory, allowing us to vividly recall the humanity that suffused this film: the drama involving briefly glimpsed but economically introduced characters while focusing chiefly on the relationship between Schanberg and his Cambodian guide and interpreter, Dith Pran (played by Dr. Haing S. Ngor, like Pran a survivor of the Cambodian holocaust and eventual Oscar winner as Best Supporting Actor for his debut role).

Pran was, owing to miscalculations by Schanberg, forced to remain in occupied Cambodia after the departure of the American journalists (including one antic photographer dazzlingly played by John Malkovich). The fate of such natives who had befriended Americans was to be herded into the countryside for "reeducation," consisting mainly of barbaric treatment and endless exposure to blatant propaganda. Intriguingly, then, first-time director Roland Joffe (a veteran of documentary filmmaking) chose his priorities carefully, refusing to invent scenes to convey the closeness between Schanberg and Pran, adding to the impact of Schanberg's unintentional betrayal of his aide and friend. Which explains why, despite the fact it existed in part to educate the moviegoing public about atrocities on a grand scale, *The Killing Fields* never broke down into polemics. First and foremost it remains a human drama.

The Killing Fields is as suspenseful, gripping and involving as a first-rate work of fiction, though never for a moment allowing us to forget this is a true tale. For instance, there's Schanberg, hailed in the press as a hero;

THE KILLING FIELDS: Al Rockoff (John Malkovich) and Sydney Schanberg (Sam Waterston) must leave his faithful friend Dith Pran (Haing S. Ngor) behind.

yet far from delivering a further embellishment of the man's legendary status, the film continually takes him to task. The movie examines Schanberg's motives, making us wonder if underneath his seemingly courageous and selfless front there existed some self-serving motivations behind his endless attempts to relocate his old friend, reasons of which he, at the time, was only dimly aware—if at all. As a character in this movie, Schanberg is neither the swiftly sketched-in protagonist of a docudrama or the uncriticized hero of a worshipful tribute, but something akin to the lead in an Ingmar Bergman drama: a man coming to conscious awareness of himself, fearful of what he may eventually have to face.

Schanberg does not, like the wish-fulfillment heroes of *Rambo II* or *Missing in Action*, strap on a pistol and march off to Southeast Asia to single-handedly free his friend; like most normal men, he remains in an office, writing letters and making phone calls, growing ever more frustrated and anxious over his inability to achieve anything at all. Schanberg's role as a journalist defined him for the movie's viewers: observer rather than active participant. To complement him, Pran was the man of action, freeing himself by making good an escape from

THE KILLING FIELDS: The evacuation, recreated in vivid detail by filmmaker Roland Joffe.

THE KILLING FIELDS: Pran's fate, after the leave taking of the Americans.

an absurdist world where reality has been subverted into a surrealistic scene, as revolutionaries, while cold-bloodedly shooting down people incorrectly identified as enemies of the state, jam along to radios playing Paul McCartney's "Band on the Run." It is during his flight to freedom that Pran comes face to face with the field that gave the film its title.

When Schanberg and Pran are at last reunited at the film's end, Joffe employed John Lennon's "Imagine"—a gesture which, though perhaps heavy-handed, nonetheless worked. Importantly, *The Killing Fields* was a message movie in tune with the Reagan era, insisting that those Americans who had politically supported the Communists during the Vietnam conflict had been naïve in believing that, once the American forces were gone, decency and order would return. The film embodied what in the late Sixties and early Seventies had been considered the reactionary attitude: only the American presence had been holding back a holocaust.

THE KILLING FIELDS: The striking cinematography of Chris Menges won one of the film's Oscars.

Romancing the Stone

A 20TH CENTURY-FOX FILM   1984

CREDITS:

Produced by Michael Douglas, Jack Brodsky and Joel
Douglas; directed by Robert Zemeckis; written by Diane
Thomas; photography, Dean Cundey; editors, Donn Cambern
and Frank Morriss; Running time, 101 min.; Rating: PG.

CAST:

Jack Colton (Michael Douglas); *Joan Wilder* (Kathleen
Turner); *Ralph* (Danny DeVito); *Ira* (Zack Norman); *Juan*
(Alfonso Arau); *Zolo* (Manuel Ojeda); *Gloria* (Holland
Taylor); *Elaine* (Mary Ellen Trainor); *Angelina, the Dream
Girl* (Kymberly Herrin).

ROMANCING THE STONE: Joan (Kathleen Turner) strikes a bargain with
Jack (Michael Douglas), who agrees to lead her back to civilization.

When *Romancing the Stone* proved to be an enormous
success in the early winter of 1984, it surprised just
about everyone, including the people at 20th Century-
Fox, gambling that this agreeable helping of old-fashioned, lighthearted Hollywood hokum would provide
enough entertainment value to lure a respectable number
of people to the box office in hopes of shaking the winter
doldrums. In fact, the film swiftly proved a runaway hit.
Romancing the Stone clicked because it offered not only
a recycling of old romance-adventure clichés, but a
perfect reinterpretation of them for the Eighties, an era
marked not only by the revival of familiar and
nostalgically recalled movie genres but also by films that
addressed the issue of movie myths and their special
meaning to audiences as, in the age of Reagan, it became
ever more impossible to distinguish between the real and
the reel.

The first onscreen image is a wild bit of action, in
which a strong, beautiful woman named Angelina
(Kymberly Herrin) finds herself caught in a near-rape
situation somewhere in the American West during the
past century, but through her strength of character and
physical stamina, she first lives out a feminist fantasy by
pummeling those holding her captive, then escaping into
the desert where she joins an ideal dream man, reverting
to a prefeminist fantasy by surrendering into his masculine arms as they ride off into the sunset. Too good to
be true, for this shortly turns out to be the concoction of
Joan Wilder (Turner), a mousy writer of romance novels

ROMANCING THE STONE: A menacing little hoodlum, Ralph (Danny
DeVito), makes life difficult for the heroes.

who creates such lusciously ludicrous tales in the privacy
of her New York apartment, then weeps out loud as she
concludes each of the stories about her alter ego, wishing
that just once in her life something exciting would
happen to her. But that will occur shortly, as Wilder
receives a frantic phone call: a girlfriend is in deep

ROMANCING THE STONE: Jack and Joan are exuberant (top) as they make their getaway, though the feeling quickly changes to panic (bottom).

ROMANCING THE STONE: Joan fends off the attentions of the sinister Zolo (Manuel Ojeda).

trouble down in Colombia, land of dictators and drug lords. Soon, she's on a plane, and presently finds herself stranded in the jungle; only the appearance of an American soldier-of-fortune, Jack Colton (Douglas), gives her the slightest hope of surviving the ordeal.

The first time we see Jack, he is silhouetted against the jungle sky, wearing the garb of a true adventurer; we sense immediately he's the living embodiment of the ideal man Joan has been writing about in her books. What gives the film such a marvelous edge of irony is that she doesn't realize this, at least not at first, anymore than she can grasp that she is, beneath her unglamorous exterior, Angelina, or at least has the potential to be. Gradually, though, Joan does come to see that Jack is the closest thing she'll ever find in real life to the dream man of her stories; better still, she undergoes a fascinating arc (beautifully pulled off by Turner) from the uptight and relatively unattractive Joan Wilder into a lady every bit as gorgeous as the fictional Angelina: reel becomes real.

In addition to that representative Eighties theme, there were other significant elements in this agreeably light-hearted adventure. *Stone* contained one of the first post-feminist jokes: When the stranded Joan and Jack first meet, she allows him to pick up her luggage and carry it for her. "Do you believe in Women's Lib?" he asks offhandedly. Like any modern woman with moderate feminist leanings, she nods that she does. "Fine," he smiles, dropping her luggage and moving on, allowing Joan—momentarily dumbfounded—to struggle with the bags herself, wondering if she perhaps prefers the pre-feminist situation, when men were gentlemen and

ROMANCING THE STONE: Juan (Alfonso Arau), a successful smuggler, gets the drop on Jack and Joan.

116

women were ladies. With its intense violence and graphic sex, the film technically should have been rated R, but in other respects it was so clearly a fun film for the family that it received a far-too-mild PG, making clear that an in-between designation was absolutely needed. When *Indiana Jones and the Temple of Doom* further confounded that problem several months later, the PG-13 rating was quickly created.

Unlike most actor-producers, who seek out starring vehicles for themselves, Douglas labored to bring to the screen a project (coproduced by his brother Joel) in which his was essentially a supporting role, proving he was less concerned with the ego trip of a star vehicle than with being a part of a worthy undertaking, for the first time taking on the kind of a role that, three decades earlier, his father Kirk would have played. As the slimy but lovable villain Ralph, Danny DeVito continued his unlikely, remarkable ascent from character actor to superstar. (The three stars were reunited for the less-charming 1988 sequel, *Jewel of the Nile*.) And Zemeckis demonstrated, in both his love for old movie clichés and the contemporary edge of irony with which he portrayed them, those qualities that established him as a key filmmaker of the Eighties.

Ghostbusters

A COLUMBIA PICTURES RELEASE   1984

CREDITS:

Executive producer, Bernie Brillstein; produced and directed by Ivan Reitman; written by Dan Aykroyd and Harold Ramis; photography, Laszlo Kovacs; editors, Sheldon Kahn and David Blewitt; Running time, 107 min.; Rating: PG.

CAST:

Dr. Peter Venkman (Bill Murray); *Dr. Raymond Stantz* (Dan Aykroyd); *Dr. Egon Spengler* (Harold Ramis); *Dana Barrett* (Sigourney Weaver); *Lovis Tully* (Rich Moranis); *Janine Melnitz* (Annie Potts); *Walter Peck* (William Atherton); *Winston Zeddmore* (Ernie Hudson).

At some point during the early-1980s, Hollywood producers became acutely aware the lion's share of their annual business happened during the summer months, when ever younger moviegoers beat the heat by relaxing in air-conditioned theatres, watching less-than-thoughtful films in general, their two favorite kinds in particu-

GHOSTBUSTERS: Ernie Hudson, Dan Aykroyd, Bill Murray and Harold Ramis in action.

GHOSTBUSTERS: Peter Venkman (Bill Murray) casts a lustful eye at his ladylove, Dana (Sigourney Weaver).

GHOSTBUSTERS: Louis (Rick Moranis), as the ghostbusters' accountant, and Janine (Annie Potts), their lawyer, were allowed a romance in the second installment.

lar: comedies about wild and crazy guys and scary films with state-of-the-art special effects. It was only logical that someone would come up with a combination of the two. *Ghostbusters* was that film and, not surprisingly, quickly topped *Tootsie* as the most popular comedy movie to date.

Effects artist Richard Edlund's ghosts appeared almost three dimensional, though special glasses were not required. The wild and crazy guys included *Saturday Night Live* alumni Bill Murray and Dan Aykroyd. The only weak link in the casting was Harold Ramis as the third member of a team of parapsychologists who go into business as "ghostbusters"—experts on alien forces who have the savvy, moxie and hardware to pull a mischievous ghost out of a hotel ballroom and some menacing ones from the apartment of a pretty woman (Sigourney Weaver). Originally, John Belushi was to have been teamed with his old cohorts, playing the brainy Spengler with Murray as Venkman, the loudmouth ladies' man, and Aykroyd as Stantz, the sincere and emotional member of the team. Such a *Ghostbusters* might have been a comedy of classic proportions. Certainly, though, audiences treated it as if it were just that, revisiting movie houses to see the film several times during its initial release, then making it an immense hit on home video as well. There were two separate Saturday morning TV cartoon incarnations, an immense array of merchandising products (everything from T-shirts to toy "slimers"), and finally an eagerly awaited if surprisingly disappointing sequel five years after the release of the original.

Ghostbusters rated as an engaging, enjoyable night out at the movies, with lots of laughs (Murray's tearful confession to his partners that a ghost "slimed me" remains a classic bit of comic delivery) mixed with solid scares. Edlund came up with everything from transparent but convincing ghosts to cute cartoonlike creatures to monsters out of mythology, which finally gathered together for a terrifying apocalypse, only to be defeated by the intrepid trio. Perhaps it's that grand finale—along with the film's basic conception—that made this such a megahit. Columbia Pictures, hoping for modest success, was happily overwhelmed by the unanticipated response. The notion that as self-concerned contemporary New Yorkers went blithely about their business, ancient forces of evil were rising to knock them out of their smug oblivion was uniquely Eighties, when spiritualism rivaled self-interest as the dominating social attitude.

Part of the appeal derived from clever bits of satire on the contemporary scene, including on-target parodies of TV advertising and current dating rituals among swinging singles; it's fascinating to note how rapidly that scene

GHOSTBUSTERS: The Ghostbusters spot a spirit.

changed, for in the 1989 sequel, Sigourney Weaver has a baby in tow and is interested in serious coupling, not casual sex. Also contributing to the appeal was a scene-stealing performance by Rick Moranis as a would-be swinger who always strikes out and Annie Potts as the firm's flaky secretary. One flaw: Ernie Hudson, as the black ghostbuster, was never portrayed as an equal member of the group (here or in the sequel) but only an inferior hanger-on.

Certainly, the combination of *SNL* performers with a storyline spoofing the then recent film *The Sentinel* seemed a modern movie conception. It's worth noting, though, that *Ghostbusters* offered a pleasant updating of past films in which great comedy teams took on the spirit world. Laurel and Hardy, Martin and Lewis, Abbott and Costello, even the Bowery Boys—all had memorable encounters with spooks. Of course, the technology for creating the spirits was, by 1984, far greater than anything possible in those old B programers, so here was a traditionally popular type of story redone with the new moviemaking technology, so true of most Eighties hits.

Finally, though, *Ghostbusters* clicked because of fine comic playing. Aykroyd is an actor who fares far bettter as part of a comic team than when trying to carry a picture on his own. Murray emerged as one of the most popular comic talents of his time, his nonchalant, nonsensical attitude toward everything and everyone around him establishing him as the comic performer who embodied the prevalent tone of the decade.

Nightmare on Elm Street

A NEW LINE CINEMA RELEASE OF A
SMART EGG PICTURES/MEDIA HOME
ENTERTAINMENT PRODUCTION   1984

CREDITS:

Executive producers, Stanley Dudelson and Joseph Wolf;
produced by Robert Shaye and Sara Risher; written and
directed by Wes Craven; photography, Jacques Haitkin;
editor, Rick Shaine; Running time, 91 min.; Rating: R.

CAST:

Freddy Krueger (Robert Englund); *Lt. Thompson* (John
Saxon); *Nancy Thompson* (Heather Langenkamp); *Tina Grey*
(Amanda Wyss); *Rod Lane* (Nick Corri); *Marge Thompson*
(Ronee Blakley); *Glen Lantz* (Johnny Depp); *Dr. King*
(Charles Fleisher); *Teacher* (Lin Shaye).

NIGHTMARE ON ELM STREET: Robert Englund as Freddy Krueger, the creature
who conveyed, within the genre conventions of a horror film, everyone's worst
fears about child molestation in a decade when this long suppressed subject at last
came out of the closet.

In the 1930s there had been Frankenstein, Dracula and
the Wolf Man; in the 1980s, there were Jason, Michael
Myers and Freddie Krueger. For the first time in half a
century, a trio of monsters made audiences shudder and
scream, then—in one sequel after another—were somehow transformed into more sympathetic characters than
their victims. If the sinister creatures of yore symbolized, on some subliminal level, the real horrors of the
Great Depression, then the movie monsters of the
Eighties likewise captured the abiding horrors of modern
society: TV news reports on child molestation, teen
suicide and the AIDS crisis all found their way into the
texture of contemporary cinematic terror.

Before *Nightmare*, viewers had experienced John
Carpenter's *Halloween* (1978) and Sean S. Cunningham's *Friday the 13th* (1980). Meanwhile, a Wes
Craven cult had been developing, composed of loyal fans
who considered him the uncrowned king of B-budget
horror. In an age when the drive-in was fast disappearing
and the movie double bill all but extinct, Craven created
cheaply produced but cleverly crafted horror films,
carrying on a great tradition of irresistibly trashy movies
harking back to Roger Corman and William Castle. The
director carved (in more ways then one) a reputation
with such gruesome landmark films as *Last House on
the Left* and *The Hills Have Eyes*. Then came the first

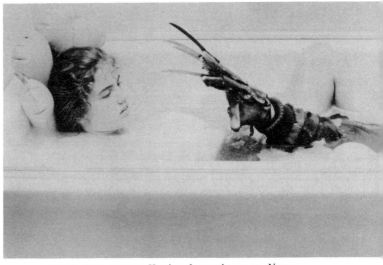

NIGHTMARE ON ELM STREET: Heather Langenkamp as Nancy
Thompson, the pretty teenager who finds her dreams haunted by
Freddy; the erotic and the violent elements were fused in such moments
as the bathtub sequence.

Nightmare, an adept little shocker containing enough
thrills and chills to keep Craven's longtime followers
happily terrified while reducing the amount of graphic

gore that had marked his first features, so *Nightmare* could comfortably play in suburban first-run theatres.

The result was a clever compromise, a horror flick featuring the sought-after scares while escaping the studied sordidness of Craven's earliest work. No one could then guess its wildly improbable popularity would

NIGHTMARE ON ELM STREET: In "The Dream Master" sequel, Freddy reveals he has no racial prejudices, first assaulting blonde Kristen (Tuesday Night) . . .

. . . then turning on a black girl, Sheila (Toy Newkirk).

lead to a series of ever more graphically brutal Freddy Krueger films and even, late in the decade, a TV series. In the unconscious transformation of the monstrous leading character from a hissable child-molesting creature to one the teen audience cheered, it also became, in view of educators and parents, an irresponsible vision.

Like all of Craven's films, *Nightmare* was strongly influenced by Freudian psychology and surrealist symbolism, set in a normal neighborhood viewed as through the distorting mirror of a carnival funhouse. This, the film implies to its young audience, is a nightmare vision of your world and yourselves. Possibly, Craven was influenced by the classic 1950s *Twilight Zone* episode "The Monsters Are Due on Maple St." Four teen neighbors discover they are experiencing an identical bad dream, in which each is pursued by Freddy Krueger, a horribly disfigured being with a three-inch-long razor at the tip of each finger. But even as the kids attempt to learn why their nightmares are recurring and identical, certain members of the group die in horrible ways. They come to understand that if the mysterious murderer manages to kill one of the kids during a dream, then the dream comes true. Or, more simply, dream that you die and you die. Gulping down vast amounts of coffee to remain awake, the surviving teenagers try to solve the secret of who this mutilated monster really is, in so doing putting an end to the dreams and the threat contained in them.

Nightmare suffered from the same defects as earlier Craven films: he isn't particularly good with actors, so the kids were nowhere as believable or convincing as those in the original *Halloween* or the first *Friday the 13th*. Even an old pro like John Saxon (as the police chief father of one girl) turned in only a perfunctory performance. Likewise, the audience sometimes saw a scare coming a mile away. More often, though, Craven proved refreshingly innovative in his approach. There were at least a dozen genuine screams in the film. More admirable still, Craven had clearly become self-assured, achieving absolute terror without actually showing much blood.

His sensibility reveals a fascinatingly ambiguous image of parents as the possible salvation but also as potential betrayers of the teen heroes. Craven featured a welcome reversal of the usual teenage-girl-as-victim syndrome, treating us to the image of the final survivor (Heather Langenkamp) effectively fighting back. *Nightmare* both transcended and transformed its genre, and if the many follow-ups were mostly junk movies of dubious quality, it's important to remember that while the Frankenstein, Dracula and Wolf Man series degenerated to some pretty embarrassing lows, the progenitor pictures were, in each case, classics of the macabre. The original *Nightmare* deserves that accolade, too.

Beverly Hills Cop

A PARAMOUNT PICTURES RELEASE OF A
DON SIMPSON/JERRY BRUCKHEIMER
PRODUCTION   1984

CREDITS:

Executive producer, Mike Moder; produced by Don Simpson
and Jerry Bruckheimer; directed by Martin Brest; written by
Daniel Petrie, Jr., from a story by Danilo Bach and Petrie;
photography, Bruce Surtees; editors, Billy Weber and Arthur
O. Coburn; Running time, 105 min.; Rating: R.

CAST:

Alex Foley (Eddie Murphy); *Det. Billy Rosewood* (Judge
Reinhold); *Sgt. Taggart* (John Ashton); *Jenny Summers* (Lisa
Eilbacher); *Lt. Bogomil* (Ronny Cox); *Victor Maitland*
(Steven Berkoff); *Mickey Tandino* (James Russo); *Zack*
(Jonathan Banks); *Chief Hubbard* (Stephen Elliott); *Serge*
(Bronson Pinchot); *Jeffrey* (Paul Reiser).

BEVERLY HILLS COP: Eddie Murphy as Axel Foley.

In 1982, Eddie Murphy was the only strong element in
a disastrous season of *Saturday Night Live*; his sassy,
irreverent persona won him a plum role in *48 HRS.* when
Richard Pryor unwisely passed (he didn't fancy taking
second billing to Nick Nolte) to do dreck like *The Toy*,
swiftly dimming his box-office appeal. Murphy, meanwhile, was elevated to superstardom, thanks to his
scene-stealing performance. All he needed was a
character that would allow him to assume center stage;
he found it in *Beverly Hills Cop*.

Initially, *Cop* was to have starred Sylvester Stallone as
Axel Foley, the street-smart Detroit police detective who
experiences culture shock while investigating the
murder of a close friend in the poshest corner of laid-
back L.A. But when Stallone dropped out (screenwriter
Daniel Petrie Jr. would not let Sly monkey with the
script, making a muddle of it as he'd already done with
F.I.S.T. and *Rhinestone*), he was replaced by the still
relatively unknown Murphy. Could a stand-up comic
possibly play a part intended for the mega-macho
Rocky? Would the role now necessarily be revamped for
the black actor? If the answer to the first question was a
happy "yes," the answer to the second was a loud "no."
Blackness is, in fact, never addressed here, making this
an antiracist film in the best sense.

BEVERLY HILLS COP: A tentative relationship develops between Axel and some
California cops (Judge Reinhold and John Ashton) with whom he forms an uneasy
alliance.

BEVERLY HILLS COP: Axel, the smart talking street black, is taken into custody by some of Beverly Hills' finest.

Murphy made Axel such a perfect incarnation of his own agreeably anarchic persona that it was impossible to imagine anyone else in the part. Whether involved in dramatic action or comic hijinks (the film deftly juggles the two), wildly riding in the back of a runaway truck or softly informing a young woman about the death of her boyfriend, Murphy provided an electric on-screen presence. He was, simply, the film's reason for existence, as well as the explanation for its phenomenal box-office success.

The film's central conceit was a clever variation on the *Coogan's Bluff* movie and the *McCloud* TV series, which pitted contemporary western lawmen (Clint Eastwood, Dennis Weaver) against Eastern big-city badmen. *Cop* merely reversed that situation. Now it was the grinning guy from the Detroit ghetto trying to survive on the elegant avenues surrounding Rodeo Drive. The contrast between Murphy, foul-mouthed and forever wearing a frayed sweatshirt, and the nattily attired men

BEVERLY HILLS COP: Axel learns to like the California scene, especially when it means driving a sports car; he returned for a hit sequel.

behind the wheels of Mercedes proved immediate and effective. First-time screenwriter Petrie (son of the veteran film and TV director) provided a sharp setup and strikingly entertaining situation, including one unforgettable sequence in which Axel confronts a gay art gallery worker a (pre-*Perfect Strangers* Bronson Pinchot).

The contrast between the unlikely hero and the unfamiliar turf, left as an implication, might have been taken further: a wealth of satiric possibilities were left underdeveloped. Besides, the mystery angle was at best functional. But no one seemed to care very much. So far

as audiences were concerned, the story was an excuse to get Murphy in L.A., then allow him to look askance at the pretensions he found there. Director Martin Brest (whose *Going In Style* remains one of the underappreciated films of the 1970s) struggled here to yoke together uncertain elements, following up a sequence of graphic violence (a man is shot point-blank in the back of the head) with scenes of silly fantasy-film fun (Murphy seeing to it that the L.A. cops assigned to tail him—Judge Reinhold, John Ashton, Ronny Cox—are served shrimp salad sandwiches by a uniformed waiter at curbside). Alternating between light escapist entertainment and a starkly honest observation of calculated crime amid the nouveaux riches, *Cop* was marked by some schizophrenic shifts in tone, mood and atmosphere. Compounding the problem was the language, so unrelentingly vile (and Murphy's performance stock-in-trade) that all but the most jaded had to wince. This created a serious problem for concerned parents, whose kids were crazy for Eddie and wanted to see his hit film.

But there, at the center, was Eddie. Fast-talking his way into an exclusive hotel, intimidating men twice his size by pretending to be an imports inspector, suddenly going soft and swishy (and, for a moment, "becoming" Little Richard) to enter a restricted restaurant, he was a marvel to behold. The ultimate irony: by the time the inevitable sequel was ready to roll Murphy could demand script control, leading to a film as awful as the first *Cop* would have been had Sly had his way. An additional irony: Eddie's leading lady the second time around was Stallone's then-wife, Brigitte Nielsen.

The Karate Kid

A COLUMBIA PICTURES RELEASE OF A JERRY WEINTRAUB PRODUCTION   1984

CREDITS:

Executive producer, R. J. Louis; produced by Jerry Weintraub; directed by John Avildsen; written by Robert Mark Kamen; photography, James Crabe; editors, Bud Smith and Walt Mulconery; Running time, 126 min.; Rating: PG.

CAST:

Daniel (Ralph Macchio); *Miyagi* (Noriyuki "Pat" Morita); *Ali* (Elisabeth Shue); *Kreese* (Martin Kove); *Lucille* (Randee Heller); *Johnny* (William Zabka); *Bobby* (Ron Thomas); *Tommy* (Rob Garrison); *Dutch* (Chad McQueen); *Chucky* (Frank Burt Avalon).

The musical score for *The Karate Kid* was by Bill Conti, who had created the magical theme for the original *Rocky*; also included was a song called "Moment of Truth" by Survivor, the group that provided "Eye of the Tiger" for *Rocky III*. The director was John G. Avildsen, who directed the first *Rocky*. Even a brief description of *KK*'s plot sounded suspiciously similar: An underdog, laughed at by everyone but the woman he loves, is trained by an elderly man who helps the

THE KARATE KID: The kid (Ralph Macchio) learns philosophy, as well as physical prowess, from Mr. Miyagi (Noriyuki "Pat" Morita).

THE KARATE KID: The final confrontation, in which Daniel must use spiritual as well as physical abilities to overcome his adversaries.

123

THE KARATE KID: Martin Kove, as the villainous karate instructor John Kreese, who wants to win the tournament and attempts to threaten the heroes.

THE KARATE KID: Miyagi and Daniel.

challenger learn to believe in himself by teaching him physical skills and self-acceptance.

In short, *The Karate Kid* allowed audiences to stand and cheer another unlikely hero. *KK* was *Rocky* reworked, now geared to a teen audience and given a martial arts backdrop, just different enough to be worth watching, though similar enough to please in the way moviegoers clearly wanted to be pleased. No wonder, then, this was the sleeper hit of the 1984 summer and, like *Rocky*, spawned a couple of inferior sequels. Like the original *Rocky*, the first *KK* revived a movie myth from which later films in the series shied away: the populist notion of the common man fighting against the power elite and (fulfilling a fantasy for frustrated viewers) winning. Like the first *Rocky*, the first *Kid* was less occupied with depicting the fights than in developing the personal relationships between a New Jersey teenager (Ralph Macchio) trying to survive in the very different Southern California lifestyle, and the people he comes in contact with: the sweet-spirited romance with a pretty girl (Elisabeth Shue), the charmingly contemporary relationship with his ever-optimistic working-class mother (Randee Heller), the growing respect and admiration he feels for an elderly benign Oriental gardener-tinkerer (Noriyuki "Pat" Morita), who begins as his karate trainer and eventually turns into a substitute father figure.

The boy, Daniel, feels he must learn karate so he can stand up to a gang of blond giants who single him out for humiliation, though one nice feature of Robert Mark Kamen's screenplay was its refusal to oversimplify martial arts, as other movies do. Instead, Kamen focused on Daniel's spiritual awakening to the subtleties of Japanese wisdom, of which fighting—even in self-defense—is but a minor part. Before he can train for the big tournament, wherein he'll eventually face off against his tormentor (William Zabka), Daniel must first learn humility, freeing him to overcome the limitation of his small frame in a way his Western-oriented ego did not.

Since it's been estimated that over half the country's karate students are under the age of 18, *KK* understandably had enormous youth appeal. But this proved one of those special youth-targeted films which, like *Risky Business*, appealed to adult audiences as well. Part of the impact derived from the way Avildsen transformed this, like the first *Rocky*, into a Frank Capra fable, updated for the Eighties, with a positive attitude about the way in which the little man can stand up to the forces of corruption and power around him, even beat them back. This was both *Mr. Smith Goes to California* and *Mr. Deeds Goes to Karate Class*. Avildsen understood that while the style of those films belonged to the past, their sentiments remained basic to the American outlook and, accordingly, he effectively updated them.

124

The drama, though highly engaging, was laced with humor that lent *KK* a special appeal. Still, there was an admirable layer of social commentary, giving the film resonance through striking contrasts of haves and have-nots. As the boy from a San Fernando Valley slum dates a girl who lives in a Beverly Hills mansion, the scene starts as an effective comedy of contrasts but concludes as borderline tragedy, a worthwhile variation on a time-tested theme. Morita finally found the character role he'd been searching for his entire life, though Mr. Miyagi grew more tiresome with each subsequent film. While Macchio was clearly the perfect choice for the part of Daniel, he, too, began to quickly grate on audiences' nerves in the silly sequels (in his late twenties by the second one, he was still playing a teenager), seeming less a likably sensitive young man, more a whining wimp. However, Avildsen had no intention of making the financial mistake he earlier had with *Rocky*, refusing to direct *Rocky II* or *Rocky III* or *Rocky IV* so as to avoid becoming a packager of worthless commercial hits. Though *KK2* and *KK3* had even less to recommend them than the *Rockys*, Avildsen was always there to helm them: doubtless to the credit of his bank account, though clearly to the debit of a lofty reputation. It's hard to believe the man who created classics like *Joe* and *Save the Tiger* would sell his soul to the sequel factory, but that's what happened.

GREMLINS: Inventor Rand Peltzer (Hoyt Axton) comes across a most unusual pet for his son Billy while in a Chinatown basement; the elderly shop owner (Keye Luke) and his grandson (John Louie) warn him, "Never get them wet."

Gremlins

A WARNER BROS. RELEASE OF AN
AMBLIN ENTERTAINMENT FILM   1984

CREDITS:

Executive producers, Steven Spielberg, Frank Marshall and Kathleen Kennedy; produced by Michael Finnell; directed by Joe Dante; written by Chris Columbus; photography, John Hora; editor, Tina Hirsch; Running time, 111 min.; Rating: PG.

CAST:

Billy (Zach Galligan); *Rand Peltzer* (Hoyt Axton); *Kate* (Phoebe Cates); *Lynn* (Frances Lee McCain); *Mrs. Deagle* (Polly Holliday); *Sheriff* (Scott Brady); *Hanson* (Glynn Turman); *Pete* (Corey Feldman); *Futterman* (Dick Miller); *Grandfather* (Keye Luke); *Gerald* (Judge Reinhold); *Deputy* (Jonathan Banks); *Corben* (Edward Andrews); *Gizmo's Voice* (Howie Mandel).

GREMLINS: Mrs. Ruby Deagle (Polly Holliday), who bears a not coincidental resemblance to the Wicked Witch of the West, enters a bank just like the one in *It's a Wonderful Life*, demanding that Billy's dog be destroyed.

125

GREMLINS: The family stands in awe as the gremlins devastate their town.

It began like *E.T.*: a nice boy, lonely but likable, cares for a cuddly creature. And for the first third of its running time, the audience accepted *Gremlins* as a good-natured, pleasantly sentimental variation on that theme. Then everything went mad: The warmth turned into terror as the cute creature was overshadowed by dozens of deadly little devils, ugly and arrogant, with snapping fangs that made them look like mini-*Alien* monsters. Their bloodlust—graphic and horrifying—changed *Gremlins* from a bright daydream into a dark nightmare. Then the movie shifted gears again as, in its final third, *Gremlins* transformed (much like the creatures it was about) one more time, ending up downright silly: a spoof of monster movies that made viewers reconsider their ever-changing reactions to the earlier portions of this daring, dazzling picture.

Producer Steven Spielberg, screenwriter Chris Columbus, and director Joe Dante took wild, wonderful risks and amazingly it all worked. In the process, they created a film that was difficult to describe, impossible to define, fitting into no preexisting categories. Clearly, though, it provided an apotheosis of everything they love best about classic "popcorn" pictures: *Gremlins* offered, among other things, an unpredictably appealing tour through Hollywood history. This was clear from the opening, a Christmas Eve sequence—complete with

GREMLINS: The young heroes (Zack Galligan and Phoebe Cates) wander through the remnants of mythical Kingston Falls, after the Gremlins have their way with the town.

126

make-believe snow falling on a patently artificial small town—which had film fans reminiscing about Frank Capra's *It's a Wonderful Life*. The key scene of *Gremlins*, like the core moment of that film, took place in a bank; to make the comparison crystal clear, the main characters in *Gremlins* later watch *It's a Wonderful Life* on TV, even as their lives begin to parallel those of the Capra characters. At one point, as they turn the channel and watch *Invasion of the Body Snatchers*, giant pods like the ones in that movie are even then popping open in their own house. What the movie implies is that Americans are so enamored of old movies, we perceive actuality in their image. Movies are not so much a temporary escape from reality as a permanent alteration of the ways people deal with the real world. No wonder, then, that when a nasty old woman (Polly Holliday) gives Billy (Zach Galligan) a hard time, he conceives of her as the witchlike lady who wanted to steal Dorothy's Toto in *The Wizard of Oz*. Or that when Stripe the Gremlin and his minimonster pals are finally overcome by Billy and the good Gizmo, they are too busy watching a movie (*Snow White and the Seven Dwarfs*) to protect themselves. Though *Gremlins* is set in the Eighties, everything about it appears to be out of the late Forties or early Fifties: the film is a perfect allegory for the politics of the Reagan years.

Gremlins was set in a small town that never existed anywhere outside a Hollywood sound stage. It so clearly took place in a make-believe movie misconception of what mainstream American life is like that it proved impossible to be offended by the sudden lapses into questionable taste, as when Mom (Frances Lee McCain) is attacked by a killer Christmas tree, then splatters one of the gremlins in a blender. *Gremlins* stands as an exercise in studied artificiality, featuring state-of-the-art special effects. The gremlins were an end-product of moviemaking imagination: Munchkins and Body Snatchers combined, *E.T.* and *Alien* yoked together. Movie lovers, familiar with all the old films, picked up on the never-ending throwaway references to a long line of beloved picture from *The Searchers* to *The Time Machine*, enjoying *Gremlins* as a summation of a great entertainment tradition. More casual moviegoers, on the other hand, did not know or care about any of that. But they knew that what they were seeing offered a great time at the movies.

Gremlins established Dante as an important filmmaker. Previously known for funky, far-fetched B horror features (*Piranha, The Howling*) Dante was a Spielberg protegé, but in many ways his polar opposite. In the previous year's *Twilight Zone—The Movie*, the Spielberg- and Dante-directed sequences were diametric. Whereas Spielberg's ("Kick the Can") offered a sweet-spirited

statement about the gentle beauty of the youthful state of old people's minds, Dante's, about a mentally ill child who possesses the terrible power to transform the world into a grotesque cartoon, conversely viewed the child state as one of monstrous moral ignorance. Amazingly, Spielberg and Dante here successfully collaborated on a film that happily combined their light and dark sensibilities.

The Terminator

AN ORION PICTURES RELEASE OF A HEMDALE PRODUCTION   1984

CREDITS:

Executive producers, John Daly and Derek Gibson; produced by Gale Anne Hurd; directed by James Cameron; written by Hurd and Cameron; photography, Adam Greenberg; editor, Mark Goldblatt; Running time, 108 min.; Rating: R.

CAST:

Terminator (Arnold Schwarzenegger); *Kyle Reese* (Michael Biehn); *Sarah Connor* (Linda Hamilton); *Traxler* (Paul Winfield); *Vukovich* (Lance Henriksen); *Matt* (Rich Rossovich); *Ginger* (Bess Motta).

THE TERMINATOR: "I'll be right back!"; Arnold Schwarzenegger gambled by taking an unsympathetic role and won big, achieving superstardom in the title role.

When Arnold Schwarzenegger essayed the title role in *The Terminator*, he was already something of a star, having appeared as himself in the documentary *Pumping Iron*, as a scene-stealing weight lifter opposite Sally Field in the romantic comedy *Stay Hungry*, and as the comic book superhero in *Conan the Barbarian*. But while Conan seemed a custom-made part for the self-effacing Atlas-like actor, most observers guessed there was nowhere for Schwarzenegger to go but into sequels (*Conan the Destroyer*) and spin-offs (*Red Sonja*), inferior films designated for a nondiscriminating audience. Then Schwarzenegger surprised everyone by crossing over to mainstream stardom, eventually proving he could be popular in a totally nonviolent comedy like *Twins*, opposite diminutive Danny DeVito.

One key step in his progress was *The Terminator*, a role Schwarzenegger took over the pleadings of advisors, who insisted that by playing a ruthless villain, he'd rule himself out for leading-man status in Hollywood. Intelligent enough to understand his ambitions were hampered by his prominent Austrian accent, Schwarzenegger wisely opted to play the almost wordless killer from the future, relying completely on his strong presence. The gamble paid off. Though shot as a relatively low-budget wall-to-wall action thriller by producer Gale Hurd and her then-husband, director James Cameron, the film propelled them, along with their then-nominal star, into the big leagues of Hollywood when this movie quickly became the most popular in the country, then a part of contemporary pop culture. When Billy Crystal is unable to kill Danny DeVito's mother in

Throw Momma From the Train, he smirks: "She's not a woman...she's 'The Terminator.'"

The saga begins a quarter century from now, when human beings and their cyborg (lifelike robot) creations have entered into a struggle for dominance, which the cyborgs seem likely to win. However, one man may rally the human race and lead them in a counterassault. Unable to locate him, the cyborgs hatch a plan: they will project one of their own, an android assassin, back through time to 1984, where this "terminator" is to kill the young woman, Sarah Connor (Linda Hamilton), who otherwise will give birth to humankind's last great hope. Luckily, the endangered future-beings learn of this and send an agent, Kyle Reese (Michael Biehn), back in time, they hope, thwart the murder.

Serious fans of science fiction were quick to note the Cameron-Hurd script bore more than marginal resemblance to a classic episode of the old TV series *Outer Limits*. But it was easy enough to forgive *The Terminator* its derivativeness considering the impressive accomplishments. *The Terminator* offered a vision of the negative-Utopia future similar to that in Ridley Scott's dazzling *Blade Runner*, but in a less pretentious manner. Though the brief opening future-world sequence could not compare with the rich texture in Scott's movie, many science fiction fans actually preferred *The Terminator* for its effective and economic use of inexpensive sets, suggesting rather than fully creating a vivid world of tomorrow. In most respects, this was a far better film than the elliptical *Blade Runner*, for the storytelling here was sharp, incisive, involving and immediate, taking off at a breakneck pace with the opening scene, then never for a moment letting up. There was not a single false move or weak moment in the entire picture.

More admirable still is that, though the film was filled with Schwarzenegger's cold-blooded killings of innocent people who get in his way, this always remained a surprisingly warmhearted movie; the body count was high indeed, yet people came away with the impression that they'd seen, not another vulgar, violent exploitation flick, but an effective human drama with a fantastical theme. The romance between Biehn and Hamilton was quite touching, and an audience truly cared about each of them as they desperately ran from the killing machine.

It was Schwarzenegger, however, who mesmerized everybody. Occasionally, his natural gift for comedy was neatly utilized: no one who has seen the film will ever forget his straight-faced delivery of the line, "I'll be right back!" to a desk clerk, returning momentarily to destroy the building by driving directly into it with his monstrous motorized vehicle. Grimacing and snarling, he and his immense frame fill the movie screen as that of his boyhood screen idol, John Wayne, did in his prime. The shoulders were so big that, when Schwarzenegger stood center screen, almost everything else was blocked from view. This was what critic Judith Crist tags a "movie-movie," visually written in the shorthand language of the cinema, its ideas carried along by nonstop, nearly wordless movement.

The Gods Must Be Crazy!

A 20TH CENTURY-FOX RELEASE OF A TLC/CAT FILMS PRODUCTION   1984

CREDITS:

Executive producer, Boet Troskie; produced, directed, written and edited by Jamie Uys; photography, Jamie Uys, Buster Reynolds and Robert Lewis; Running time, 108 min.; Rating: PG.

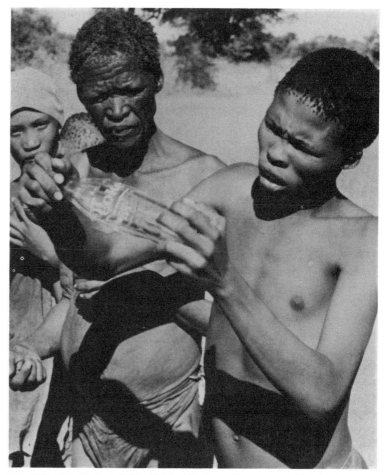

THE GODS MUST BE CRAZY!: The Kalahari Bushmen discover a soft drink bottle, dropped by a passing airplane, and believe it to be a gift from the gods.

THE GODS MUST BE CRAZY!: Xi (N!xau) journeys to what he believes to be the end of the world in order to toss the crazy gift back to the gods.

THE GODS MUST BE CRAZY!: Andrew Steyn (Marius Weyers) does his best to halt his advancing, brakeless jeep.

CAST:

Andrew Steyn (Marius Weyers); *Kate Thompson* (Sandra Prinsloo); *Xi* (N!xau); *Sam Boga* (Louw Verwey); *Mpudi* (Michael Thys); *Reverend* (Jamie Uys); *Jack Hind* (Nic de Jager); *President* (Ken Gampu).

The story of this film's success—its metamorphosis from an all-but-unknown and barely released imported item into a cinematic legend—is every bit as fascinating as the story told by the movie itself. Completed in 1981, *The Gods Must Be Crazy* did not immediately find wide distribution in the United States, in part because the old art-house circuit had all but disappeared, in part because of a growing disdain for anything perceived of as being from South Africa, land of apartheid. Technically, though, the film was a product of Botswana, and while the writer-producer-director, Jamie Uys, was white, his film's contents made clear this was anything but prejudicial. When *Gods* finally received wide American release, moviegoers discovered this diamond in the rough and swiftly made it the highest grossing foreign language film ever distributed in the United States.

It was, simply, a one-of-a-kind film, wonderfully wacky and so original it all but defied simple description. The movie begins with a quasidocumentary tone, resembling a *National Geographic* special (complete with somber-voiced narration) about a tribe of African bushmen who inhabit a stretch of the Kalahari so remote that civilization has never brushed against their primitive lifestyle. Next there follows a brutal depiction, right out

130

THE GODS MUST BE CRAZY!: Kate Thompson (Sandra Prinsloo) attempts to abandon a runaway jeep in the wilds of the Kalahari.

of a Charles Bronson shoot-'em-up, of violent revolutionaries pursued by police. Finally, a pretty blonde, Kate Thompson (Sandra Prinsloo), is seen journeying into the jungle to teach deprived children there, instead finding herself traveling through the bush with a bumbling microbiologist (Marius Weyers) as, in the tradition of a romantic road comedy such as *It Happened One Night*, the two gradually realize their initial antipathy is giving way to tentative true love.

With a blatant disregard for such aesthetic niceties as balance, proportion, or consistency of tone, *The Gods Must Be Crazy* than leaps (with an outlandish energy unseen since Preston Sturges's *Sullivan's Travels*) from one story to the next, exhibiting the wild abandon of Benny Hill and Clint Eastwood dueling to the death in the middle of a Disney "True Life Adventure." The title derived from an incident in which a bush pilot, flying low over isolated territory, finishes a bottle of Coca-Cola, then mindlessly tosses it out his window. Down below, this bit of litter causes a major catastrophe when an easygoing bushman (N!xau) stumbles upon it, rushing back to his tribe with the object they decide must come from the gods. But to what purpose? At first, they can't figure out what to do with the Coke bottle (which somehow landed unbroken) but worship it. Then they come up with too many possible functions, causing the once happily complacent people to become jealous and greedy as everyone hopes to possess it. At last, Xi decides to take on the immense responsibility of march-

ing to the edge of the world and throwing this enchanted but apparently evil object into the abyss, thereby returning it to the gods, who clearly must have been crazy to rain it down on them in the first place.

During his journey, the bushman comes in contact with those violent revolutionaries and the comically romantic couple, not to overlook some other assorted oddballs wandering about the darkest continent, including a flaky reverend, played by filmmaker Uys. All this mayhem and madness added up to a remarkable example of black humor (no pun intended) as Uys captured on film the innocent charm of a tribal fable crashing head-on into a screwball comedy. Perhaps *Gods* was meant as an allegory of sorts, scrutinizing the ways in which even the least significant element of our overly commercialized culture is enough to totally blight a beautiful primitive civilization; perhaps it was supposed to be a wry discourse on the way in which any civilization reads great religious significance into any unknown object, however mundane. But whatever one sees as the true meaning, *Gods* impressively presented an antiracist vision. The bushman is a noble figure indeed, marching steadfastly on his single-minded mission with the self-assurance of one who has lived a simple life, close to the earth. Compared to him, the white characters are a bit dotty, but other than the vicious terrorists, they are decent enough sorts, trying to exist without harming anyone, as much the victims of their own consumer culture as is the tribe that brushes up against them. *The Gods Must Be Crazy*, like the Australian *"Crocodile" Dundee* and the independently produced American sleeper-hit *Eating Raoul*, proved that even during a decade marked by a return to the formula films of the past, audiences could still be lured into the theaters by agreeable oddities that really did provide something entirely different.

Amadeus

AN ORION RELEASE OF A SAUL ZAENTZ CO. PRESENTATION   1984

CREDITS:

Executive producers, Michael Hausman and Bertil Ohlsson; produced by Saul Zaentz; directed by Milos Forman; written by Peter Shaffer from his play; photography, Miroslav Ondricek; editors, Nena Danevic and Michael Chandler; Running time, 158 min.; Rating: PG.

AMADEUS: Tom Hulce as Wolfgang Amadeus Mozart.

CAST:

Antonio Salieri (F. Murray Abraham); *Wolfgang Amadeus Mozart* (Tom Hulce); *Constanze Mozart* (Elizabeth Berridge); *Emanuel Schikaneder* (Simon Callow); *Leopold Mozart* (Roy Dotrice); *Katerina Cavalieri* (Christine Ebersole); *Emperor Joseph II* (Jeffrey Jones); *Parody Commendatore* (Kenny Baker).

They said it couldn't be done: Turning Peter Shaffer's marvelous stage piece *Amadeus* into a movie would produce only another talky failure on the order of *Royal Hunt of the Sun* and *Equus*, earlier live-theatre works by this critically acclaimed playwright that had suffered when transferred to the screen. But therein lay the problem: they'd only been "transferred," whereas *Amadeus* was totally transformed, and the distinction proved more than merely semantic. Rather than hire a Hollywood screenwriter to "open up the play" (custom-arily retaining the original dialogue but constantly switching the locations), producer Saul Zaentz (*One Flew Over the Cuckoo's Nest*) hired Shaffer. Instead of protecting his play, Shaffer slashed away at it, cutting out not only important dialogue and scenes but even his original conception. The result, a script about Mozart (1756-91) every bit as brilliantly cinematic in conception as the play had been in tune with the possibilities and limitations of live theatre.

Onstage, the focus remained on Antonio Salieri, the Italian composer-conductor who enjoyed favored status at the Viennese Court of Joseph II, Hapsburg emperor, until the young upstart Mozart arrived, threatening to show up Salieri's essential mediocrity. The duel between journeyman and genius was, onstage, seen through Salieri's eyes, Mozart remaining a distant, secretive, even secondary figure, appreciated or envied from afar: a romanticized portrait of the artist as sensitive and self-destructive. The film, however, turned that concept inside out: Here, Salieri (Oscar-winning F. Murray Abraham, little known to moviegoers prior to this, but a respected New York stage actor) was only an inroad, a handy means of introducing Mozart (Tom Hulce), who quickly assumed the pivotal part.

Onstage, *Amadeus* may have been a meditation on the madness of true talent, perceived through the awestruck eyes of the self-acknowledged ordinary man; on screen, *Amadeus* emerged as an awesome appraisal of greatness, employing the second-rate talent as a foil to reveal the shimmering style and impressive substance that, on those rare occasions when they come together in one person, lead to true greatness. This, then, was a film with two heroes and no villains: Salieri may at first seem a cynical, manipulative Iago to Mozart's naïve, trusting Othello, but under Milos (*Ragtime*) Forman's firm though delicate directorial hand, something quite special transpired. Despite what Salieri does, he wins our sympathies. He may be weak, but he is not evil.

In his time, Salieri enjoyed immense popular success by strictly following all the rules, though he was doomed to realize his work was fading, even forgotten, before his own life drew to a close. Mozart, flouting convention at every turn, knew full well the public failure that regularly visits artistic innovators, while the status of his work grew with each passing year. If Mozart's tragedy is that he cannot temper brilliance with moderation, Salieri's is that he cannot rise above convention to achieve the ultimate aim of any artist, inspiration. In Forman's vision, they are less like Othello and Iago than Thomas Becket and Henry II, locked in an agonizing life-death struggle that drags the dazzled audience through an intellectual battering and emotional brutalizing that's ultimately cathartic. Viewers left the movie houses drained and delighted, exhausted and enlightened, sen-

AMADEUS: An ill Mozart is "cared for" by his seeming friend/actual enemy Salieri (F. Murray Abraham); as the lighting in this sequence indicates, the focus was subtly shifted from Salieri to Mozart for Peter Shaffer's film version.

AMADEUS: Tom Hulce, as Mozart, conducts an orchestra at a command performance.

AMADEUS: The Emperor (Jeffrey Jones) and his court attend a Mozart performance.

sing they'd vicariously experienced the highs and lows of creative conflict.

To make clear this was no simple biography of a past master but a more universalized assessment of every artist's plight, the filmmakers daringly decided on a modern tone for this costume film. Despite the 18th century trappings (Forman shot *Amadeus* in his native Prague, his first film there in more than 15 years), Shaffer insisted his characters speak not in the stilted style of period-piece pictures but in contemporary slang. Hulce played "Wolfie" as a gleeful variation on the frat rat he created in *National Lampoon's Animal House*, a giddy punk rocker with an idiot's laugh that belied his masterful ear. Had the chemistry not clicked, the result would have been a disaster of mammoth proportions, a failed epic on the order of Ken Russell's ludicruous *Lisztomania*. Thankfully, that was not the case: *Amadeus* proved a mesmerizing, invigorating movie, as constant a delight for the eyes as for the ears. Mozart's music (*Don Giovanni*, *The Magic Flute*), a mere given in the stage play, correctly assumed its position as the core of this Oscar-winning Best Picture of the Year.

Lost in America

A WARNER BROS. RELEASE OF A DAVID GEFFEN CO. PRODUCTION   1985

CREDITS

Executive producer, Herb Nanas; produced by Marty Katz; directed by Albert Brooks; written by Albert Brooks and Monica Johnson; photography, Eric Saarinen; editor, David Finfer; Running time, 91 min.; Rating: R.

CASTS:

David Howard (Albert Brooks); *Linda Howard* (Julie Hagerty); *Casino Manager* (Garry Marshall); *Employment Agent* (Art Frankel); *Paul Dunn* (Michael Greene); *Brad*

Tooley (Tom Tarpey); *Pharmacist* (Ernie Brown); *Patty* (Maggie Roswell); *Highway Cop* (Charles Boswell).

LOST IN AMERICA: Off to search for America: Julie Hagerty and Albert Brooks as two mid-Eighties yuppies who try and rediscover the lost innocence of their late-Sixties yippie-youth by taking off on an *Easy Rider* adventure—not on motorcycles, but in a comfortable camper.

Like Camembert, capers, caviar and cranapple cocktail, the comic sensibility of Albert Brooks is an acquired taste. To call his humor "dry" is to understate the situation as drastically as describing Death Valley that way: The belly laughs in a Brooks film are as rare as oases on the great American desert. That is not meant as criticism, but as a backhanded compliment. While Brooks is not easily accessible, he's worth making the effort to understand. In the mid-1970s, Brooks enjoyed his first exposure as a regular feature on the original *Saturday Night Live*, though his short films were eventually dropped (in favor of others by Gary Weis), too intellectually esoteric in a context of off-the-wall. At least he had the last laugh, finishing his run as their in-house avent-garde filmmaker with a mock documentary in which Brooks conducted man-on-the-street interviews to determine why the *SNL* audience didn't find him funny.

After that, Brooks wrote, directed and starred in a pair of nervous comedies, *Real Life* and *Modern Romance*, the latter described by one critic as "*Annie Hall* without mainstream appeal." That about sums up Brooks: his writing approach is akin to that of Woody Allen, his screen persona more on the order of Charles Grodin. Then, in 1985, came *Lost in America*, which many reviewers hailed as his breakthrough/crossover film. The story might have been subtitled "love among the yuppies," focusing on two highly successful Los Angeles businesspeople, advertising executive David Howard (Brooks) and his career-bent wife, Linda (Julie Hagerty). Creature comforts collect in their house, though neither feels particularly satisfied with their relatively luxurious lifestyle. He's unable to sleep at night, wrestling with demons of unfulfilled ambition; she can't concentrate at work, wailing on the telephone to friends about their mounting marital problems. They symbolized the yuppie couple incarnate: slick and sophisticated on the surface, anxious and distraught underneath. But Brooks's main objective here was not a simple observation of their troubles. When his David is denied a long-promised promotion, he flips out and gets himself fired. Somehow he persuades Linda they should go out into the real world ("Touch Indians," he keeps repeating) and make contact with the common folk. They will shortly learn, though, that reality is difficult to locate and even harder to hold.

The film contains few gags in the traditional sense; anyone expecting a comedy that could compete with the laugh quota of *Ghostbusters* came away considering this

LOST IN AMERICA: At a Nevada gambling casino, Linda hopes to win enough to finance their on-the-road adventures, soon losing every penny the couple has.

LOST IN AMERICA: Garry Marshall, best known as a TV producer (*Happy Days*) and movie director (*The Flamingo Kid*), provided a memorable cameo performance as the casino owner who can't fathom David's bizarre notion that all the money lost by the couple ought to be returned to them.

an absolute disaster. But Brooks's brand of humor is as intriguing as it is unique; better still, there's even an edge of importance to it. He's a demanding and difficult comic artist, easier to admire than to like. A kind of American Molière, Brooks perceptively observes the foibles of people attempting to live up to false standards they've created for themselves. In particular, *Lost in America* addresses the issue of the ghost of the Sixties haunting those who live in the Eighties: here, middle-aged people, who have learned to love the upscale life, wander out into the world at large with an image of themselves as incarnations of *Easy Rider's* Captain America and Billy the Kid, a conceit neatly created by a sound track echoing rock music from that landmark Peter Fonda-Dennis Hopper film, here ironically set against the disastrous journey of these RV yuppies.

A typical situation had Brooks losing all his money in a Vegas casino, then desperately attempting to convince the dumbfounded manager (played by TV producer-movie director Garry Marshall) that he ought to return it all as a grand gesture which can be exploited for positive publicity. The scene is all setup, no punch line, but if one can only latch on to Brooks's circular sense of humor, it's quite clever. Brooks has the courage to try and redefine humor, the chutzpah to ask an audience to watch an ostensible comedy in which a belly laugh is unthinkable, a smile the best that can be hoped for. He created a plum

LOST IN AMERICA: Linda and David still maintain a shell of their yuppie life-style while on the road, in their trailer: characters caught between their romanticized notion of the late-1960s and their comfortable but unsatisfying existence in the mid-1980s would provide the basis for such other memorable films as *The Big Chill*.

part for Hagerty, a remarkable actress with a flair for comedy who enjoyed success in the early Eighties with *Airplane!* and Woody Allen's *Midsummer Night's Sex Comedy*, then found few vehicles to properly showcase her talent. Brooks's ambiguous attitude toward his characters added to the impact: though they seem silly, they remain worthy of sympathy. While few yuppies attempted, like these characters, to revisit the Sixties' on-the-road lifestyle, many could understand the desire to do so: inside every middle-aged yuppie, there was still a yippie struggling to work its way free again.

Back to the Future

A UNIVERSAL RELEASE OF AN AMBLIN ENTERTAINMENT FILM   1985

CREDITS

Executive producers, Steven Spielberg, Frank Marshall and Kathleen Kennedy; produced by Bob Gale and Neil Canton; directed by Robert Zemeckis; written by Bob Gale and Robert Zemeckis; photography Dean Cundey; editors, Arthur Schmidt and Harvey Keramidas; Running time, 116 min.; Rating: PG.

CAST:

Marty McFly (Michael J. Fox); *Dr. Emmett Brown* (Christopher Lloyd); *George McFly* (Crispin Glover); *Lorraine Baines* (Lea Thompson); *Jennifer Parker* (Claudia Wells); *Biff Tannen* (Thomas F. Wilson); *Mr. Strickland* (James Tolkan).

Released without fanfare, *Back to the Future* quickly became a sleeper hit and one of the most popular box-office attractions of the decade. In the process, it proved fledgling filmmaker (and Steven Spielberg protégé) Robert Zemeckis's phenomenal success the previous year with *Romancing the Stone* had been no fluke, while allowing Michael J. Fox (of TV's popular *Family Ties*) to demonstrate movie star potential. This was a sweet and sassy science fiction flick, taking a clever premise and transforming it into a charming work of lighthearted entertainment.

Marty McFly (Fox) is a contemporary teenager who self-importantly skateboards his way around his small town, devoting himself to dating pretty girls and playing rock 'n' roll with an aspiring band. Marty tolerates his

BACK TO THE FUTURE: Marty McFly (Michael J. Fox) and Dr. Emmett Brown (Christopher Lloyd) witness the first test of the Doc's time machine in the shopping mall parking lot.

lovable loser parents (Lea Thompson and Crispin Glover) while befriending an eccentric inventor, "Doctor" Brown (Christopher Lloyd). One day, though, Doc comes up with his pièce de résistance, a refurbished DeLorean capable of whisking the driver into the past. When Marty subsequently finds himself stranded for a week back in 1955, his situation grows sticky. For the young beauty who must grow up to be his mother falls for him at first sight. This intrusion into the natural order of events causes Lorraine to miss her fateful meeting with George. Before long, the time traveler is dissolving, sensing that unless he can repair the damage his presence has done to the past, his parents will never marry, and he will cease to be—in fact, never be born.

Essentially, *Future* was a summertime diversion with a bizarre Oedipal theme, a family film that flirted with incest. It worked because, beneath the veneer of hip entertainment, this was a moral fable with a strong value system at work. "It's been educational," the hero here

BACK TO THE FUTURE: Marty's Dad (Crispin Glover) likes the young visitor from the future, though he isn't sure why he feels he knows Marty already.

BACK TO THE FUTURE: Doc Brown fears that time is running out.

BACK TO THE FUTURE: Marty brings rock 'n' roll back to 1955 with him.

says of his experiences in 1955, and his word was well-chosen. For at the final fade-out, when Marty is whisked back to the future, the audience did believe he'd learned something from what he'd gone through, that he was a better person for it. Which is why the mother-son romance, which could easily have strayed into tastelessness, came off instead as heartwarming. Zemeckis was up to other things as well. One marvelous bit concerned a rerun of *The Jackie Gleason Show* the family watches in 1985, which Marty subsequently sees broadcast live when he slips back to 1955. There the viewers laugh as heartily as they do when seeing it for the umpteenth time three decades later, proving true classics transcend the limits of time. Other aspects of our immediate pop-culture environment, however, may briefly divert us but do not likewise survive the natural selection process. A key theme of the movie was the way in which certain performers or styles are hooked into a limited time frame, of intense but passing interest, and are thus incomprehensible to anyone outside it. Calvin Klein's 1985 designer fashions are as temporal in impact as were the Davy Crockett coonskin caps of 30 years ago, whereas the appeal of Chuck Berry's music or The Honeymooners' humor is a joy forever—past, present or future.

Understandably, then, the film's best gag concerned Fox's frenzied attempt to persuade the disbelieving Doc Brown of 1955 that he is a friend of Doc's from 30 years later. "If you're from 1985, then who's the President then?" the wily Doc asks. "Ronald Reagan," Marty answers. A wide-eyed Doc, now convinced this kid is absolutely crazy, scoffs: "You mean the cowboy on TV? Hah! Who's the vice-president, Jerry Lewis?" in many respects, *Back to the Future* was the ultimate film about America's long-standing (if somewhat inexplicable) nostalgia craze for the 1950s: when Fox goes back in time to that period, he was fulfilling a fantasy of most Americans who lived out that desire by attending this film. And as the movie gently acknowledges, the election of President Reagan may have had less to do with the man's political philosophy than with a mass desire to return to the simpler way of life that Reagan, in his bearing and manner, symbolized. When Marty McFly returns to the Fifties, he was something more than a character in a charming film: Marty was a child of the Eighties returned to the Fifties, literally doing what Americans had emotionally and intellectually done.

Early on, Zemeckis established the tone as fairy tale, with Dean Cundy's cinematography capturing a near-bucolic image of a dreamily recollected period. How sad that the long-planned 1989 sequel (actually, two followup films were shot by Lemeckis back to back) turned out to be nothing more than a high-tech roller coaster ride of a film, with great special effects but no charm at all, the poignancy replaced with pyrotechnics.

Rambo—First Blood, Part 2

A TRI-STAR PICTURES RELEASE   1985

CREDITS:

Executive producers, Mario Kassar and Andrew Vajna; produced by Buzz Feitshans; directed by George P. Cosmatos; written by Sylvester Stallone and James Cameron from a story by Kevin Jarre; photography, Jack Cardiff; editors, Mark Goldblatt and Mark Itelfrich; Running time, 92 min.; Rating: R.

CAST:

John Rambo (Sylvester Stallone); *Major Trautman* (Richard Crenna); *Murdock* (Charles Napier); *Co Bao* (Julia Nickson); *Podovsky* (Steven Berkoff); *Ericson* (Martin Kove); *Tay* (George Kee Cheung); *P.O.W. Banks* (Andy Wood).

The advent of the Reagan era demanded a single screen hero able to embody and project the decade's macho mentality: a strong, simple, ruggedly individualistic man of action who would in deed express the traditional ideas the public had reembraced. The actor who embodied the country's contemporary conception of itself was Sylvester Stallone, ironically achieving his initial fame in the mid-Seventies playing Rocky Balboa, a populist hero and lovable loser in a pessimistic anti-Establishment film which insisted the American Dream was only an unattainable illusion. Future films in that series, however, reversed the politics, as Rocky emerged a winner in the social Darwinistic arena of the boxing ring. But it was as John Rambo, self-styled Superman and avenger of America's soiled post-Nam reputation, that Stallone captivated the public's fancy by conveying

RAMBO: Rambo (Sylvester Stallone) confers with the pretty Cambodian guide (Julia Nickson) who will lead him to the MIAs; shortly, she will die, leaving Rambo to fight them all alone.

RAMBO: Colonel Trautman (Richard Crenna) gives Rambo his orders to go in and get the guys out, killing as many commies as he can on the way; Rambo is proud and happy to comply.

the general attitude that patriotic flag-waving was once more in fashion.

Rambo was introduced in the 1982 film *First Blood*, an uneven but popular movie about a scruffy Vietnam vet hassled by a small-town sheriff (Brian Dennehy). The film suffered from the conflict between its director, the serious-minded Ted Kotcheff, attempting to make a relatively realistic tale, and Stallone, who clearly wanted Rambo to emerge as a superhero. That film's unexpected commercial success allowed Stallone to completely control the content of the sequel. During the intervening time, Stallone endulged in cosmetic surgery and bodybuilding, also announcing that, in his estimation, the ideal film would have only one line of dialogue: "Yo!"

The plot had John Rambo rescued from hard labor by his former Green Beret commander, Major Trautman (Richard Crenna), who enlists the finest soldier he ever knew for a daredevil mission, slipping into Cambodia as a one-man army. His mission: rescue the MIAs still held captive there, with only a beautiful young Cambodian woman (Julia Nickson) as his guide. She was killed off quickly, so time would not be wasted on the niceties of romance, allowing Rambo-Stallone to waste his enemies without distraction. He realizes, while accomplishing his mission, that he's been betrayed by his superior (Charles Napier), representing the government's desire not to bring the boys home but to close the book on them once and for all.

At the finale, Stallone delivered an impassioned albeit claptrap speech about the plight of American vets. Up until then, though, the action film played beautifully as a combination of *Road Runner* cartoon and *Two Fisted Tales* comic book, thanks to George Cosmatos's flashy, frenetic, fast-forward direction, and Stallone's undeniably commanding presence in the lead. *Rambo* tapped into the national nightmare (which had recently come to full consciousness thanks to magazine articles and TV news reports) about the possibility Americans were still being held prisoner. That fear so dominated the public psyche that Chuck Norris was able to make it the subject of a similar (though considerably cheaper) film, *Missing in Action*, which also did brisk business, while *First Blood*'s Kotcheff's treated the subject in *Uncommon Valor*. Those films likewise touched the country's open nerve of social conscience about the missing Americans in Southeast Asia, but none hit with the impact of *Rambo*, which whirred through an exhaustingly fast-paced ninety minutes of murder and mayhem, wherein the muscular hero danced around enemy rockets and bombs, and dodged bullets but never missed when he fired back, and single-handedly saved the POWs.

He was clearly a fantasy figure, right out of the kinds of action-adventure movies President Reagan had long ago starred in. Briefly, some Vietnam veterans—who had never been happy with the way they were depicted on film—rallied around *Rambo*. Quickly, though, their more intelligent spokesmen (like Senator John Kerry) began speaking out against the film, which implied Sylvester Stallone could, in one day, get a job done at which the armed forces had failed, an unintentional put-down of our fighting men. Ultimately, Rambo was most

. . . or with a knife.

Peterman; editors, Daniel Hanley and Michael J. Hill; Running time, 117 min.; Rating: PG-13.

CAST:

Art Selwyn (Don Ameche); *Ben Luckett* (Wilford Brimley); *Joe Finley* (Hume Cronyn); *Walter* (Brian Dennehy); *Bernie Lefkowitz* (Jack Gilford); *Jack Bonner* (Steve Guttenberg); *Mary Luckett* (Maureen Stapleton); *Alma Finley* (Jessica Tandy); *Bess McCarthy* (Gwen Verdon); *Rose* (Herta Ware); *Kitty* (Tahnee Welch); *David* (Barrett Oliver); *Susan* (Linda Harrison); *Pillsbury* (Tyrone Power Jr).

appreciated by subteens who had been too young for Vietnam and enjoyed seeing it reduced to a comic book level of fantasy action, a contemporary cowboys-and-Indians yarn. *Rambo* captured the spirit of a country that was passing this decade with a chip on its shoulder, gloatingly looking for a war (and finding it in Grenada) that could handily be won.

Cocoon

A 20TH CENTURY-FOX RELEASE OF A ZANUCK/BROWN PRODUCTION   1985

CREDITS:

Produced by Richard D. Zanuck, David Brown and Lili Fini Zanuck; directed by Ron Howard; written by Tom Benedek, from a novel by David Saperstein; photography, Don

With *E.T.*, Steven Spielberg proved audiences would enjoy watching sweet-spirited aliens intermingling with innocent children. But would moviegoers likewise enjoy seeing such charming extraterrestrials mixing with old people? In the Eighties, the U.S. population was proportionally growing older, reflected in the choice of our President, so viewers did respond to a film which treated the problems of a graying America with sensitivity and humor. *Cocoon* started realistically enough, with three old-timers, retired to Florida, where they have everything they need in life except a sense of purpose. So when the adventurous Art (Don Ameche), the cantankerous Ben (Wilford Brimley), and the ever lustful Joe (Hume Cronyn) suggest to the authorities running their old folks' home that the new next-door neighbors may be visitors from another planet, people only shake their heads, shrug their shoulders, and mutter something about senility. But the boys know what they're talking

COCOON: The famous logo-shot, which captured the magical quality of this special film.

about. The recent arrivals on the block are returning visitors from the galaxy, come back to Earth to collect a cocoon left behind long ago.

The three old gents dizzily whizzed about their city after being physically and spiritually revived by a dip in the enchanted swimming pool housing the life-force cocoon. Ron Howard—shaping up as a director to be reckoned with after the success of *Splash!*—pulled off precisely the kind of whimsically melancholic magic Spielberg had tried for and failed to achieve in his similar "Kick the Can" episode of *Twilight Zone—The Movie*. The sequence in which the elderly gentlemen swim away their years might easily have been cloying, but clicked with cleverness and warmth. Most impressive, Young Howard created senior citizen characters without slipping into either of the two possible pitfalls. He avoided not only the condescension of playing them as saints and seers, but also the caricaturization in satirizing geriatric stereotypes. Working from a story by Tom Benedek and David Saperstein, Howard presented an intriguing assortment of people who have one thing, and one thing alone, in common: they are all seventysomething. Some proved likable, others less sympathetic; some were insightful, others oblivious; some engaging, others insufferable. Together, they formed an ensemble of meticulously defined characters able to play off one another and react to the weird but amiable aliens, as well as their grim-looking but benevolent leader (Brian Dennehy).

Though the focus remained on the trio of young-at-heart seniors (Jack Gilford was also memorable as their frightened friend), there were also lovely roles for the women in their lives, played with charm and complexity

COCOON: The beautiful young extra-terrestrial Kitty (Tahnee Welch) finds true love, earth style, in the arms of the sympathetic boat captain Jack (Steve Guttenberg).

143

COCOON: The mysterious and cryptic Walter (Brian Dennehy), leader of the Antarean expedition, rents a boat from the genial Jack, as Pillsbury (Tyrone Power, Jr., rear) and Kitty look on.

by Jessica Tandy, Gwen Verdon and Maureen Stapleton. The film faltered only when the focus shifted away from the old-timers to the subplot, a contrived love story between a bumptious young charter-boat captain (Steve Guttenberg, just then graduating from the *Police Academy* comedies) and a beautiful alien (Tahnee Welch, daughter of Raquel). Their entire romance seemed an afterthought, added to the film to "round it out" and insure that youngish audiences would find characters they could relate to. Their midnight swim sequence was the most contrived moment in the movie: intended as saucy-but-sweet, agreeably erotic though strictly within the limits of family film. Likewise, a final chase sequence over a Florida waterway (in which the old people attempt to leave Planet Earth with their alien friends, slipping off to the stars) came off as an obligatory compromise, necessary for a blockbuster, but dramatically contrived.

Cocoon, a grand idea for a ninety-minute art film about three old guys encountering aliens, was expanded into a major movie with something to offer every portion of the immense summertime moviegoing audience. Ultimately, though, what was good about *Cocoon* easily overrode such commercial considerations. While the young people were on screen, viewers could head for the refreshment stand, returning with popcorn and candy just in time to see veteran Don Ameche doing a break-

dance. The film earned him a Best Supporting Actor Oscar and (along with *Trading Places*) revived his long-dormant acting career. If *Close Encounters* had been the perfect science-fiction film for the Seventies and the posthippie era, when we still believed only the young possessed the innocence necessary for metaphysical experiences, *Cocoon* rethought that notion for the Eighties (although the 1989 sequel reuniting most of the cast neutralized the concept) and an age in which we, as a maturing society, were necessarily coming to grasp the value of the elderly.

The Breakfast Club

A UNIVERSAL PICTURES RELEASE OF AN A&M FILM   1985

CREDITS:

Executive producers, Gil Friesen and Andrew Meyer; produced by Ned Tanen and John Hughes; written and directed by John Hughes; photography, Thomas Del Ruth; editor, Dede Allen; Running time, 97 min.; Rating: R.

CAST:

Andrew (Emilio Estevez); *John/"Bender"* (Judd Nelson); *Claire* (Molly Ringwald); *Brian* (Anthony Michael Hall); *Allison* (Ally Sheedy); *Vernon* (Paul Gleason); *Carl* (John Kapelos).

Titles for *The Breakfast Club* appeared as simple white print against a black background, just as one would expect at the beginning of an Ingmar Bergman film and a far cry from the wild, colorful credit sequences of youth-exploitation flicks like *Porky's*. The basic plot was likewise distant from those breathlessly frantic teen films: Five high school friends spend a long, revealing Saturday in a detention hall, where they tear into each other's defenses, then make sudden stabs at confession, finally realigning their basic loyalties and forming unexpected relationships. Such moments made this seem less like another *Fast Times at Ridgemont High* than an underage *Who's Afraid of Virginia Woolf?* While the kids were not exactly in a *No Exit* situation (all leave, for better or worse, at afternoon's end), it was easy to see the film's message as a paraphrasing of Jean-Paul Sartre: Hell is other high-schoolers.

As uneven as it was ambitious, too often pretentious

when it tried to be poignant, *The Breakfast Club* none-theless rated as a watershed film. Arriving at mid-decade, it spelled an end to the predominance of vulgar, superficial teen comedies, establishing John Hughes as the writer-director who approached the young audience without condescension. Also, *Club* introduced young performers who would shortly attain prominence as the dominant force during the decade, known (to their chagrin) as The Brat Pack.

Hughes's film demanded that audiences accept the comedy-drama as an uncompromising portrait of the dark side of being a teenager. A lofty and worthwhile attitude, to be sure, but his vision often failed to live up to its own worthy ambitions, the film was filled with fine moments of antic humor and dramatic angst in-congruously, ineffectually placed side by side with blatant, banal silliness. Even the premise was contrived: the detention teacher, Vernon (Paul Gleason), assigned to watch over a thug (Judd Nelson), a jock (Emilio Estevez), a deb (Molly Ringwald), a wimp (Anthony Michael Hall) and a shrinking violet (Ally Sheedy), almost imme-diately leaves them to their own devices to work on required essays. Naturally, they instead spend the time talking to each other. We are asked to believe the teacher would aimlessly, endlessly, wander the halls, never guessing that the kids might take turns destroying the library and one another's psyches. In fact, the teacher leaves the room not because he really would do so, but because the screenwriter Hughes wanted, needed, him to: that is, and always has been, the difference between believable drama and contrived melodrama.

THE BREAKFAST CLUB: Enter The Brat Pack: (from left, rear) Ally Sheedy, Judd Nelson, Anthony Michael Hall, Emilio Estevez and Molly Ringwald, aspiring young actors who were suddenly catapulted to superstardom.

THE BREAKFAST CLUB: Claire, Bender and Andy (Emilio Estevez) warily confront one another as they begin their long morning of detention.

THE BREAKFAST CLUB: Claire (Molly Ringwald) searches through Bender's wallet while Bender (Judd Nelson) examines the contents of her purse; like most John Hughes films, *The Breakfast Club* dealt with young people learning about one another—and themselves.

As if that weren't bad enough, Hughes continued to create implausible (and in some cases, impossible) situations. The cocky Bender, placed in a solitary confinement area, crawls out, crashing through a ceiling to rejoin the others, while Vernon never appears to notice; the entire pack of kids rushes out of the library and through the school without his catching on. Hughes

145

THE BREAKFAST CLUB: Claire, Brian (Anthony Michael Hall) and Bender watch the offscreen Andy perform wild stunts on the balcony; the film faltered only when writer-director Hughes concocted unbelievable stunts to keep *The Breakfast Club* from bogging down in talk.

seemingly feared the audience would grow bored if something (other than talk) didn't happen, but too much of the action was forced. Still, many individual moments were fine, including individual passages that briefly did yield a powerful study of youthful anxiety, circa 1985.

One bit stands out in memory: a soliloquy in which Andy confides to the others he's in detention owing to a cruel joke he played on a weakling classmate, perpetrated because he believed it might impress his bullying father. The moment played as natural and touching, communicating a greater truth about how all teenagers, however outwardly swaggering and self-assured they may seem, are inwardly confused, ironically trying to please the very parents whose values they despise. But the integrity of such a sequence (there was one for each character) proved brief, sparkling gems showcased in cheap plastic rather than 24 karat gold: having Vernon return to the room with toilet paper hanging out of the rear of his trousers was the most unpleasant of many such cheap shots. A bizarre, unrelated and unresolved subplot had the school's janitor (who could speak like a moron or a messiah, depending on Hughes's preference at any moment) trying to blackmail the teacher. Everything worked out too conventionally at the end: the prom queen take up with the hoodlum for the flimsiest of reasons, the jock falling madly in love with the recluse

merely because she changes her hairstyle. For all its obvious failings, though, *The Breakfast Club* did deeply touch the teen audience in a way *Rebel Without a Cause* had an earlier generation. However artistically imperfect, this film, alternately predictable and perceptive, said something important to the young people it was both for and about, while its box-office success paved the way for the more serious-minded youth films, including Hughes's own superior *Pretty in Pink*.

Witness

A PARAMOUNT PICTURES RELEASE   1985

CREDITS:

Produced by Edward S. Feldman; directed by Peter Weir; written by Earl W. Wallace and William Kelley; photography, John Seale; editor, Thom Noble; Running time, 112 min.; Rating: R.

CAST:

John Book (Harrison Ford); *Rachel* (Kelly McGillis); *Schaeffer* (Josef Sommer); *Samuel* (Lukas Haas); *Eli* (Jan Rubes); *Daniel* (Alexander Godunov); *McFee* (Danny Glover); *Carter* (Brent Jennings); *Elaine* (Patti LuPone).

Witness, when it came down to it, sounded like an updating of that old John Wayne western *Angel and the Badman* combined with key elements from the Alfred Hitchcock formula. An attractive Amish widow (Kelly McGillis) and her little boy (Lukas Haas) find themselves in the wrong place at the wrong time. About to board a train in Philadelphia, Samuel sees a murder in the railroad station's men's room. Shortly, a dedicated policeman, John Book (Harrison Ford), questions the child in the precinct building, though none of the mug shots shown the lad match the face of the killer glimpsed briefly. Then the youngster happens to notice a framed photograph of an award-winning police officer, clearly the murderer. Realizing he may have stumbled onto a drug-related conspiracy within the force, Book tells only his immediate superior, planning a secret sting operation. But when Book is nearly killed the next day, he realizes his superior must be the ringleader. Desperate and wounded, Book has nowhere to go but into that uniquely American subculture, the Amish community,

WITNESS: The two faces of John Book, urban police inspector and Amish farmer; Harrison Ford proved his range and intensity as an actor, quickly making audiences forget the comic book super-hero antics of Han Solo and Indiana Jones, convincingly portraying a decent but vulnerable man.

hiding with Rachel (whom he soon learns to love) and the child witness, Samuel. Book senses that, owing to the power and prestige of his enemy, the killer can track Book down while hiding behind a shield of respectability. Though the wrong man, Book appears to be guilty.

Fascinatingly, Australian director Peter Weir worked against the grain of his material. His previous movies (*Picnic at Hanging Rock, The Last Wave*) were enigmatic and understated: Weir set up the basic framework of a conventional thriller only, to subvert, with perverse delight, all the rules of the genre, resulting in films which told relatively conventional stories in unconventional ways. In so doing, Weir redeemed the thriller form. In *Witness*, viewers assumed that, in the Hitchcock tradition, they would constantly be made aware of the forces of evil closing in, with the Amish setting employed as a colorful, original backdrop to the suspense story. Weir chose to do the opposite, making a thriller with very few obvious thrills. Early on, it became apparent Weir was not much interested in the mechanics and devices of the traditional suspense story, instead employing the film as a study of cultural dissociation.

There was only one cheap, easy, obvious gag: early on, the child-witness confuses a Hassidic Jew with one of his Amish friends. Otherwise, the humor proved humane, including one beautiful moment when, while still on his turf, Book introduces the woman and child to the joys of deli food, then tries to accommodate to their habit of praying in public; conversely, in a later scene, on her

WITNESS: Kelly McGillis, Lukas Haas and Jan Rubes pull the wounded police detective Book from their hay wagon and provide him with refuge; movie buffs were quick to note the plot similarities to *Angel and the Badman*, an old Republic western with Gail Russell and John Wayne.

turf, the widow explains to Book that Amish children are brought up to shun violence. That moment, the subsequent plot development in which the good man who has lived with violence all his life must protect an innocent community from an encroaching evil force, had more in common with the classic western *Shane* than with a typical Hitchcock thriller, while the final

147

As that man, Ford—heretofore so identified with the comic-book-level antics of *Star Wars'* Han Solo and *Raiders'* Indiana Jones—did a remarkable job of distancing himself from his previous invincible, epic-style heroes, delivering a sympathetic portrait of a strong-willed but entirely vulnerable man caught in an offbeat situation and trying to survive; Ford wisely reminded his audience that he was an actor as well as a star. Following her work in the not widely seen gem *Reuben, Reuben,* Kelly McGillis made clear she was star material. To type *Witness* (the screenplay for which Wallace and Kelley won Oscars) as one of the decade's best thrillers is to miss the point. Like Weir's earlier films, this one transcended the ordinary limits of its genre, turning the usual material into a unique moviegoing experience.

WITNESS: A gentle romance develops between the Amish farm girl (Kelly McGillis) and the big city policeman (Harrison Ford); Peter Weir brought the delicate qualities of his art-house Australian films like *Picnic at Hanging Rock* to Hollywood's popular cinema, creating a happy compromise between the two.

duel between Book and the trio of killers who arrive in town (with the Amish morally confused as to whether they should help Book or not) featured echoes of *High Noon.* Though set in the East, *Witness* was in many respects a western.

Weir avoided playing to an audience's expectations. Viewers assumed the sophisticated big-city man to be the sexual aggressor, though it was the simple, soft-spoken woman who took on that role; expected a jealous Amish farmer (dancer Alexander Godunov) would emerge as Book's chief enemy, though he instead turned out to be his best friend; guessed the final confrontation between Book and his superior would feature a duel to the death, though Weir absolutely refused to supply that. Under the guise of making a simple thriller, he instead created a cinematic essay about the Amish: a perceptive, unconventional study of a special people and one "normal" man's adjustment to an esoteric lifestyle.

WITNESS: With her wan eyes and wistful appearance, Kelly McGillis entered the project an unknown and left it a star.

Kiss of the Spider Woman

AN ISLAND ALIVE RELEASE   1985

CREDITS:

Executive producer, Francisco Rancalho, Jr.; produced by David Weisman; directed by Hector Babenco; written by Leonard Schrader, based on the novel by Manuel Puig; photography, Radolfo Sanchez; editor, Mauro Alice; Running time, 119 min.; Rating: R.

CAST:

Molina (William Hurt); *Valentin* (Raul Julia); *Leni Lamaison/ Marta* (Sonia Braga); *Warden* (Jose Lewgoy); *Gabriel* (Nuno Leal Maia); *Greta* (Pat Bisso).

At first, potential moviegoers were thrown by the title, which sounded like something fit for a drive-in double bill. In fact, *Kiss of the Spider Woman* had nothing to do with the kind of lurid, low-budget horror flicks its name conjured up, playing more like *Midnight Express* turned into a buddy-buddy film, Sartre's *No Exit* set in contemporary South America, *The Purple Rose of Cairo* stripped of its gentle whimsy and transferred to a Third World prison. *Kiss* proved to be a movie about many things: personal love and public loyalty, narrow self-interest as opposed to broader commitments, the fantasy of reality vs. the reality of fantasies, supposed beliefs set

KISS OF THE SPIDER WOMAN: Valentin (Raul Julia) and Molina (William Hurt) are mismatched cellmates, one imprisoned for his public politics, the other for his personal sexual preferences.

KISS OF THE SPIDER WOMAN: Sonia Braga as Marta, The Spider Woman, in the film within the film, rushing through the streets of Nazi-occupied France; Molina loves the old movie's style and elegance, while Valentin believes it may present a repressive political point of view.

KISS OF THE SPIDER WOMAN: The glamorous Marta is romanced by a German army officer in the film within a film; like Woody Allen's seminal film *Purple Rose of Cairo*, Hector Barbenco's *Kiss of the Spider Woman* conveyed the Eighties notion of real and reel becoming ever more confused and inseparable.

against seeming betrayals. Most profoundly, though, it was—like most representative films of its era—a motion picture about motion picture fantasies and their intrusion into real life.

There was but one kiss in *Spider Woman*, shared by Valentin (Raul Julia), a seething political activist, and Luis (William Hurt), a flamboyant homosexual. Cellmates, Valentin is incarcerated for revolutionary attitudes, Luis for molesting a child. They endlessly argue about each other's values or lack of them, entering into a verbal sparring match more brutal than physical combat. Yet when one is given an opportunity to walk out into the world a free man, both understand that mutual animosity has somehow transformed into mutual affection. They are diametrically opposed, psychologically and philosophically, but the possibility of permanent separation forces them to face the fact they've been dancing around for some time: they love each other.

To describe this as the screen's most sensitive, unsensationalized homosexual love story is to be correct while missing the point. Babenco, a filmmaker from Argentina, shot his film (based on a cult classic by Argentine novelist Manuel Puig) in Brazil, but the specific setting of this totalitarian state is left unspecified, adding to an effectively Kafka-esque aura of ambiguity. Though the prison confines and surrounding world appear realistic as portrayed on screen, well within the contours of believability, Babenco subtly lent his film a surrealistic edge. Every scene was played for heightened effect,

KISS OF THE SPIDER WOMAN: The battle of wills: Valentin and Molina argue heatedly over the message of the imperfectly remembered movie, while the viewer understands that ultimately, all movies exist not onscreen but in an audience's mind.

150

through lighting effects and acting techniques, forcing the viewer to sense that at some point, the movie reached beyond naturalism, spilling over into allegory.

The performances effectively added to growing awareness that these people are employed as pawns in a story ripe with resonance. So Hurt (Oscar-winning Best Actor for his role) and Julia neatly played their parts on a fine line between human melodrama and moral fable. Yet there was another remarkable portrayal: the title character, exquisitely incarnated by Sonia Braga. To pass the time and survive their unbearably sordid surroundings, Luis creates for them an alternative fantasy world. At great length, he relates to Valentin the story from an old World War II-era film, about a fascinating mystery woman involved in political intrigue and romantic adventure. At first, Valentin resists, insisting such Dream Factory fabrications represent decadent escapism. Worse still, he fears the film being described may be a work of Nazi propaganda, in which the Nazis are the heroes and the French Resistance the villains. To Valentin, everything is political.

The apolitical Luis cannot comprehend such concepts. Never having considered the film's political implications, he has enjoyed it only for the shimmering evening gowns and the elegant black-and-white photography. One man sees only the thematic substance in art, the other only the surface-sense of style. What we see on screen is remarkably complex, for Babenco visualizes not only scenes from the old film—or even the film as recalled (embellished and distorted through nostalgia) by Luis—but the film as finally envisioned by Valentin. We may think we share films as a common experience, allowing audiences a sense of collective entertainment/ art, but all of us recreate every movie for ourselves in our own minds, shaping it (and personalizing it) even as we experience the movie.

That's true of the movie that the characters in *Spider Woman* are obsessed by, and of the movie we watch them walk through, too. At the very end, the barrier between the world on screen and the world of the viewer is broken down in much the same manner it was in Woody Allen's exquisite *Purple Rose of Cairo*. There the effect was brittle, bittersweet comedy; here it edges up to fullblown tragedy. The two films can be perceived as unintentional companion pieces, each dealing in its own distinct way with the fact that the kind of movie they don't make anymore still haunts us. Each offers a unique enough variation on a common theme to rate among 1985's most impressive films.

The Color Purple

A WARNER BROS. RELEASE OF AN AMBLIN ENTERTAINMENT FILM   1985

CREDITS:

Executive producers, Peter Guber and Jon Peters; produced by Steven Spielberg, Kathleen Kennedy, Frank Marshall and Quincy Jones; directed by Steven Spielberg; written by Menno Meyjes, from the novel by Alice Walker; photography, Allen Daviau; editor, Michael Kahn; Running time, 152 min.; Rating: PG-13.

CAST:

Celie (Whoopi Goldberg); *Albert Johnson* (Danny Glover); *Shug* (Margaret Avery); *Sofia* (Oprah Winfrey); *Harpo* (Willard Pugh); *Nettie* (Akosua Busia); *Young Celie* (Desreta Jackson); *Old Mr.* (Adolph Caesar); *Squeak* (Rae Dawn Chong); *Miss Millie* (Dana Ivey); *Pa* (Leonard Judison); *Swain* (Larry Fishburne).

From his initial successes in the mid-1970s (*Jaws, Close Encounters*), admiration for Steven Spielberg was accompanied by an implicit criticism: Would he ever be capable of making a movie about human relationships that would not, by the end, be overwhelmed by the magic of special effects? His best pictures suggested Spielberg was an overgrown child, Peter Pan with a moving picture machine, enthralling us with elaborate entertainment, but giving us a little food for thought. No one likes being typecast, so Spielberg hungered to prove everyone wrong. Bringing Alice Walker's Pulitzer Prize-winning novel to the screen appeared the perfect opportunity.

Walker artistically analyzed the maturation of varied female Southern blacks on their journey toward self-realization. Her focus was on Celie, who journeys from a state of sexual, emotional and mental abuse as a child by a man she calls "Pa," to similar treatment by the husband she knows only as "Mister." Walker's book spanned some 40 years (1906-1947) in Celie's life, studying relationships with relatives (especially the sister torn from her) and friends, including Shug (Margaret Avery), the blues-singing mistress of Celie's husband. Her contact with other women inspires a growth in Celie's consciousness, making Walker a writer of feminist as well as minority sensibility.

The book's narrative device is a series of letters written over the years by Celie. Walker gradually revealed Celie's spiritual and mental development through

THE COLOR PURPLE: Whoopi Goldberg as Celie: the self-conscious quality of this image made clear director Steven Spielberg's intense desire to be taken seriously as a filmmaker.

her growing command of language: As her mastery of words improves, so does the width and depth of her viewpoint. This is uniquely literary, a storytelling style that all but defied transfer to the screen. But Spielberg tried valiantly, and for once in a Spielberg film, viewers concentrated on the actors. As Celie, stand-up comic Whoopi Goldberg had audiences laughing one moment and crying the next, earning her a Best Actress Oscar nomination. Sadly, she then diminished her career by appearing in an succession of pointless potboilers. The uniformly fine cast also included Adolph Caesar, playing with marvelous shadings Celie's garrulous father-in-law, and Oprah Winfrey (the TV talk-show star in her acting debut), providing a perfect counterpoint for Celie as Sofia, who degenerates from spirited woman to virtual slave. Spielberg also collaborated effectively with producer/musical supervisor Quincy Jones, who paralleled Celie's changing fortunes with his own interpretation of the evolution of black music, providing not just another background score but an aural history encompassing African ethnic influences, church music and blues, which at the film's end all finally meshed into what Jones perceives as the unique American black musical culture: jazz.

But this rich film ultimately suffered from an abundance of riches. Walker's relatively short novel was

THE COLOR PURPLE: The mayor and his wife (Dana Ivey, Philip Stone) confront the aging Sofia (Oprah Winfrey, in an Oscar nominated performance); as in Alice Walker's novel, whites are portrayed as ruthless and heartless.

THE COLOR PURPLE: Shug (Margaret Avery) heats up the action at Harpo's Juke Joint with a rousing rendition of a blues number.

THE COLOR PURPLE: The film drew its title from the beautiful purple flowers in which the significant conversations between Nettie (Akosua Busia) and Celie take place.

THE COLOR PURPLE: Mr. (Danny Glover) tears Nettie away from the side of young Celie (Desreta Jackson).

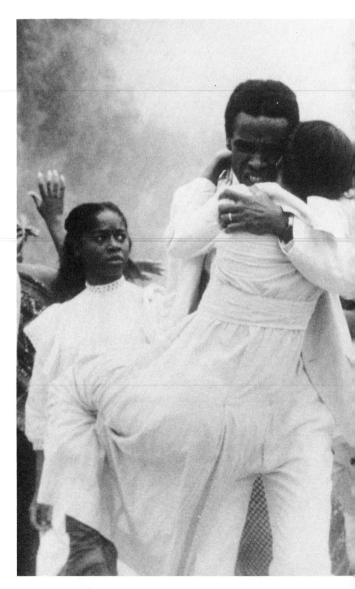

THE COLOR PURPLE: Forced by soldiers from the ravaged African village where they have served as missionaries, Rev. Samuel (Carl Anderson) cradles his wife Corinne (Susan Beaubian) in his arms, while their assistant Nettie (Akosua Busia) looks on in fear, far from the side of the beloved sister who eagerly awaits the letters which are kept from her by the heartless man she has married.

turned into a 2½ hour movie, which seemed too long yet not long enough. In telling the story of eight interrelated characters, Spielberg and screenwriter Menno Meyjes left large holes in the narrative (Rae Dawn Chong's scene-stealing scamp "Squeek" seemed shortchanged), suggesting this might have worked better as a TV mini-series. Tone and technique posed a greater problem: whereas Walker had written a grim, no-nonsense book which begged for a bleak, subdued color scheme, Spielberg shot in glorious hues, diminishing the power by prettifying everything. He seemed less than comfortable with Walker's unapologetically romantic lesbian scenes, playing them rather as tender, innocent cuddlng. The film was anticlimactic, appearing ready to end a half dozen times before it finally did.

Black men bitterly complained they were simplistically and stereotypically portrayed, there being not a single positive image of a male in the entire movie. In print, as Alice Walker's personal point of view, that presented no problem. But a movie objectifies everything, so what hadn't been a problem in words posed a very real problem in public performance. Spielberg proved, in his work with the cast, that he was indeed a fine director of actors; but in his overall vision of the story, he also revealed an inability to grasp, much less communicate, the finer points of Walker's portrait. Little wonder, then, that when the Academy Award nominations were announced, he was passed over for Best Director, though the film scored in numerous other categories. Essentially, the film represented Spielberg's total misconception of what it was like to be poor, black and female in the Deep South during the Depression.

Out of Africa
A UNIVERSAL PICTURES RELEASE   1985

CREDITS:

Executive producer, Kim Jorgensen; produced and directed by Sydney Pollack; written by Kurt Luedtke, based on writings by Isak Dinesen, Judith Thurman and Errol Trzefinski; photography, David Watkin; Editors, Fredric Steinkamp, William Steinkamp, Pembroke Herring and Sheldon Kahn; Running time, 150 min.; Rating: PG.

CAST:

Karen (Meryl Streep); *Denys* (Robert Redford); *Bror* (Klaus Maria Brandauer); *Berkeley* (Michael Kitchen); *Farah* (Malick Bowens); *Kamanto* (Joseph Thiaka); *Felicity* (Suzanna Hamilton); *Lady Belfield* (Rachel Kempson); *Delamere* (Michael Gough).

Based on diverse works of literature—Isak Dinesen's book of the same title, Judith Thurman's well-regarded biography of Dinesen (1885-1962), letters never intended for public consumption—this cinematic interpretation of the enigmatic, well-heeled, iconoclastic literary lady of the Dark Continent transformed all those words into a visual experience. Throughout the nearly three-hour film, almost nothing "big" happened; the high point, a dangerous lion hunt employed to sell the film via TV commercials, hardly represented the subtle, dreamlike, reserved tone permeating this picture. *Out of Africa* seduced its audience not through grand-scale happenings (a World War I battle proved all the more effective when played offstage) but by making the audience concentrate on what was truly important in life: the look that briefly flashes across an Englishman's eyes when he inadvertently thinks in racist terms about the primitive people his country has conquered; the manner in which a husband and wife reveal the changing chemistry of their

155

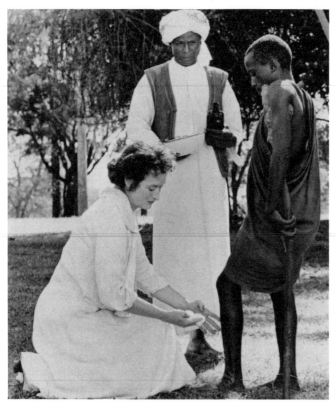

OUT OF AFRICA: Karen tends to the infected leg of Kamante (Joseph Thiaka) as Farah (Malick Bowens) looks on.

relationship less through what they say than the positioning of their bodies as they discuss mundane matters; how an affair can be charted not through purple-prose dialogue or long, loving kisses but by the special smiles lovers reserve for one another.

In this case, the love was that between Baroness Karen Blixen (later to assume the nom-de-plume Isak Dinesen), a European dilettante who journeyed to Africa in 1913 with plans of managing a farm with her agreeably worthless husband Bror, and Denys Finch Hatton, the English aristocrat-turned-adventurer who offered her love on his own terms, an open-ended emotional commitment unhampered by the vagaries of official stamp. For Finch Hatton, permanence was not something that could be insured through a marriage license, a point the baroness's own failed marriage aptly proved. For her, Victorian-era values were not so eroded by a life lived close to nature that she could ever completely cease hoping for a more conventional approach to their unconventional romance. The strikingly re-created Africa of the century's early years served as a sumptuous backdrop—a huge, detailed curtain surrounding (but never suffocating) the intimate drama.

That approach qualified *Out of Africa* as epic-romance, a tale of a singular love set against an important period of great social upheaval. Director Sydney Pollack, working with screenwriter Kurt Luedtke (his collaborator for 1981's *Absence of Malice*) here adapted an eliptical style that reached far beyond the respectable, straightforward storytelling technique of earlier Pollack films (*Jeremiah Johnson, The Electric Horseman*). Thankfully, this proved not to be a screen version of Dinesen's totally unfilmable book (part essay, part memoir, part fiction, part philosophy), but a movie inspired by her life and works, a screen interpretation of how she came to write what she did. Some critics carped that Robert Redford, as Finch Hatton, didn't even attempt an English accent. Yet to do so would have drawn attention to himself, giving the role a forced quality. Instead, his Denys emerged as less a recreation of a specific man than a dramatization of the values and the spirit Denys represented. Meryl Streep worked in precisely the opposite manner. She is, paradoxically, an American actress at perhaps her best when playing a character with a foreign accent. Pollack allowed Streep none of the whining self-indulgence other directors disastrously granted her in the name of genius, so she provided the perfect screen incarnation of Dinesen: a woman who arrives in Africa as the result of a cavalier whim and transforms, during the course of the story, into an enlightened person capable of the most harrowing commitments to a land, its people, and the individual man she has come to truly love. German actor Klaus

OUT OF AFRICA: Karen and Bror (Karl Maria Brandauer) exchange wedding vows in Nairobi.

OUT OF AFRICA: When Bror fails to help, Karen takes on the responsibilities of cultivating their coffee plantation.

Maria Brandauer appeared effortlessly effective at revealing a shallow man's considerable appeal, playing her handsome, affable but boring husband.

Leisurely in approach and deliberate of pace without ever growing long-winded or interminably slow, *Out of Africa* contained enough clipped, clever dialogue to rate as an appealing entertainment of the sort Spencer Tracy and Katharine Hepburn, or Errol Flynn and Olivia de Havilland, would have relished starring in a half century earlier. Likewise, it featured enough undercurrents of ideas to remind viewers of an import from Europe. Like all the best movies, *Out of Africa* combined entertainment and art; for those who wanted a night out at the movies, it was just that; anyone looking for serious cinema found what they wanted, too. The film deserved its Oscar for Best Picture of the Year.

Salvador

A HEMDALE FILM   1986

CREDITS:

Executive producers, John Daly and Derek Gibson; directed by Oliver Stone; written by Richard Boyle and Oliver Stone; photography, Robert Richardson and Leon Sanchez Ruiz; editor, Claire Simpson; Running time, 123 min.; Rating: R.

CAST:

Richard Boyle (James Woods); *Dr. Rock* (James Belushi); *Ambassador Thomas Kelly* (Michael Murphy); *Maria* (Elpedia Carrillo); *John Cassady* (John Savage); *Major Max* (Tony Plana); *Morgan* (Colby Chester); *Cathy Moore* (Cynthia Gibb); *Colonel Hyde* (Will MacMillan); *Pauline Axelrod* (Valerie Wildman); *Archbishop Romero* (José Carlos Ruiz); *Col. Julio Figueroa* (Jorge Luke).

Made independently on a relatively small ($5 million) budget, *Salvador* packed a big wallop for the few who saw it. From the unsympathetic hero it introduces during its opening moments to the upsetting ending Oliver Stone insisted on, *Salvador* provided a harsh slap to the face. Featuring a controversial combination of docudrama and didacticism, the film preaches as well as portrays, making little attempt to conceal Stone's anti-Reagan bias. Richard Boyle (who wrote the screenplay with Stone, and is played by James Woods, emerging in the Eighties as one of the most versatile actors and one of

SALVADOR: As real-life photojournalist Richard Boyle, James Woods offered such a well-rounded and complex performance that he was nominated for Best Actor—a rarity in the case of a film unsuccessful at the box office.

the most underrated) is an out-of-work stringer for various news services. In 1980, he takes off for troubled Salvador in desperate hope of finding work and living cheap. Accompanying him is Dr. Rock (Jim Belushi), an aging rock 'n' roll disc jockey and "compendium of everything left over from the Sixties." Shortly, they are forced to confront unthinkably harsh realities, including the wanton killing of citizens by a corrupt, fascistic regime our government supports.

Although the people in power insist the massacres are the work of leftist rebels, Boyle comes across evidence that the Salvadoran death squads are actually in the service of the right wing power structure. Which is why the American-ambassador (Michael Murphy) and various U.S. military advisors, adamant on maintaining the anti-Communist status quo, refuse to acknowledge the damning evidence Boyle and a photojournalist friend (John Savage) gather. Boyle's Salvadoran mistress (Elpedia Carrillo) and her brother are marked for death, along with liberal Archbishop Romero, who employs the Catholic church to urge revolution; also targeted is a

SALVADOR: James Belushi, as a wacky radio D.J. who joins two photojournalists (James Woods and John Savage) in Salvador, proved he was far more than just the late, legendary John's little brother—this was one of the year's most striking supporting-actor performances.

nurse (Cynthia Gibb) and three nuns caring for children mutilated in the constant violence.

The assassination of the archbishop and rape-murder of the women are stories anyone who regularly follows the news had already encountered. The power and importance of *Salvador* derived from its effective humanizing of the headlines, making grim drama out of cold facts. Despite the heaviness of the subject, Stone miraculously avoided heavy-handedness with his harrowing sense of humor. At the least likely moments, Dr. Rock reminds everyone his pet dog was put to sleep by do-gooders back home. And Woods's playing of a scene in which Boyle makes his first confession in 32 years was classic enough to win him a Best Actor Oscar nomination. Sadly, such statuettes are rarely awarded to films that fail at the box office, however brilliant.

And in a smug know-nothing decade, when the political attitudes of Stone were damned as coming too close to the dreaded "L word," audiences did not bother to put themselves through the excruciating experience of *Salvador.* For those few who chose to see it, the movie's message was conveyed through the moral education of its far-from-likable hero. At first a glib, noncommittal loser, Boyle enters the country strictly out of self-interest. Early on, he wanders through a dump of dead bodies, unconcerned with the victims as people, intrigued only with the possibility of winning a Pulitzer for his pictures. During the course of the story, he grows in understanding of the larger, human issues. When we see him last, he has unconsciously shifted to deep concern for the ravaged population in general, a family

SALVADOR: Elpedia Carrillo (left) as the local woman who becomes involved in the political turmoil owing to her relationship with the Americans (James Woods and James Belushi); filmmaker Oliver Stone emerged here as the last great screen muckraker.

159

SALVADOR: The political uprising explodes around the journalists (John Savage and James Woods); though the film failed at the box office at a time when audiences still hungered for escapist entertainment, filmmaker Stone's serious and socially oriented approach to moviemaking would find a large audience only months later, with the release of *Platoon.*

Star Trek IV— The Voyage Home

A PARAMOUNT PICTURES RELEASE OF A HARVE BENNETT PRODUCTION   1986

CREDITS:

Executive producer, Ralph Winter; produced by Harve Bennett; directed by Leonard Nimoy; written by Harve Bennett, Steve Meerson, Peter Krikes and Nicholas Meyer, from a story by Leonard Nimoy and Harve Bennett; photography, Don Peterman; editor, Peter E. Berger; Running time, 119 min.; Rating: PG.

CAST:

Kirk (William Shatner); *Spock* (Leonard Nimoy); *McCoy* (DeForest Kelley); *Scotty* (James Doohan); *Sulu* (George Takei); *Chekov* (Walter Koenig); *Uhura* (Nichelle Nichols); *Amanda* (Jane Wyatt); *Gillian* (Catherine Hicks); *Sarek* (Mark Lenard); *Lt. Saavik* (Robin Curtis); *Klingon Ambassador* (John Schuck).

of three in particular, and the American government's secret participation in the horrors happening around him.

No one described this (or any other Stone film) as subtle. But here—as in his subsequent *Platoon, Wall Street* and *Born on the Fourth of July*—Stone hardly appeared interested in establishing himself as an understated artist. Working in the admirable tradition of the muckrackers who flourished at the turn of the century, Stone sometimes slipped into preachiness, but—like the protagonist of this picture—redeemed himself through a final commitment written in blood, sweat and tears. Though some critics objected to the strong political slant Stone gave to this study of actual events, *Salvador* achieved a stirring, stinging, searing vision. Like all great films, it rated as an upsetting experience, demanding to be seen and debated. If Stone chose to upset rather than appease audiences, then his film served as a healthy reminder that popular cinema has a responsibility to do something besides soothing viewers into a belief that all's right with the world.

When Trekkies last saw Admiral James Kirk and crew, they were stuck in a foreign ship, apparently unable ever to return to Earth. That humiliation extended to the cast, as well as the characters, for 1984's *Star Trek III: The Search for Spock* had been a disastrous and dull galactic journey. But by the end of *The Voyage Home*, the crew would reclaim their beloved Enterprise, and Trekkies the world over would rejoice, for this—by far, the best installment—would redeem the *Star Trek* movie series. Beyond that, *Voyage* satisfied as a unique and all but irresistible adventure even for those who had never become hooked on the series. You didn't have to be a Trekkie to love *Voyage*, which clicked both as a science fiction film (and worked wonderfully as that) and as polished light entertainment, also enthralling those who believe the only good movie is one with a message. Though the filmmakers never became overtly didactic, they did make an environmentalist theme the basis for their concept.

As Kirk and company, now out of favor with the interplanetary political alliance, approach Earth in the 23rd century, they are made aware of an imminent danger that may destroy the planet. A deep space probe is sending out signals to a species which the probe's computers believe to exist on Earth. But the species—the humpback whale—has been extinct for nearly 200 years. The ceaseless—and ever more intense—attempts to communicate are throwing the Earth's systems into chaos. Master of logic Spock (Leonard Nimoy) devises a desperate but feasible solution: travel back in time, pick up several humpback whales, and deposit them in the ocean of the future, so the probers will make contact, be satisfied, and leave. The crew wanders like virtual aliens around the America of 1986, coming in contact with all manner of contemporary problems, from punkers with loud boomboxes to medical malpractice.

It isn't surprising that the city they visited happened to be San Francisco, as the script was written in part by Nicholas Meyer, who in addition to directing in 1982 the excellent second "Star Trek" film, *The Wrath of Khan*, also penned *Time after Time*, a laudatory late Seventies sci-fi flick in which H. G. Wells's time machine traveled to mid-1970s Frisco. As in that film, this one featured a woman of the present who must choose to stay on Earth in an era ill-suited for her, or journey with the man she loves to another unknown period of time. Here, the woman is Gillian (Catherine Hicks), a Sea World worker specializing in whales, who doesn't want to lose her humpbacks any more than she wants to see Kirk beam up and out of her life forever. The human element—the sweetness and believability of the loving friendship that develops between them—lends this film its poignancy. Shatner—an unexciting actor, who always felt constricted by the role of Kirk but should consider himself

STAR TREK IV: Kirk (William Shatner) and Spock (Leonard Nimoy) try and adjust to life in the 1980s after traveling through time; by portraying aspects of everyday life in our time as they would be perceived by outsiders, the filmmakers were able to satirically comment on the Eighties and make moviegoers more aware of our current eccentricities by forcing us to view them from the point-of-view of "visitors."

STAR TREK IV: The crew of the Enterprise embark on their greatest cinematic adventure.

161

STAR TREK IV: Trekkers Sulu, Scotty and Bones find themselves in a hostile environment—earth, 1986!

lucky to have been cast and thankful for the career it gave him—rose to the occasion, holding his own against Hicks, a dynamo of an actress who has yet to receive due recognition.

Always, just under the film's diverting surface, was the writers' more serious intention: Save the Whales,

though as in all good science fiction, they scored their points through implication, satire and studied observation rather than shrill direct statements. Everyone involved understood that the audience could be given a rousing good time while being infused with a heightened awareness of the magnificence of these animals and the horrors inherent in their possible extinction: *Voyage* was a heavy cautionary fable disguised as lightweight diversion, seducing the movie-hungry audience while gently educating viewers about the need for ecological commitment.

On the level of entertainment, *Voyage* balanced a clever sense of humor with striking suspense. The give-and-take one-upmanship between Spock and McCoy (DeForest Kelley) was never quite so acerbically appealing as here, while the trials of Chekov (Walter Koenig) as he finds himself in deadly serious problems aboard an Enterprise of our own time had viewers on the edges of their seats. Redeeming himself after *The Search for Spock*, which he also helmed, Nimoy's directorial work made clear his considerable talent, shortly reasserted in both comedy (*Three Men and a Baby*) and dramatic (*The Good Mother*) projects. Sadly, Shatner had a contract clause stating that if Nimoy got to direct, he would have that option, too. The fifth film, *The Final Frontier*, was

STAR TREK IV: Movie and TV veteran Jane Wyatt made a return to the big screen as aging Queen of Outer Space Amanda; Mark Lenard (left) plays Sarek.

162

by far the worst, receiving a critical (and Trekkie) drubbing, flopping at the box office, dimming the chances that this series would continue, and proving Shatner was little better behind the camera than in front of it.

Mona Lisa

AN ISLAND PICTURES RELEASE OF A
HOMEMADE FILMS PRODUCTION   1986

CREDITS:

Executive producers, George Harrison and Denis O'Brien; produced by Stephen Woolley and Patrick Cassavetti; directed by Neil Jordan; written by David Leland and Neil Jordan; photography, Roger Pratt; editor, Leslie Walker; Running time, 104 min.; Rating: R.

CAST:

George (Bob Hoskins); *Simone* (Cathy Tyson); *Mortwell* (Michael Caine); *Thomas* (Robbie Coltrane); *Anderson* (Clarke Peters); *Cathy* (Kate Hardie); *Jeannie* (Zoe Nathenson); *Max* (Sammi Davis); *Torry* (Rod Bedall); *Dawn* (Pauline Melville).

The public which had elected a relic from old movies to the presidency turned increasingly nostalgic not only for films from his Hollywood period but also for recordings that set memories dancing through the listener's mind. Movie producers quickly seized on the possibilities of using such immediately identifiable songs for their films, creating an instantaneous audience recognition: *Peggy Sue Got Married, Blue Velvet, Stand By Me.* Sometimes the song was not integrated into the storyline, grafted on as an afterthought, but *Mona Lisa* proved the exception. This superb, gritty British film was about what the song meant to those who listen to it, as well as about music in general and its ability to program people into perceiving reality in romanticized ways. Tragedy occurs when the hero can no longer mentally resolve his sentimental pop-culture sensibility with the grim reality he encounters.

In that rare role capable of turning a quirky character actor into an offbeat leading man, Bob Hoskins (*The Long Good Friday*) was cast as a small-time London thug named George, just out of stir after seven years as a

MONA LISA: Cathy Tyson made a smashing debut as Simone, a glamorous and mysterious call girl; "Are you warm, are you real, Mona Lisa/Or just a cold and lonely, lovely work of art?"

fall guy for his slimy SoHo boss (Michael Caine in an against-type villain role). On the outside, George's life consists of rekindling a relationship with his teenage daughter while working again for the thankless Mortwell in a new capacity. George is paid to drive a high-priced call girl, Simone (Cathy Tyson), to and from her appointments. The instinctual enmity between the short, stocky man in cheap suits and the tall, chic black hooker bedecked in gowns gradually mellows into a warm friendship. Before long, she's confident he can be entrusted to locate her lost girlfriend, last seen working as a teenage prostitute: a girl, George notes, the same age as his own daughter.

Messy, matter-of-fact and occasionally mean-spirited, there could be no less likely a candidate for romantic hero than this near-caricature of Cockney complacence. Except for one detail: whenever George finds himself alone in the limo, he inserts a tape onto the deck and listens to Nat King Cole. "Are you warm, are you real, Mona Lisa?" the song asks about the fascinating, unknowable woman in the famed painting and, George believes, about Simone, "or just a cold and lonely, lovely work of art?" There's a secret, romantic side to this dark, dreary lowlife. Before long, he's obsessed with Simone, confusing her with the woman in the pop song. Worse, George assumes she will live up to the role of goddess he has assigned her; though their relationship is perhaps the only platonic one she engages in, George comes to

163

MONA LISA: A strange relationship develops between Simone and her ex-con Cockney driver, George (Bob Hoskins), who comes to believe he is the only man Simone really trusts—despite the fact he's about the only man she isn't sleeping with.

MONA LISA: Mortwell (Michael Caine in a rare villain and rare supporting role) convinces George to gather some damaging information; director Neil Jordan created a *film noir* atmosphere while using the most contemporary styles in British moviemaking.

MONA LISA: Bob Hoskins as George.

believe this makes him special in her view, that he's the only man she really loves. Certainly, Simone says little things that would indicate this is the case; George cannot grasp that Simone tells a man what he wants to hear so he'll emotionally crumble and do anything she asks.

Heading into the neon nightlife, George picks his way through the punker prostitutes walking London's mean streets. A tarnished knight on an unlikely quest, George will eventually realize the Simone he loves is not the actual woman but an image he has created in his mind, a mental reconstruction of the real girl. Neil Jordan related George's sometimes comic, sometimes violent, sometimes sad, always absorbing story through an effective combination of low-key acting and high-style cinematography, calling attention to the similarities between this tale and the fabulous Hollywood *films noir* they emulated. In so doing, he implied George was something more than just a specific character. In his wholesale acceptance of romantic myths about women—and his difficulty in seeing beyond those myths to grasp the real woman before him—George emerged as a symbol for the modern moviegoing male.

None of this was overstated. On the surface, *Mona Lisa* remained a fascinating murder mystery, filled with involving if unlikely plot twists and marvelously detailed decors in which the classy title lady entered into endless tawdry situations. Jordan (who had attracted critical attention with his earlier *The Company of Wolves*, a Freudian interpretation of "Little Red Riding Hood") captured the essence of a classic Forties thriller, restyling it for contemporary audiences. In the process, he culled terrific performances from his cast: Caine, one of those rare superstars willing to play supporting roles in worthwhile projects, was particularly impressive in an unsympathetic role. Newcomer Tyson appeared elegantly enigmatic as the woman everyone (save poor George) has but nobody really knows. Ultimately, though, this was Hoskins's film: Moviegoers vividly recall his anger when the dream girl is really threatened, his anguish when the real girl before him cannot live up to his dream.

Blue Velvet

A DE LAURENTIIS ENTERTAINMENT GROUP RELEASE 1986

CREDITS:

Executive producer, Richard Roth; produced by Fred Caruso; written and directed by David Lynch; photography, Joe Dunton; editor, Duwayne Durham; Running time, 120 min.; Rating: R.

CAST:

Jeffrey Beaumont (Kyle MacLachlan); *Dorothy Vallens* (Isabella Rossellini); *Frank Booth* (Dennis Hopper); *Sandy Williams* (Laura Dern); *Mrs. Williams* (Hope Lange); *Ben* (Dean Stockwell); *Paul* (Jack Nance); *Raymond* (Brad Dourif); *Aunt Barbara* (Frances Bay); *Detective Williams* (George Dickerson); *Mrs. Beaumont* (Priscilla Pointer).

Blue Velvet was the brainchild of David Lynch, who had established himself with the cult classic *Eraserhead* (1978), went mainstream with *The Elephant Man* (1980), then stumbled with his big-budget disaster *Dune* (1984). Retreating from commercial compromise, Lynch attempted a balance between the two types of pictures he'd earlier succeeded with: *Blue Velvet* was a major studio release, but one with a New Wave sensibility, focusing on sadomasochistic sex but doing so with a purposefully inappropriate monotone approach. Watching *Blue Velvet* is a little like seeing a Brian De Palma plot (*Body*

Double) as filmed by Ken Russell (*Crimes of Passion*), a labyrinthian murder mystery played as arch, ugly black comedy.

If Lynch's intention was to astound and outrage, he accomplished his goals. Stylistically, *Blue Velvet* was unquestionably dazzling enough to enthrall anyone who appreciated avant-garde approaches; Such moviegoers consider *Blue Velvet* a kinky, iconoclastic "midnight movie." For traditional audiences, attracted by the schmaltzy title tune, *Blue Velvet* proved a nasty viewing experience.

The young hero, Jeffrey (Kyle MacLachlan, also the hero of Lynch's *Dune*), is an average young man living in

BLUE VELVET: Isabella Rossellini as Dorothy Vallens, the mysterious, haunting, and sometimes off-key cabaret singer in David Lynch's bizarre quasi-Hitchcockian thriller.

BLUE VELVET: Dorothy threatens Jeffrey Beaumont (Kyle MacLachlan), though she may in fact be faking in order to calm her dominating lover, Frank (offscreen), watching them carefully.

an idealized small town which looks suspiciously like Disneyland's Main Street, U.S.A. During the course of the story, Jeffrey is plunged from the happy oblivion of his total acceptance of the good, ordered everyday world around him into a realization of an alternative existence he never noticed, lurking just around the edges of the brightly lit village: a dark, terrifying nightworld of chaos and absurdity that's always been there, though seldom seen—at least not by nice people such as himself. This is the story of how an accidental occurrence sends Jeffrey for a walk on the wild side, a journey which destroys his all-American innocence.

On his way home one day, Jeffrey chances upon something gross in the grass: a decomposing human ear, covered with ants. Rushing to people in power, Jeffrey's shocked to learn everyone in authority is for mysterious reasons reticent about doing anything. Accompanied by Sandy (Laura Dern), the pretty teenage daughter of a cop too stupid or too corrupt to help, Jeffrey sets off to solve the crime on his own. But he's inadvertently set in motion events that will touch almost all the "good folks"

BLUE VELVET: Dorothy swears to Jeffrey that she really cares for him and isn't a bad girl . . .

166

in the community. Ultimately, the key to the mystery is Dorothy (Isabella Rossellini), a fascinating, enigmatic saloon singer.

At times, the movie appears to be talking place in the mid-Fifties, when the Bobby Vinton song that lends this film its title was first released. At other moments, it seems set in the mid-Eighties. Ultimately, the story occurs in a surreal combination of past and present, cleverly commenting on our contemporary obsession with Fifties, kitsch culture. The presence of ubiquitous Dennis Hopper (as an overbearing bondage-and-discipline molester) and Dean Stockwell (as his transsexual but no less frightening friend) cinches that connection, for both actors are living pop-art icons from the Fifties. Early on, Jeffrey finds himself trapped in Dorothy's closet, helplessly watching Frank (Hopper) force Dorothy to submit to unspeakably twisted sex acts. At this point, Jeffrey became Lynch's symbol for moviegoers: consciously putting themselves in the position of peeking through their fingers at what attracts and repels them in the most voyeuristic of all entertainment forms. Much

of what followed was purposefully and self-consciously "bad," just like Dorothy's singing. The plot grew ever more ridiculous (a virtual burlesque of Hitchcock's *Shadow of a Doubt*); the dialogue—recited in monotone, composed of outrageous clichés—elicited guffaws.

Importantly, the awfulness was intentional. Lynch was not making a bad movie but an oftentimes brilliant movie about bad movies, a work of high-art cinema concerned with the banality of our popular junk culture. That view worked well enough during the film's first half, when the intensity of Lynch's vision carried the viewer along. But the concept can only be stretched so far. Unable to sustain itself, *Blue Velvet* curdled in mid-movie when Jeffrey was viciously beaten by the villains. The experience was rendered in too intensely realistic a manner: at that point, it was impossible to tell whether Lynch was kidding or not. What began as a black comedy was still black—but was it a comedy? Some critics hailed *Blue Velvet* as hypnotic, while others insisted it was horrible. In fact, this movie began as the former and ended as the latter.

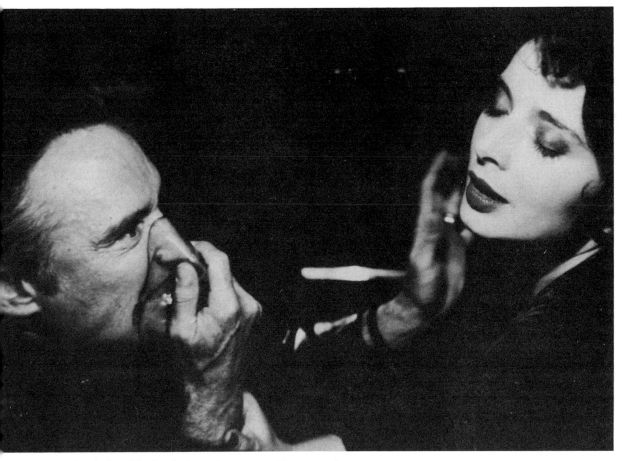

... though she willingly submits to the ever more bizarre sexual-fantasy games of Frank (Dennis Hopper).

167

Stand by Me

A COLUMBIA PICTURES RELEASE OF AN ACT III PRODUCTION   1986

CREDITS:

Produced by Bruce A. Evans, Raynold Gideon and Andrew Scheinman; directed by Rob Reiner; written by Bruce A. Evans and Raynold Gideon, based on *The Body* by Stephen King; photography, Thomas Del Ruth; editor, Robert Leighton; Running time, 87 min.; Rating: R.

CAST:

Gordie Lachance (Wil Wheaton); *Chris Chambers* (River Phoenix); *Teddy Dechamp* (Corey Feldman); *Vern Dechamp* (Jerry O'Connell); *Ace Merrill* (Keifer Sutherland); *The Writer* (Richard Dreyfuss).

Stand by Me begins as a writer (Richard Dreyfuss), struggling to hold back his tears, studies a newspaper headline announcing a man's death. The writer is not seen again until the film's end, though his narration provides a knowing, cynical, warmhearted counterpoint to recollections of the boyhood friends with whom the writer shared his first horrifying, humbling experience with the reality of death. Now, the death of one of those friends stirs him to nostalgia and, beyond that, serious self-consideration: his own personal Big Chill.

In the story proper, a treehouse provides the meeting place of four 1950s preteen pals who, like everyone else in the area of Castle Rock, Oregon, follow radio reports on the disappearance of another child. Then one member makes a startling announcement: he's overheard his hoodlum brother talking about having found the dead body alongside railroad tracks in the forest. The brother and his roughneck friends didn't report the discovery as they were in a stolen car at the time, but they plan to go back shortly and turn the body over to the police, emerging as local heroes. Meanwhile, the teenage pals—bored by a long, hot, uneventful summer—decide to win celebrity status for themselves by getting there first. Under the pretense of taking an overnight camping trip, they set out; this is the story of their journey—toward that body, though ultimately also toward a greater understanding of themselves.

Filmmaker Rob Reiner, following up on his previous impressive pictures, including *This Is Spinal Tap* and *The Sure Thing*, guided a quartet of young, relatively inexperienced performers to striking performances. Chris (River Phoenix), slightly older than the others, is a tough kid with untapped potential but seems destined to become a juvenile delinquent himself. Teddy (Corey Feldman) has a physical disfigurement caused by his mentally unstable father, though the boy clings to an

STAND BY ME: The young adventurers (Wil Wheaton, River Phoenix, Jerry O'Connell and Corey Feldman) spot "the body."

idealized notion of his dad. Vern (Jerry O'Connell) is overweight and always frightened, joining the adventure only because he's afraid of being tagged a coward. Gordie (Wil Wheaton) has to deal not only with the death of his older brother, a much-loved local football star he cannot measure up to, but also with his father's unstated though obvious lack of interest in his surviving son. Gordie's means of handling that situation is to constantly weave stories designed to amuse his friends.

There is a dark side to each of Gordie's yarns. It made sense, then, that Gordie represents popular horror novelist Stephen King, the writer of "The Body," the novella on which *Stand by Me* was based. King here forsook ghosts, goblins and ghoulies to concentrate on real-life terrors, traumas and truths: fathers who scar their sons, the intense bond of friendship one knows for only a fleeting moment in youth, the acceptance of death as an unavoidable part of life, the painful process of turning one's own psychological torments into tales for others to read and enjoy.

Heavyweight themes, to be sure. Yet director Reiner juggled them with such a disarmingly light touch that the film never became depressing or didactic. Apparently, this was emotionally autobiographical for him, as well as for King and screen adapters Raynold Gideon and Bruce A. Evans, all of whom dredged up repressed fears, frustrations and fantasies from childhood, solidifying them in a single story line. It touched similar chords in the audience, emerging as that most special item, a unique tale told in such a way that it stirred

STAND BY ME: At his word processor, "The Writer" (Richard Dreyfuss) creates popular fiction from his personal experiences after learning about the death of his boyhood best friend.

STAND BY ME: Chris (River Phoenix) sums up his courage to confront the town tough, Ace (Keifer Sutherland).

169

STAND BY ME: Daredevil Teddy (Corey Feldman, back to camera) wants to dodge the approaching train, though his friends try and dissuade him.

CAST:

Micky (Woody Allen); *Elliot* (Michael Caine); *Hannah* (Mia Farrow); *April* (Carrie Fisher); *Lee* (Barbara Hershey); *Hannah's Father* (Lloyd Nolan); *Hannah's Mother* (Maureen O'Sullivan); *Dusty* (Daniel Stern); *Frederick* (Max Von Sydow); *Holly* (Dianne Wiest); *The Architect* (Sam Waterston); *Mickey's Friend* (Tony Roberts); *Bobby Short* (Himself).

universal emotions. *Stand by Me* rated as yet another variation on a favorite theme for films of the Eighties.

Though the popular song by Ben E. King and The Drifters was pleasantly employed, it still seemed more an afterthought than anything else: the words and music had less to do with the emotions of the movie than setting a time and a place, so this was one more case of a film's being presold by connecting it in the public's mind to a musical standard. That was a minor complaint, though, as was the rough language spoken by a mean teenager (Keifer Sutherland), which caused the film to be slapped with an R rating. Most observers felt *Stand by Me* was as positive an experience for 12-year-old viewers who identify with the young Gordie as for those in their forties who, like the adult Gordie, drew strength and inspiration in the present from the triumphs and losses they survived in the past.

Hannah and Her Sisters

AN ORION PICTURES RELEASE OF A JACK ROLLINS AND CHARLES H. JOFFE PRODUCTION   1986

CREDITS:

Executive producers, Jack Rollins and Charles H. Joffe; produced by Robert Greenhut; written and directed by Woody Allen; photography, Carlo Di Palma; editor, Susan E. Morse; Running time, 115 min.; Rating: PG-13.

Ever since he began making movies back in the mid-Sixties, Woody Allen has insisted that comedy strikes him as an insignificant form, however talented he may be at eliciting laughter. The films that most impress him are Ingmar Bergman's existential works, created in the style of such Chekhov plays as *Three Sisters*, on the surface dealing with the psychological interactions of fascinating, varied women within a single family and the confused men who relate to them, on a deeper level dealing with such themes as the meaning of life, the value of art, and the possibility of moral action in a seemingly chaotic universe. The only problem has been that whenever Woody tried being Woody the Auteur—*Interiors, September, Another Woman*—the critics dismissed him derivative and humorless. The solution was to lighten up, creating a film filled with his unique, quirky twists on traditional Jewish humor, balancing that

HANNAH AND HER SISTERS: The neurotic Mickey (Woody Allen) tries to communicate with his ex-wife Hannah (Mia Farrow).

HANNAH AND HER SISTERS: Hannah and her sisters: Barbara Hershey as Lee (center), Oscar winner Dianne Wiest as Holly.

HANNAH AND HER SISTERS: Screen legends Lloyd Nolan (in his last role) and Maureen O'Sullivan portrayed Hannah's parents, a pair of former Broadway stars; as O'Sullivan was Farrow's real-life mother, this gave the film an extra edge of "family affair" for Allen, Farrow's leading man offscreen as well as on.

element with the serious themes he really wanted to cover. In *Hannah and Her Sisters*, Allen struck that delicate balance (even managing to cast Bergman's favorite actor, Max Von Sydow, in a key role), providing one of the decade's film masterpieces.

Hannah (Mia Farrow) is a successful artist, assured of her own talent and therefore assured in her relations with men; her sister Holly (Dianne Wiest) has all the angst of an artist but none of the necessary talent to create; Lee (Barbara Hershey), the beauty of the family, is assumed to be superficial by everyone, though that turns out not to be true. The men in their lives include Mickey (Allen), a mass media celebrity who fears his fame is

only fleeting; Elliot (Michael Caine), a man of commerce who desperately, obsessively attempts to seduce every attractive woman he meets; and Frederick (Max Von Sydow), the glum solipsist-artist who lives and works as an island unto himself. Hannah takes place over a two-year period, opening on a Thanksgiving celebration and closing on a similar one; though relationships have changed and marriages shuffled in strange ways, there is a sweet, almost sentimental sense of well-being as the characters come together for their traditional feast.

In public, Woody Allen has always spoken out loudly against the politics of Ronald Reagan in particular, Republicans in general, but his films actually reveal a far

HANNAH AND HER SISTERS: Ingmar Bergman's favorite star, Max Von Sydow (second from left), cinched the connection between this film and the existential works of that Swedish master, so admired by Allen; Barbara Hershey, Daniel Stern and Michael Caine confer with "Frederick."

more traditional sensibility than he might care to admit. Indeed, considering Allen's warm nostalgia and near reverence for the culture of the late Forties and early Fifties—old movies, popular music, etc.—his films were in tune with the country's mood during the early Eighties. His character here, Mickey, is an inveterate moviegoer, *Duck Soup* being his favorite; when he wants music, Mickey tends to favor Bobby Short elegantly doing Cole Porter. Critic David Denby noted that in the West Side apartment of *Hannah*, we notice "furnishings that offer the memory of a slower, more gracious and simpler style of New York life." There is an abiding desire to recapture the past in Woody Allen films of the period (as in his *Purple Rose of Cairo* and *Radio Days*), an urge that is beautifully captured in *Hannah* (the casting of Lloyd Nolan and Maureen O'Sullivan heightens that effect), and is a reflection on the time when this film was made.

Certainly *Hannah* offers much more than was to be found in many of the nostalgia feasts. But in making a movie about an artistically inclined family, studying the way in which people act in real life as well as when they are playing characters, Allen's film commented on the Eighties and the age of the Acting President. Allen's characters must here decide between art and life as of primary importance, as Frederick turns his back on the human community while Hannah gives up her acting in order to spend more time with her children.

As in previous Allen films, reaching all the way back to his first screenplay, *What's New, Pussycat?*, there is a *La Ronde* situation in which everyone is pursuing someone he or she can't have, quite sure the forbidden fruit will be tastiest. Allen sees the world as populated by endless romantics, all questing after anything they do not possess and growing bored with it the moment that the impossible dream becomes a tangible reality. If the Woody Allen vision remained essentially the same, his range as an artist had clearly grown considerably. In its depth of character and richness of understanding, *Hannah and Her Sisters* made clear that, his occasional failures notwithstanding, Woody Allen remained America's most mature and meaningful filmmaker.

The Fly

A 20TH CENTURY-FOX RELEASE OF A BROOKSFILM PRODUCTION   1986

CREDITS:

Produced by Stuart Cornfeld; directed by David Cronenberg; written by Charles Edward Pogue and David Cronenberg, from a story by George Langelaan; photography, Mark Irwin; editor, Ronald Sanders; Running time, 100 min.; Rating: R.

CAST:

Seth Brundle (Jeff Goldblum); *Veronica Quaife* (Geena Davis); *Stathis Borans* (John Getz); *Tawny* (Joy Boushel); *Dr. Cheevers* (Les Carlson).

172

One disarming aspect of 1980s nostalgia was the remaking of science-fiction classics from the 1950s: *The Thing, Invaders From Mars* and *The Blob* were elaborately redone, the results generally lacking the appeal of the originals. Critics and audiences soon believed any state-of-the-art remake of a Fifties horror classic would fail dismally, improving on the quality of special effects while missing the essence of the original story. Then there appeared the striking exception to that rule: David Cronenberg's *The Fly.* The Canadian filmmaker, who achieved a cult following with such disarming if thoughtful horror items as *Rabid, The Brood* and *Videodrome*, provided something special. His film was not, like the others, a sequel, a prequel, or a remake in the strictest sense of the term. Instead, it offered a total reconceptualization of the source material. This was another movie entirely, with new characters, a new plot, and new ideas to express. The only thing in common with the original was the scientific principle from which the fiction proceeds: the teleportation of matter by breaking down the molecular structure of an object and reassembling it elsewhere.

In the 1958 film, David Hedison played the first human guinea pig. Unfortunately, a housefly slips into the teleportation device with him; when he emerges on the other side, he has the head of a fly, causing all his colleagues to frantically search for the fly with a human head. Once considered frightful, the movie is pure silly fun; costars Vincent Price and Herbert Marshall have admitted publicly they had to bite their lips in order not to laugh out loud while playing some of the scenes. A remake that remained true to the original would have to be played as a wacky comedy.

Which is why Cronenberg took a different route entirely. The scientist, Seth Brundle (Jeff Goldblum), emerges from the disastrous experiment seemingly unchanged, though his genetic structure has been totally blended with that of the fly who accompanied him into the teleportation device. Most of the movie concerns the triangular romantic relationship involving this brilliant, well-intentioned, obsessive workaholic; Veronica (Geena Davis), the attractive journalist who initially approaches Brundle with a reporter's cool attitude on a potentially prizeworthy story, then gradually falls deeply in love with her subject; and Stathis Borans (John Getz), her former lover and current editor. The script did not approach the three as stereotypical characters clearly earmarked for a science-fiction film, but as real people, able to attract us with admirable characteristics, offend us with unsympathetic attitudes. Our loyalties switch several times during the competition, as the characters' emotions grow so intense viewers occasionally forget completely this is all taking place within the context of a

THE FLY: Jeff Goldblum as Seth Brundle, "The Fly."

THE FLY: Seth sets the controls of his matter transportation device; David Cronenberg's rethinking of the Fifties camp classic proved to be the rare case of a remake being better than the original.

173

THE FLY: Brundle realizes he is turning into "Brundle-fly."

morphosis. Such literary illusions are hardly imposed on the picture, for as a student at the University of Toronto, Cronenberg switched his majors back and forth between science and literature. Since then, his films have revealed the duality of his interests, with *The Fly* blending the two as completely as Brundle and the fly become mixed together in the movie. Offering none of the mayhem and fast-paced excitement fans of high-tech horror expected, the film left many disappointed; moviegoers interested in films with an existential attitude found it a surprisingly ambitious and impressive work, purposefully slow-moving and effectively bleak. *The Fly* proved a fascinating contradiction in terms: the first thinking-man's gross-out movie.

THE FLY: Veronica (Geena Davis) is terrified to find herself trapped inside the telepod transporter.

horror tale. *The Fly* offered human melodrama short-circuited by a scientific experiment gone awry.

The acting, then, was never campy but realistic, and it was regrettable that Goldblum failed to receive an Oscar nomination. This demanding drama moved at a deliberate pace toward the key moment when Brundle's newly arranged DNA factors wreak havoc on his physical being. Then the special effects by Christopher Walas proved as stunning as they were stomach churning. What audiences saw as the mutant species "Brundlefly" took shape was as grotesque visually as anything glimpsed in George Romero's *Dawn of the Dead* or Cronenberg's earlier *Scanners*. Yet fans of previous gross-out flicks did not particularly like *The Fly*, for while it ultimately did deliver, there were none of the reassuring elements of conventional horror-exploitation flicks. The creature did not terrorize the countryside, barely venturing out of his room. There he paced, Hamlet-like, pondering his identity and existence, even while his body continually transformed, like something out of Kafka's *Meta-*

A Room With a View

A CINECOM INTERNATIONAL FILMS
RELEASE OF A MERCHANT IVORY
PRODUCTION   1986

CREDITS:

Produced by Ismail Merchant; directed by James Ivory;
written by Ruth Prawer Jhabvala, based on the novel by E.
M. Forster; photography, Tony Pierce-Roberts; editor,
Humphrey Dixon; Running time, 115 min.; Rating: R.

CAST:

Charlotte Bartlett (Maggie Smith); *Lucy Honeychurch*
(Helena Bonham Carter); *Mr. Emerson* (Denholm Elliott);
George Emerson (Julian Sands); *Cecil Vyse* (Daniel Day
Lewis); *Reverend Beebe* (Simon Callow); *Miss Lavish* (Judi
Dench); *Freddy Honeychurch* (Rupert Graves); *Mrs.
Honeychurch* (Rosemary Leach); *Mr. Eager* (Patrick
Godfrey).

ROOM WITH A VIEW: The ultra-Victorian Charlotte Bartlett
(Maggie Smith, right) drags her pretty young charge, Lucy
Honey-church (Helena Bonham Carter), on what's intended as a
tour of Italy that will aesthetically broaden the young lady's
horizons; instead, the girl finds herself steeped in passion and
romance.

In *Sweet Liberty*, Alan Alda's film about filmmaking
in the 1980s, a hack Hollywood director explains there
are three things you must now have the characters do:
defy authority, destroy property and take off their
clothes. Otherwise, a film can't get financed. For
anyone of moderate intelligence, that formula seemed
terrifying. In fact, though, there was yet hope for the
movie industry. For even within the limits of that idiotic
little coda, great things could still happen. *A Room with
a View*, a classy art-house item derived from E. M.
Forster's 1908 novel, provided a case in point, maintaining a delicate balance between respect for its literary
origin and appreciation for the unique method of cinematic storytelling.

At the time of its initial release, the exquisite *Room*
provided upscale, discriminating audiences with nearly
two hours of sophisticated viewing. Surprisingly
enough, though, it managed to adhere to those three
cardinal rules of contemporary moviemaking. The central character was the very proper Miss Honeychurch
(Helena Bonham Carter), youthful product of the Edwar-
dian era and representative 20th century female in
embryo. Forster worked in the forefront of serious
writing and thinking, so, like his contemporary D. H.
Lawrence's Constance Chatterley, Miss Honeychurch

represses her innate if full sexuality just as she's been
taught by church, state and family—until she meets an
iconoclastic man able to set her off on a total abandon-
ment to the senses. Like Henry James's Daisy Miller, the
very proper but potentially wanton hussy finds herself
questioning all the proper post-Victorian rules and
regulations she spent her early years learning while
traveling through Italy, whose lush countrysides and
eternal art make her realize there's more to life than the
stiff, stodgy attitudes she heretofore uncritically ab-
sorbed. Even her name is something of a paradoxical
joke, "honey" suggesting the worldly pleasures to which
she would love to succumb, "church" a reminder of her
orderly Establishment origins.

Taking his cue from Forster, filmmaker Ivory wisely
played this woman's inner tension for humorous rather
than melodramatic effect, demonstrating that an adaptation of a literary classic should be puckish, not pon-
derous, best introducing a modern audience to the joys
of yesterday's masterworks by sharing their sense of
surface fun as well as the more demanding subtext of
ideas. *Room* radiated with a disarming light, almost
frivolous tone, reaffirming to the viewer that film's

175

ROOM WITH A VIEW: When she's with Cecil (Daniel Day Lewis), Charlotte responds to his aura of civilization by acting like a proper little lady . . .

. . . but when she's with the non-conformist George (Julian Sands), she quickly finds herself becoming unconventional.

ROOM WITH A VIEW: Early on, Lucy is portrayed by filmmaker James Ivory in imagery suggesting she is an observer of life; before the film is over, she will have become an active participant.

primary function was simply to provide a fabulous time at the movies.

To achieve that, Ivory found clever ways to turn Forster's literary conceits into cinematic devices. Forster employed cynical titles for the heroine's manipulations of the men in her life ("Lying to George," "Lying to Cecil") as chapter heads. Ivory kept the words intact, adapting them to film by presenting the phrases as title cards one might have experienced in a silent movie circa 1908. Throughout, the screenplay by Ruth Prawer Jhabvala found nuances of naughtiness in Forster's seemingly straightforward story. Previous Ivory-Jhabvala projects (*Heat and Dust*) played the period-piece confrontations as solemn occurrences, a theatrical version of sorts of PBS's *Masterpiece Theatre*; on the other hand, *Room* was wonderfully, ever so slyly, wicked. Therefore, the recreations of the past—from the vital streets of Florence to the subdued British countryside—never appeared remote from the modern moviegoing audience but magically immediate and important to us. Though the canvas here was considerably smaller than that of David Lean's 1984 adaptation of Forster's *A Passage to India*, this was the more successful film, capturing not only the surface of Forster's world but, more significantly, the essence of the author's vision.

For gourmets of top-notch acting, *Room* provided a feast. Standouts included Maggie Smith, as the heroine's chatty chaperone, and Denholm Elliott, as a prospective seducer's quirky father. Intellectuals and academics marveled: how did such an intelligent, refined film get made in the age of Schwarzenegger and Stallone? Simply turn back to those three cardinal rules: Miss Honeychurch is a teen who defies authority; her rule-breaking boyfriend George Emerson (Julian Sands) does indeed get naked in front of proper people; and if physical property was not destroyed "Animal House" style, then at least some social baggage gets gleefully demolished. *Room* proved, then, that even within the lamentably limiting rules governing filmmaking in the mid-Eighties, there was yet room for great screen art.

Top Gun

A PARAMOUNT PICTURES RELEASE OF A DON SIMPSON/JERRY BRUCKHEIMER PRODUCTION   1986

CREDITS:

Executive producer, Bill Badalato; produced by Don Simpson and Jerry Bruckheimer; directed by Tony Scott; written by Jim Cash and Jack Epps, Jr.; photography, Jeffrey Kimball; editors, Billy Weber and Chris Lebenzon; Running time, 110 min.; Rating: PG.

CAST:

Maverick (Tom Cruise); *Charlie* (Kelly McGillis); *Ice* (Val Kilmer); *Goose* (Anthony Edwards); *Viper* (Tom Skerritt); *Jester* (Michael Ironside); *Cougar* (John Stockwell); *Wolfman* (Barry Tubb); *Slider* (Rick Rossovich); *Merlin* (Tim Robbins); *Sundown* (Clarence Gilyard); *Hollywood* (Whip Hubley); *Stinger* (James Tolkan); *Carole* (Meg Ryan).

For a modern variation of the old chicken-or-the-egg riddle, try this: Which came first, Tom Cruise's superstar status or the phenomenal success of *Top Gun*? It's hard to say: Though Cruise was already a major draw after *Risky Business*, his charisma didn't bolster the box office of *Legend*, an expensively mounted epic-fantasy dud. Still, *Top Gun's* producers insisted on signing Cruise before moving ahead with production. They got him, and with him the perfect meeting of performer and project: the image of a macho Eighties youth, arrogantly

sitting in a fighter plane's cockpit, wearing military garb and winking at the audience while giving the "thumbs up" sign, presold the film when it appeared as the basis of the publicity campaign.

Simply, *Top Gun* was a High Concept movie in all respects, from the canny casting of Cruise to the sly if superficial exploitation of our (then)-current Gung Ho! national mindset, from the trendy MTV style music-mix set against rapid-fire editing techniques to the post-feminist romantic plot about a modern liberated professional woman happily surrendering to an old-fashioned man of action, from the early 1940s formula-film plotting to the late 1980s approach to gritty language and intense sex scenes. Producers Bruckheimer and Simpson, previously responsible for *Flashdance*, continued their decade-long reign as the packagers who most fully comprehended the country's current mood and were able to swiftly fashion the films (retrograde in plot and attitude, state of the art for sight and sound quality) that

TOP GUN: Kelly McGillis and Tom Cruise: the modern liberated woman meets an old-fashioned macho man, as each discovers there's ample room for old-fashioned romance, Hollywood-style.

TOP GUN: Val Kilmer as Ice, one of Maverick's chief competitors for the title of Top Gun.

TOP GUN: Anthony Edwards as the scene-stealing Goose, the lovable but doomed nice guy; if James Cagney would have been a natural for Maverick in a Forties version of this story, then Ronald Reagan would have been a shoe-in for Goose.

TOP GUN: Tom Cruise, revealing the magnetism that would make him the new Paul Newman: ambitious actor as well as sex symbol.

insured box-office (if not critical) success by tapping into the collective sensibility of the Reagan years.

The producers admitted the script was a scant 80 pages, screenplays ordinarily ranging between 120 and 150 pages. That's because the scenario was but a thumbnail sketch for what appeared on screen, as Maverick (Cruise), a talented if hotshot flyer with a chip on his shoulder and a deep need to prove himself, enters the prestigious training school at Miramar Naval Air Station in San Diego. His best buddy, Goose (Anthony Edwards), is soon involved with pretty local girl Carole (Meg Ryan), though Maverick has his sights set on their beautiful "older woman" astrophysics instructor, Charlotte Blackwood (Kelly McGillis). Life in the fast lane or unfriendly skies includes their romance as well as Maverick's competition as "Top Gun" with Ice (Val Kilmer), though Maverick seeks advice from the rugged but understanding flight instructor (Tom Skerritt) who knew Maverick's father, reputedly a coward; Viper helps Maverick overcome the deep anxieties which the youth covers with his ultramacho pose. Eventually Maverick proves himself by shooting down several Russian aircraft, in a strange sequence which offhandedly gave the impression that the U.S. and the Soviets were already engaged in an all-out shooting war.

Though director Tony Scott certainly created a flashy visual scheme set against insistent music, his approach here (as in the equally loud, no-let-up *Beverly Hills Cop II*) is more commerce than creativity, aping the striking surfaces found in the films of his more ambitious brother Ridley (*Alien, Blade Runner*) without offering any of their deeper resonances of meaning. *Top Gun* was not a director's personal expression, but a product designed by the producers. Watching it was not unlike looking at an air force recruiting advertisement done in the style of a rock video; if that sounds outrageous, not that the Air Force observed the film's popularity and had their ad agency create new TV commercials that looked almost identical to *Top Gun*, tapping into the trendiness among youth of the military, so disparaged during the Sixties but now at new popularity, the highest since the patriotic Forties. At the time, youthful Cruise was doubtless unaware of the film's Reagan-era implications, heatedly defending the movie as nothing more than a romance/entertainment sent against a flashy training school backdrop. A few years later, when he filmed *The Color of Money* with Paul Newman, his consciousness was expanded by his liberal costar. Later, hearing that Oliver Stone was preparing a film version of Ron Kovic's antiwar autobiography, *Born on the Fourth of July*, Cruise called Stone directly and begged for a chance to read for the part. In his eventual role as Kovic, Cruise considered himself vindicated for what had been (for him, at least) the unintended prowar implications of *Top Gun*.

Something Wild

AN ORION RELEASE OF A RELIGIOSO PRIMITIVA PRESENTATION   1986

CREDITS:

Executive producer, Edward Saxon; produced and directed by Jonathan Demme; coproducer, Kenneth Utt; written by E. Max Frye; photography, Tak Fujimoto; editor, Craig McKay; Running time, 113 min.; Rating: R.

CAST:

Charles Driggs (Jeff Daniels); *Audrey Hankel* (Melanie Griffith); *Ray Sinclair* (Ray Liotta); *Irene* (Margaret Colin); *The Country Squire* (Tracey Walter); *Peaches* (Dana Preu); *Larry Dillman* (Jack Gilpin); *Peggy Dillman* (Su Tissue); *Tracy* (Kristin Olsen).

In a film by Jonathan Demme, things do not happen quite the way they do in real life; for that matter, they don't even happen the way they do in other people's movies. His earlier *Handle With Care* and *The Last Embrace* and later *Married to the Mob* straddle the gap between cult-film sensibility and mainstream movie mentality. Demme's works begin in what looks, more or less, like the real world we all share, then shortly sweep their unsuspecting characters off on a whirlwind tour of a terrain as alien and unpredictable as *The Twilight Zone*, one that looks vaguely like our own everyday landscape as perceived in the slightly distorted reflection of a funhouse mirror. Submitted for our approval: characters to consider with fascination. With an ironic eye for the tackiest of contemporary sights and a perceptively funny ear for the funky sounds of the very best rock 'n' roll, Demme's films are the cinematic equivalent of a Talking Heads concert; indeed, it's no coincidence that Demme once documented that iconoclastic, idiosyncratic, intellectual group in *Stop Making Sense!* or that the group's leader, David Byrne, contributed the opening song to *Something Wild*.

The film dealt, in Demme's eccentric, seemingly offhand manner, with the two distinct lifestyles which emerged during the Eighties: the decade's characteristic counterculture, the punk scene, and the decade's representative Establishment culture, the yuppie syndrome. For Demme, it was a natural to tell an unlikely love story between representatives of each group. While on a lunch break from the Manhattan firm where he works, yuppie Charles Driggs (Jeff Daniels) allows himself to be picked up by a beautiful punker, Audrey Hankel (Melanie Griffith) running off (to the tune of the hard-rock classic "Wild Thing") for an exciting, illicit, guilt-ridden afternoon of forbidden pleasure, constantly calling his office from the New Jersey motel room where Audrey is handcuffing him to the bed, giving his secretary ever more preposterous reasons why he can't return to the office. Before long, he's sucked ever deeper into Audrey's bizarre demimonde, as superstraight Charles helps her to steal cars and rip off restaurants and liquor stores, loving every minute of it even as he senses, in a sweaty state of near-panic, he may never be able to go home. While Audrey brings out the wild side of Charles, he helps her to reveal her softer side. She has,

SOMETHING WILD: Yuppie Charles Driggs (Jeff Daniels) falls for the New Wave bombshell Audrey (Melanie Griffith) . . .

. . . only to discover she'd really love to be a nice girl, given the chance.

like many other girls, a conservative mother living in a small town whom she wants to visit, and would like Charles to accompany her to the high school class reunion for which she doesn't yet have a date. Charles passes himself off as Audrey's husband, until he runs into a seductive girlfriend (Margaret Colin) of Audrey's, a jealous old lowlife boyfriend (Ray Liotta), and his own coworker from the office (Jack Gilpin).

The film changes tones as often as it does story direction. Part sex farce, part mellow love story, part thriller, it confused those few people who caught up with it on the initial theatrical release. However, *Something Wild* became an immense hit on cable and home video, where repeated viewings allowed ever more mesmerized viewers to realize the film's funky rhythms were really something special indeed, played on the cutting edge of satire. The anarchic Demme sees the everyday world as a nuthouse in which zanies bounce off the walls as though existing in some living cartoon. With *Something Wild*, it was a case of no holds barred: anything could happen, and most anything did. Demme was always easier for the mainstream to take than, say, John Waters (*Pink Flamingos* or *Polyester*) because he's less interested in outraging the straights. Rather than gross anyone out, Demme only wants to playfully confuse them a bit, gently ruffling their feathers.

None of his films yet has broken through and become a major hit, not even *Married to the Mob*, which boasted radiant Michelle Pfeiffer and an Oscar-nominated Dean Stockwell. Demme might simply be too hip for most moviegoers; his films are to movies what *Late Night*

180

With David Letterman is to television, attracting an intensely loyal if not massive following. Demme's films stand as an offbeat array of left-of-center items, movies which seem strange, scintillating, and vaguely unsatisfying on initial viewing but which grow with each subsequent one. Perhaps the great Demme film would have been *After Hours* if he, rather than a misplaced Martin Scorsese, had been allowed to direct. If *Something Wild* is not necessarily Demme's best, it is clearly his most representative.

'Crocodile' Dundee

A PARAMOUNT PICTURES RELEASE OF A RIMFIRE PRODUCTIONS FILM   1986

CREDITS:

Produced by John Cornell; directed by Peter Faiman; written by Paul Hogan and Ken Shadie; photography, Russell Boyd; editor, David Stiven; Running time, 102 min.; Rating: PG-13.

CAST:

Mick Dundee (Paul Hogan); *Sue Charlton* (Linda Kozlowski); *Wally Reilly* (John Meillon); *Richard Mason* (Mark Blum); *Sam Charlton* (Michael Lombard); *Nevile Bell* (David Gulpill).

Paul Hogan, host in the early Eighties of a popular Down Under talk show and spokesperson for Australian tourism on stateside TV advertisements, had fashioned *'Crocodile' Dundee* as a showcase for himself. There was no reason to believe its enormous homegrown box-office success would repeat itself in America. On a gamble, Paramount bought the American rights and unceremoniously released it as "filler" in fall 1986. The rest is movie history.

Throughout the Eighties, numerous American film-makers attempted to revive the western, assuming a public which had elected an old-time TV–movie cowboy president was ripe for such a screen renaissance. All

'CROCODILE' DUNDEE: Between two worlds: Mick Dundee (Paul Hogan) stares down a bull in the wilds of Australia...

... then faces off with pseudo-sophisticated Manhattanites.

less) man she meets there, eventually learning to appreciate him as a Rousseau-style "Natural Man" whose back-to-back basics life-style conveys his simplicity and sincerity. The cowboy proves himself superior to the cultivated urban men she has known and previously accepted, but now recoils from. Cowriter Hogan openly admitted his indebtedness to American western films and other adventure classics, insisting he'd always preferred them to such arty Australian movies as *Picnic at Hanging Rock*, which had delighted highbrow critics but had little impact on the wider Aussie audience Hogan spoke to and for.

Dundee clicked because it was the logical Aussie version of the wild man–civilized woman theme, entertainingly serving up this age-old tale in a new (and just right for the Eighties) guise, for our fascination with anything Australian proved as intense during this decade as America's infatuation with anything British had been in the late 1960s. Dundee wore a cowboy hat, carried an oversize Bowie knife, even looked a bit like Clint Eastwood, last of the great cowboy stars, cinching his connection to the western; yet his Australian accent made him the perfect contemporary counterpart to those traditional heroes of bygone books and movies.

A number of name actresses (Morgan Fairchild among them) had passed on the chance to play Sue Charlton, assuming this was a small movie that would do nothing for their careers; unknown Linda Kozlowski won by default the part of an American reporter, searching the bush for a mythic man named Mick, who reportedly fights crocodiles with his bare hands, headstrong but helpless in a place where her Bloomingdale's

attempts seemed to have missed the essence of the western motif that Reagan had so brilliantly manipulated for political purposes. Ostensibly a "foreign" film, *Dundee* captured the true spirit and flavor of the great western works, including Owen Wister's *The Virginian*, with its philosophically romantic theme featuring a civilized woman who journeys into the wilds, at first frightened by the rough-'n'-ready (and apparently name-

'CROCODILE' DUNDEE: At first, reporter Sue Charlton (Linda Kozlowski) is wary of Mick . . .

. . . but like the civilized heroine of such American frontier classics as *Last of the Mohicans* and *The Virginian*, she soon melts while in a primitive setting, in the company of the last natural man.

charge card is worthless. Feminist critics charged *Dundee* was a reactionary film, a return to the notion that every independent modern woman's secret fantasy is to find a real man—unenlightened by Women's Lib—who is called upon regularly to save her while she helplessly stands about and screams like Fay Wray in *King Kong*, waiting to be ritualistically rescued by her protective male. Essentially true, though also true to the spirit of the Eighties and its return to old-fashioned attitudes about women.

In fact, Mick finds himself as lost as Kong when he accompanies her to Manhattan, and on her turf is treated like an anachronism, something from out of the primitive past to be derided by pseudosophisticates, while the blonde Sue now clearly sees his essential nobility in contrast to such crass reactions. The film was imperfect: though an early sequence involving Mick's subduing a dangerous beast implied he had strange spiritualist powers owing to his innocent life close to nature, other bits confusingly suggested he was something of a phoney. Sue's family and friends in New York, too broadly caricatured to be very effective, were vulgar (rather than vivid) stereotypes; it would have been far more interesting to see Mick win her away from a more likable New Yorker rather than the clichéd stuffed shirt she's going with. The final sequence, in which hero and heroine are reunited in a subway station while symphonic music built, too obviously anticipated a *Rocky* type reception from the audiences—which turned out to be legion.

Yet if critics carped, audiences didn't care. The breathtaking photography of the outback and strong chemistry between the leads helped; more significant, though, were the ideas just beneath the surface of this film, and of so many other critically drubbed but commercially successful ventures that in their time touched something deep and basic: *"Crocodile" Dundee*—and its sequel, which returned Mick and Sue to Australia—tapped the same wellspring of popular attitudes that Wister previously employed as the basis for his popular classic.

Platoon

AN ORION RELEASE OF A HEMDALE FILM
PRESENTATION   1986

CREDITS:

Executive producers, John Daly and Derek Gibson; produced by Arnold Kopelson and A. Kingman Ho; written and directed by Oliver Stone; photography, Robert Richardson; editor, Claire Simpson; Running time, 120 min.; Rating: R.

CAST:

Sgt. Barnes (Tom Berenger); *Sgt. Elias* (Willem Dafoe); *Chris* (Charlie Sheen); *Big Harold* (Forest Whitaker); *Rhah* (Francesco Quinn); *Sgt. O'Neill* (John C. McGinley); *Sal* (Richard Edison); *Bunny* (Kevin Dillon); *Junior* (Reggie Johnson); *King* (Keith David); *Lerner* (Johnny Depp); *Tex* (David Neidorf).

When *Platoon* was awarded the Oscar as Best Picture of the Year, it seemed less an acknowledgment of the movie's qualities (considerable) than its timely expression of long-overdue angst about Nam and the men who fought the war. Vividly based on Oliver Stone's own experiences, *Platoon* surveyed Southeast Asia, circa 1968. The film was told from the shifting point-of-view of a young volunteer named Chris (Charlie Sheen). In the grim opening, newcomers disembark from the transport plane, passing body bags—destined for back home—containing the dead soldiers they're replacing, a rough image for an audience used to *Rambo*-romanticizations.

As Chris wanders through jungles filled with unseen snipers and omnipresent insects, Stone employed state-of-the-art moviemaking techniques to rub our collective nose in the experience, forcing us to see and hear the war as his central character does. In time, the untested Chris finds himself forced to make a moral choice, dramatized by the two characters who vie for his soul and sanity: Barnes (Tom Berenger), a facially and spiritually scarred combat veteran, survives the madness of jungle war by embracing violence; Elias (Willem Dafoe), also battle-hardened, clings to a code of decent conduct even as the entire world around him appears absurd. In his mixture of exposé and old-fashioned morality play, Stone effectively employed Barnes and

Elias both as realistically drawn figures and symbols for evil and good; in choosing between them, Chris will either sell his soul or save it.

The film so effectively dramatized Stone's ideas that there was no reason to state them in words. Unfortunately, he chose to do so anyway, through Chris's comments in his voice-over letters home and, at movie's end, as Chris neatly tabulates all he (the real character and the real director) has learned and wants us to learn from the film. How subtly effective the film might have been had we been allowed to decipher this for ourselves, without the overobvious lecture.

Still, *Platoon* overcame such momentary lapses by stunning the viewer's senses with realistic recreations of war. Best of all is the ambiguity: Stone uncompromisingly captured the horror of death in combat, but also pinned down the exultation of battle. We're never quite sure how our hero will react in any given situation, showing a surprising propensity for cruelty and violence one moment, a decency that causes him to recoil from brutality a second later. Chris appears both real and representational, a unique person who also conveys the potential for darkness and light in all men. Stone revived stereotypical war movie situations, then neatly undercut them, throwing his audience off balance by refusing to play to the expectations he raised. We assume a particularly lovable soldier will die when he jubilantly boards an early helicopter out, but the explosion we expect never comes. We assume a nice kid could never pull the trigger on his own noncom, but he casually blows away his superior. Perhaps the key to the film's abiding greatness derives from the fact that like the men in the platoon, we're never certain, while watching, whether the village they devastate is or is not a Cong hideout. To have insisted either way would have been to give us a distance audiences expect, but Stone wanted us to feel a member of the platoon, sharing their limited knowledge, their tunnel vision. With its stunning array of brief but exquisitely etched character roles (Keith David as a confused black recruit and Kevin Dillon as a nasty wise guy stood out), *Platoon* was to Vietnam what *A Walk in the Sun* was to World War II: the film that most vividly captured and convincingly conveyed the experience of the common fighting man.

Stone spent ten difficult years getting the movie financed; considering the Rambo mentality of the early Eighties, it's possible that if *Platoon* had been made and released a few years earlier, it might not have been so perfectly in touch with the times. By 1986, most moviegoers were scoffing at the simplistic war histrionics they'd enjoyed at the height of the Reagan era, instead getting ready to view and analyze Nam as the complex, ambiguous page in history that it was. Stone

PLATOON: Every Oliver Stone movie is structured as a morality play; here, evil Sgt. Barnes (Tom Berenger, left) and Christ-like Sgt. Elias (Willem Dafoe, who would play Jesus shortly thereafter for director Martin Scorsese) struggle for the souls of the men, while a confused serviceman (Mark Moses) looks on.

PLATOON: The insane Barnes threatens the life of a child in an incident not unlike the one at My Lai.

PLATOON: Chris (Charlie Sheen, left) and Rhah (Francesco Quinn) help a wounded comrade (Chris Pedersen) back from the front.

may have made this movie to exorcise his own personal demons, but for the audience—especially those viewers who had served in Nam—*Platoon* served as a movie mantra, an experience upon which, along with Stone's subsequent *Born on the Fourth of July*, the audiences invested emotions in excess of what the filmmaker could ever have hoped for.

PLATOON: Conflict within the ranks: Charlie Sheen, Cory Glover, Chris Pedersen, Willem Dafoe, Forest Whitaker and Keith David struggling with Barnes' cruelty.

Tin Men

A BUENA VISTA RELEASE OF A
TOUCHSTONE PICTURES PRESENTATION
IN ASSOCIATION WITH SILVER SCREEN
PARTNERS II   1987

CREDITS:

Produced by Mark Johnson; written and directed by Barry
Levinson; photography, Peter Sova; editor, Stu Linder;
Running time, 112 min.; Rating: R.

CAST:

Bill "BB" Babowsky (Richard Dreyfuss); *Ernie Tilley*
(Danny DeVito); *Nora Tilley* (Barbara Hershey); *Moe* (John
Mahoney); *Sam* (Jackie Gayle); *Gil* (Stanley Brock); *Cheese*
(Seymour Cassel); *Mouse* (Bruno Kirby); *Wing* (J. T. Walsh);
Carly (Richard Portnow); *Bagel* (Michael Tucker).

TIN MEN: Tin man Bill "BB" Babowsky (Richard
Dreyfuss) discovers a fender bender and quickly is feuding
with . . .

. . . rival tin man Ernie Tilley (Danny DeVito) in an
accelerating and ever-escalating comedy of vengeance.

The title refers to aluminum siding salesmen in 1963 who earn their commissions by duping homeowners. Cool manipulator Bill Babowsky (Richard Dreyfuss) pretends he's a photographer from *Life* magazine. Setting up a camera on some poor soul's front lawn, he convinces the resident and neighbors he's looking for a house to feature in a story about aluminum siding. When informed that his or her home will be a "before" shot, the pigeon eagerly purchases siding to qualify for an "after" picture. Ernie Tilley (Danny DeVito), who compensates for his slight stature with an overly aggressive approach, practices another scam. He gives away the siding, then sends in his partner to convince the unsuspecting that Tilley will lose his job unless the unwary customer's decent enough to pay. In their ploys, the two men prove the old adage that there's a sucker born every minute.

Babowsky and Tilley are the best tin men of their day but, like the best of them, fierce rivals. In the opening scene, something happens to render impossible any friendly competition. The two meet for the first time when a distracted Tilley, driving to work, has a fender bender with Babowsky's new Cadillac. In their world of sleazy sales and vulgar displays of status, nothing is more valued than a high-priced car. Shortly, the accident escalates into all-out war between the two. And this is

TIN MEN: Barbara Hershey as Nora Tilley, unsuspecting pawn in the feud; written off as a glamour girl during the Seventies, Hershey reemerged as one of the heavyweight actresses of the Eighties.

TIN MEN: BB seduces Tilley's wife to exact the cruelest sort of revenge.

187

the key to writer-director Barry Levinson's humor. Working within a comic tradition that has its roots in *Big Business*, arguably the finest of Laurel and Hardy shorts, *Tin Man* grabs the audience with a slow, seething escalation of anger and ever more aggressive acts of vengeance. First, Babowsky feels the need to get even, purposely damaging his rival's car slightly more seriously than his own. That leads to Tilley's counter-vengeance, until the situation spirals into an all-consuming case of reciprocal destruction. Levinson neatly shifts gears, moving into a more subtle, satiric, poignant form of comedy. When the cars are all but demolished, Babowsky decides on an insidious course, setting out to seduce Tilley's wife. In the male value system that emerges as the serious subject of this deceptively light-hearted film, women are not people to be appreciated but objects to be possessed, and Tilley's beautiful spouse Nora (Barbara Hershey) is clearly the Cadillac of housewives.

Fortunately, Levinson did not allow the men to remain arch characters. Babowsky, in time, shows us a vulnerable, unfulfilled side. After gleefully forcing his arch enemy to understand that he, Babowsky, has seduced Tilley's wife, he is decent enough to take the woman in when she has nowhere else to go. Tilley ultimately lets us see the sad, threatened psyche that makes him so dedicated to sales success, so oblivious to what's really happening around him. Despite a cartoonish quality that heightens the comedy immensely, this is a film we can respond to emotionally: the characters are real, as is their anguish.

That's especially true with Nora. The scene in which she returns home to discover Tilley has thrown all her clothes out of the house—a simple, verbal statement that he knows she's cheated on him—effectively stops the laughter (at least temporarily) to give us a glimpse of the sadness of a woman whose entire life has been decimated for the thrill of a romantic escapade. As in Woody Allen's *Hannah and Her Sisters*, Hershey displayed with élan a magical transformation from glamour girl to heavyweight actress, while the diminutive DeVito continued to click in just the right roles, making him the least likely giant star of the Eighties, and Dreyfuss continues his amazing turnaround and successful comeback from admitted drug abuse and poor career moves.

Without ever defending or justifying the self-serving schemes of Babowksy and Tilley, Levinson made these desperate men seem totally sympathetic. As a director of comedy, his work was surefire: every gag clicked, skillfully eliciting the proper response, from giggle to all-out guffaw. As a writer, his ear was remarkable: the supporting characters, including other salesmen who heatedly argue over breakfast in a diner about TV's *Bonanza* as though it were the central cultural experi-

ence of their lives, deftly convey the rhythms and absurdities of everyday conversation. Ultimately, though, Levinson focused on the American male's macho mentality and the changing of our lifestyle in the Sixties. Thus, the film ends where it has to: Babowsky and Tilley have, almost reluctantly, become the best of friends, even as their way of life has disappeared, owing to government regulation of sales. Confused by the shifting values around them and unable to adjust, they finally drive off together, dreaming up new schemes, sad but strangely sympathetic relics of a pre-1963 value system that is with us still.

Lethal Weapon

A WARNER BROS. RELEASE   1987

CREDITS:

Produced by Joel Silver; directed by Richard Donner; written by Shane Black; photography, Stephen Goldblatt; editor, Stuart Baird; Running time, 110 min.; Rating: R.

CAST:

Martin Riggs (Mel Gibson); *Roger Murtaugh* (Danny Glover); *Joshua* (Gary Busey); *The General* (Mitchell Ryan); *Michael Hunsaker* (Tom Atkins); *Trish Murtaugh* (Darlene Love); *Rianne Murtaugh* (Traci Wolfe); *Amanda Hunsaker* (Jackie Swanson); *Nick Murtaugh* (Damon Hines); *Carrie Murtaugh* (Ebonie Smith).

To that small number of films about tough cops which truly rate as classics—*Bullitt, Dirty Harry* and *The French Connection*—in 1987 movie lovers added *Lethal Weapon*. Likewise, it stood as a prime example of the Eighties buddy-buddy film. This briskly paced, crisply photographed, convincingly acted genre piece stands as a flawless example of how to make a film that barrels ahead, pausing briefly for bursts of brutality and comedy bits, at last leaving the viewer with a sense of having experienced a touching human tale rather than one more dehumanizing wallow in violence for violence's sake.

Certainly *Lethal Weapon* contained scenes of violence every bit as graphic as those in, say, Sylvester Stallone's *Cobra*, including the sadistic torture of a teenage girl. The key to an appreciation was that audiences never sensed it was excessive or exploitive, but rather a legitimate part of the storytelling, director Richard

LETHAL WEAPON: The greatest buddy-buddy team of the Eighties: Danny Glover as conservative Roger Murtaugh and Mel Gibson as wild man Martin Riggs.

LETHAL WEAPON: Gary Busey as the albino bad guy Joshua.

Donner effectively employing the violence to reveal the lengths to which the film's villains were willing to go; without this, it would have been impossible to make an audience accept some of the vigilante tactics to which the heroes ultimately resort.

Lethal Weapon begins with a deceptively benign tone, the camera breezing about Los Angeles in an aerial shot while that good-time Christmas song "Jingle Bell Rock" creates a bouncy mood. Suddenly, the mood is undercut as the camera slips into a high-rise building, coming to rest on a beautiful blonde snorting cocaine. She rises, goes to the window and, too high to comprehend her actions, leaps. The following morning, a mismatched pair of cops investigate the death. The senior detective, Roger Murtaugh (Danny Glover), is a conservatively dressed, ultrarespectable family man, whose greatest worries appear to be his daughter's decision to wear a revealing dress to a New Year's Eve party, and the fact that he's just hit the big five-O. The younger, Martin Riggs (Mel Gibson), is a self-destructive wild man, dressing like a street person, busting drug dealers with manic glee, barely restraining himself from venting his inner anger by killing them. Riggs spends long, lonely nights, desperately crying over his deceased wife's portrait while weighing the pros and cons of suicide.

LETHAL WEAPON: Riggs tries to prevent Len McCleary (Michael Shaner) from committing suicide.

189

LETHAL WEAPON: Riggs and Murtaugh form an uneasy alliance.

Initially, each man is antagonistic toward his new partner. But as they proceed with the case, which proves ever less routine, their shock at the enormity of the ugly situation they've unwittingly uncovered draws them together, first out of necessity, then from a bond of friendship that grows without either cop's intention or awareness.

Glover realizes the deceased girl is the daughter of an old friend who attempted to contact him only a short time before the "accident." The lab reports indicate that, had the girl not overdosed or jumped, she would have died shortly thereafter anyway, since the drug had been purposely poisoned. The attempt to discover the source of that murder and its motivations thrusts the two into conflict with a deadly secret conspiracy, which they ultimately challenge in a bloody arena. The action sequences, some of them stylized in slow motion, were all first rate—especially memorable was the episode involving a low-flying helicopter and a high-stretching mansion—so that *Lethal Weapon* could be enjoyed at the same level as lesser films of its order, in which the story exists mainly to string together a succession of exciting moments. But there was more to *Lethal Weapon* than just that. Properly understood, it was a melodrama about the relationship of opposite individuals who come to understand and appreciate each other, with the heavy emotional elements effectively undercut by wry, dry humor.

At movie's end, a mellow Christmas celebration neatly underscores, despite all the shooting, that what we've witnessed is not a shallow action flick but a sensitive (though fortunately never sentimental) "people picture," a redemption saga with Gibson craftily playing a man who has lived too long on the edge but makes his perilous way back to hearth and home. Gibson finally found the role to showcase his superstar status. Glover

offered a less flamboyant but no less fascinating portrait, with Gary Busey providing a neat turn as an albino hit man. The film clicked, as did its 1989 sequel, thanks to a perfectly packaged combination of state-of-the-art action sequences, contemporary off-the-wall comedy, convincing suspense, buddy-buddy chemistry, and the ability to touch an audience's emotions while providing an impressive pyrotechnical virtuosity.

Dirty Dancing

A VESTRON PICTURES RELEASE 1987

CREDITS:

Executive producers, Mitchell Cannold and Steven Reuther; produced by Linda Gottlieb; directed by Emile Ardolino; written by Eleanor Bergstein; photography, Jeff Jur; editor, Peter C. Frank; Running time, 97 min.; Rating PG-13.

CAST:

Baby Houseman (Jennifer Grey); *Johnny Castle* (Patrick Swayze); *Jake Houseman* (Jerry Orbach); *Penny Johnson* (Cynthia Rhodes); *Max Kellerman* (Jack Weston); *Lisa Houseman* (Jane Brucker); *Marjorie Houseman* (Kelly Bishop); *Neil Kellerman* (Lonny Price); *Robbie Gould* (Max Cantor); *Tito Suarez* (Charles Honi Coles); *Billy* (Neal Jones).

Yet another time-worn tale was taken out of the attic trunk and allowed a new lease on life in *Dirty Dancing*, an unexpected runaway hit period-piece romance which proved the old formulas of dance-musicals like *42nd Street* still had life—especially if set in the early Sixties, that last moment of innocence before the Kennedy assassination and America's entrance into its confused, radical period. Here, a familiar line was given a revitalized appearance, though the plot remained clichéd and predictable: young lovers from different social classes, kept apart by the interference of a traditional blocking figure, the girl's meddling if well-intentioned father. Eventually, the two sweethearts win him (and everyone else) over by proving the depth and sincerity of their feelings.

Such a summation fails to communicate the humor and charm with which screenwriter Eleanor Bergstein defined her characters, the vividness with which director Emile Ardolino brought to life a unique place at a

DIRTY DANCING: Patrick Swayze and Jennifer Grey as Johnny Castle and Frances "Baby" Houseman. Vestron, the company which had achieved overnight success with the marketing of videotapes, took its first major stab into movie production with this sleeper hit. But any hope that the company would soon become a "major" dissipated when its other films flopped and it swiftly went out of business.

specific point in time, or, best of all, the sensational sensual approach of choreographer Kenny Ortega. Their combined work transformed what could easily have been a pat, predictable movie into an uncommon dramatic musical, a sleeper hit for the summer of '87, and even a TV series (however brief).

Set at a Catskills resort run by the abrasive Max (Jack Weston), *Dirty Dancing* concerned one of the borsht belt retreats that catered in the Sixties exclusively to an upper-middle-class Jewish clientele. Among the guests are Dr. Houseman (Jerry Orbach) and his family, including the older daughter, 17-year-old Frances (Jennifer Grey), nicknamed "Baby." A classic example of the Jewish American Princess, she is plain, pampered and patronizing. But her potential to evolve into a more caring, sensitive person is tapped the moment she meets Johnny Castle (Patrick Swayze), a sexy dancer performing at the club with his partner, Penny (Cynthia Rhodes). Before long, Frances and Johnny are in love, though such fraternization between staff and guests is strictly forbidden. The course of their true love, like that of Romeo and Juliet, never does run smooth: When the pregnant Penny has an abortion, Baby's father mistakenly thinks Johnny is the man responsible, holding that against the innocent boy.

There's never any doubt the mistake will be cleared up at the last possible moment, with Johnny's reputation salvaged and the identity of the actual would-be father revealed. What was impressive is the way in which a young woman's unwanted pregnancy was handled, with

DIRTY DANCING: Johnny dances at the Catskill Mountain Resort with his pretty partner, Penny Johnson (Cynthia Rhodes); though she's pregnant, he's not the culprit, despite what Baby's father thinks.

191

DIRTY DANCING: The show must go on: Penny and Johnny teach Baby the intricacies of the mambo.

far more compassion than might be expected from a work of popular entertainment, with the abortion issue presented in a powerful manner and the young moviegoers of today forced to watch a woman's painful trauma in the days before such an operation was legal.

The film's strong appeal, though, derived directly from the chemistry between the two young stars. Grey neatly made Frances's step-by-step emotional growth visible to the viewer, giving us a character we gradually learned to like. Swayze revealed himself to be the most masculine dancing star since the golden days of James Cagney and Gene Kelly. The dancing here was "dirty" in the sense of being overtly sexual; ironically, this was a film in which the bedroom scenes were milder than those sequences in which the main characters, fully clothed, step—in the sensational mode of the previous decade's *Saturday Night Fever*—onto the dance floor. The choreography was neither simple nostalgia nor modern interpretations, but an effective appreciation of past dancing styles as filtered through (and reinterpreted for) a modern sensibility. That balance proved impressive enough to satisfy older moviegoers longing to rediscover past dancing styles and also younger moviegoers desiring to see trendier ones.

In the tradition of *42nd Street*, there was even the last-minute necessity of bringing novice Baby on to dance in place of leading lady Penny when the latter was unable to go on; one could almost hear the ghost of Bebe Daniels

DIRTY DANCING: Johnny and Baby, doing the "dirty dancing" of the title.

encouraging wide-eyed Ruby Keeler to knock 'em dead, while Warner Baxter intoned: "The lives and careers of everyone in the cast is depending on you. You're going out there a youngster, but you've got to come back a star!" Such irresistible kitsch made its comeback during the Reagan years, but was palatable only when given a contemporary edge. So enough "realism" was added (the abortion problem, prejudice—in this case ironically from Jews toward Gentiles rather than the other way around—rougher language and a more honest attitude about sex than would have been possible in the old films) to make the beloved fantasies seem real.

RoboCop

AN ORION PICTURES RELEASE   1987

CREDITS:

Executive producer, John Davison; produced by Arne Schmidt; directed by Paul Verhoeven; written by Edward Neumeier and Michael Miner; photography, Jost Vacano; editor, Frank J. Urioste; Running time, 103 min.; Rating: R.

CAST:

Murphy/RoboCop (Peter Weller); *Lewis* (Nancy Allen); *Jones* (Ronny Cox); *Clarence* (Kurtwood Smith); *Morton* (Miguel Ferrer); *Sgt. Reed* (Robert DoQui); *Old Man* (Daniel O'Herlihy).

The incredible amount of violence almost earned it an X rating, but the slightly trimmed and still stunningly violent *RoboCop* was the sleeper hit of the summer 1987, a surprisingly sharp-witted retro-future film. *Dirty Harry* by way of *Blade Runner* with a touch of *Repo Man* thrown in for good measure, *RoboCop* rated as a flipped-out action film that captivated not only cult fans but the mainstream audience as well. Its plot was straight out of a Marvel Comic or a TV adventure series, with the unique vision of director Paul Verhoeven adding an element of art: in a day-after-tomorrow future, dedicated street cop Murphy (Peter Weller) is blown away while he and his partner Lewis (Nancy Allen) pursue street criminals. His remains are rushed to a lab, where Murphy is transformed into a cyborg—part human, mostly robot. He/it is then sent back to the streets, human enough to harbor decent instincts but as indestructible as any other high-tech machine. What made

ROBOCOP: Peter Weller as RoboCop.

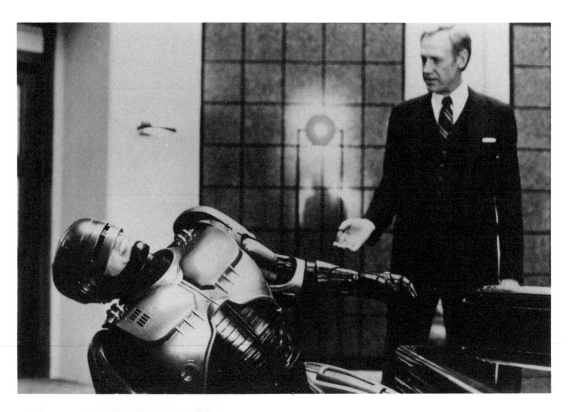

ROBOCOP: Jones (Ronny Cox) studies the half-human, half machine supercop (Peter Weller).

the movie so impressive was the way the filmmakers fleshed out this idea, injecting the kind of incisive satire that distinguished Stanley Kubrick's classic *Dr. Strangelove* while adding enough graphic brutality to satisfy the action-adventure audience. *RoboCop* rated as a rarity: a loud, fast-paced popular hit with enough smarts and style to captivate even the toughest critics.

RoboCop could be enjoyed as futuristic escapism or as a serious-minded film with plenty to say about the present, scoring its points by taking the most terrifying tendencies at work in the world today and exaggerating them to render a frightfully possible nightmare portrait of the future. Set in Detroit, identified as the crime capital of America, the film depicted a downtown area that's become such a wasteland it will be razed to make room for "Delta City," America's most ambitious urban development program ever. The police are controlled by something called Security Concepts, Inc., a subsidiary of OmniConsumer Products, the megaconglomerate about to initiate construction on the Delta project. We discover just how far the OmniConsumer influence reaches: the most violent criminals in the inner city are actually secret operatives for the corporate executive (Ronny Cox) assigned to develop "enforcement droids" to police the era.

ROBOCOP: Scott Thompson, Donna Regan, and Bill Schockley as denizens of the ruined futureworld who find themselves under the shadow of Robocop.

Early on, we catch brief glimpses of the grotesque world at large, in which South Africa has the Bomb, while vacationers in Acapulco must skirt gun-wielding rebels operating out of the international airport. We perceive these people and places through the logical extension of today's headline-news networks, a televised vision of the world for viewers whose attention spans have been systematically shortened. "Give us three minutes; we'll give you the world," the pretty, banal anchorwoman gleefully comments. She was played by Leeza Gibbons, weekend hostess for TV's *Entertainment Tonight*, one of the Eighties shows that really did presage the kind of television *RoboCop* warned its audience about. In the future, *RoboCop* implies, hard news will be reduced to the level of fluff; indeed, in the age of Geraldo Rivera and *A Current Affair*, that was already the case.

Yet for all the on-target satire, *RoboCop* remained remarkably poignant. Murphy is glimpsed only briefly before the shooting and subsequent transformation, yet Weller managed to suggest a believable, likable person. The relationship with Lewis was quickly but effectively sketched in, allowing us to understand her desire to rekindle their friendship even though (in his cyborg guise) his memory has been blanked. Some of the best moments occur when RoboCop finds his memory buds stirring, returning to the home where he once lived with his family. Audiences were surprisingly touched, as bits proved warmhearted in a way not expected from a film otherwise filled with savage satire and savage action.

Rob Bottin (*The Thing*) did a first-rate job of creating the look of RoboCop himself. Other special-effects artists and production designers collaborated to create a vivid visualization of the near future as a place of moral,

cultural and architectural contradictions, where inner cities have become social cesspools surrounded by sleek, sophisticated high-rise structures from which corporate yuppies rule the world. Dutch filmmaker Paul Verhoeven (*Soldier of Orange, Spetters*) superbly tied all the film's disparate elements together into a fast-paced tour of a high-tech future that terrified its audience because it appeared all too possible a nightmare scenario for where we were apparently headed. While being viewed, *RoboCop* entertained. But when viewers left the theater and found themselves unable to shake the experience afterward, they realized this film was also able to enlighten.

Fatal Attraction

A PARAMOUNT PICTURES RELEASE OF A JAFFE/LANSING PRODUCTION   1987

CREDITS:

Produced by Stanley R. Jaffe and Sherry Lansing; directed by Adrian Lyne; written by James Dearden; photography, Howard Atherton; editors, Michael Kahn and Peter E. Berger; Running time, 119 min.; Rating: R.

CAST:

Dan Gallagher (Michael Douglas); *Alex Forrest* (Glenn Close); *Beth Gallagher* (Anne Archer); *Ellen Gallagher*

FATAL ATTRACTION: Michael Douglas as happily married Dan Gallagher dawdles with Glenn Close as "liberated" Alex Forrest in the first post-feminist, post-AIDS thriller: The "enlightened" woman is a maniac, while a one night stand can come back and kill you.

(Ellen Hamilton Latzen); *Jimmy* (Stuart Pankin); *Hildy* (Ellen Foley); *Arthur* (Fred Gwynne); *Joan Rogerson* (Meg Mundy); *Howard Rogerson* (Tom Brennan); *Martha* (Lois Smith).

When this erotic thriller opened in September 1987, it quickly broke box-office records for a fall release, shortly emerging as the hot movie not only in sophisticated New York, where the story was set, but all around the country. People responded, less to the relatively simple story (not all that different from past pictures like *Play Misty for Me*) but to unstated implications in the plot and a masterpiece of timing, which allowed this intense work of entertainment to function also as a nightmare vision and cautionary fable about sex in the late-Eighties.

Dan (Michael Douglas) is a happily married New Yorker, with a beautiful wife (Anne Archer) and a child, enjoying an envious upscale lifestyle in the trendy corners of Manhattan. One of the people with whom his career brings him into contact is Alex (Glenn Close), an attractive, aggressive lady executive. While Dan's wife is out of town, a late evening business dinner he has with Alex concludes and she invites him to her place. Hesitating briefly, he decides to take her up on the offer; he is a bit bored, Alex is appealing, and he's a product of the post-Sexual Revolution generation, conditioned to believe there's nothing all that wrong with a brief fling just so long as he's completely honest with the lady involved, making certain she knows he's married.

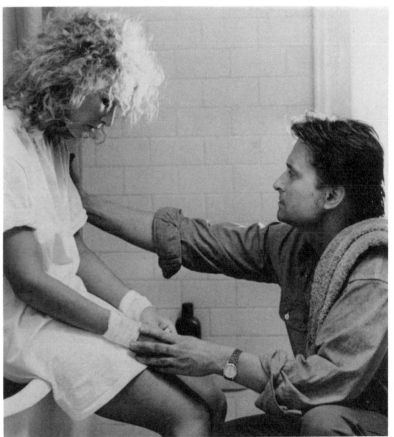

FATAL ATTRACTION: Dan consoles the self-destructive Alex; in the original (and dramatically correct) version, Alex ultimately commits suicide in such a way as to implicate Dan.

197

FATAL ATTRACTION: "I will not be *ignored!*"; Glenn Close as Alex, an intense, erotic, brilliant performance—up until the shrill, screeching, knife-wielding finale, which Close was forced to return and film.

The weekend comes to an end, and Dan has his first sense that Alex is not the strong, modern liberated woman she pretends to be when she grows despondent, possibly suicidal, at the thought of his walking out the door. Soon, she's calling him at his office regularly, assuming they've entered into a continuing relationship; Dan tries to make it clear, hopefully without hurting her, he had assumed something different, enjoying the weekend as an extended one-night stand. Alex insists on another meeting, at which time she informs Dan she's pregnant. Though he's stunned that she didn't use birth control, he's quite willing to pay for the abortion, but is shocked to learn Alex has no intention of going that route. She expects Dan to marry her and, when he firmly tells her to stay away, begins calling his house, then makes personal contact with his wife. Terrified that if the truth comes out he'll lose his family, Dan jumps in fear every time the phone rings. Such moments are brilliantly played: audiences literally leaped out of their seats at the sound of the phone suddenly ringing.

Originally, the film—based on a 45-minute British independent production called *Diversion*—had Alex (who constantly listens to *Madame Butterfly*) commit suicide, leaving behind enough circumstantial evidence to implicate Dan in her death. That's de rigueur for an art-house item, but *Fatal Attraction* was intended as a mainstream blockbuster; when audiences at preview showings complained of being let down by the grim conclusion, producers Sherry Lansing and Stanley R. Jaffe called back cast and crew, filming a more conventional third act: Alex stalks Dan and his family, like a pregnant female version of Jason from *Friday the 13th*, even rising out of a tub of water (shrieking as she wields a knife, her eyes bulging), in which she's seemingly been drowned, to try and kill again.

Which is all well and good in a genre piece, but *Fatal Attraction* had, until that point, shaped up as far less facile than that: a powerfully realistic and highly moral (though never simplistically moralistic) movie on the subject of extramarital affairs, brilliantly played by a marvelous cast: Douglas (curiously not an Oscar nominee here, although a winner the same year for *Wall Street*) made Dan both an individually drawn character and a universal symbol for the contemporary male; Oscar-nominated Close, usually associated with sensitive roles, was sexier than anybody suspected she could be, keeping Alex sympathetic even when she does terrible things; Archer (also Oscar nominated) played what could have been a stereotyped stay-at-home wife in such a striking way that the lady emerged as impressive and, in the end, strong. But the public lapped it up, apparently loving the new, garish ending. More than for the romance and thrills (which can be found in a dozen other sexy suspense movies that didn't click), *Fatal Attraction* attracted audiences with a timeliness of theme: by implication, this was the first AIDS film, even though that dread disease was never mentioned. The point of *Fatal Attraction* was that a one-night stand could come back to haunt you, even kill you; that the age of promiscuous sex was over simply because it had become deadly. There is no longer any such thing, *Fatal Attraction* made powerfully and painfully clear, as casual sex.

Good Morning, Vietnam

A BUENA VISTA RELEASE OF A
TOUCHTONE PICTURES
PRESENTATION   1987

CREDITS:

Produced by Mark Johnson and Larry Brezner; directed by Barry Levinson; written by Mitch Markowitz; photography, Peter Sova; editor, Stu Linder; Running time, 120 min.; Rating: R.

CAST:

Adrian Cronauer (Robin Wiliams); *Edward Garlick* (Forest Whitaker); *Tuan* (Tung Thanh Tran); *Lt. Steven Hauk* (Bruno Kirby); *Trinh* (Chintara Sukapatana); *Marty Lee Dreiwitz* (Robert Wuhl); *Sgt. Major Dickerson* (J. T. Walsh); *Gen. Taylor* (Noble Willingham); *Pvt. Abersold* (Richard Edson); *Phil McPherson* (Juney Smith).

Good Morning, Vietnam rates as a significant film of the Eighties in a number of respects. First, it was yet another in the string of good, mediocre and bad Vietnam war movies that peppered the decade, as America at last tried to put that conflict behind it through the ritualistic act of watching every facet of the Nam experience on the screen. Second, it stood as part of the significant 1980s', tendency to base popular entertainment on actual events, retaining the names of real characters while playing fast and loose with the facts. Third, it allowed stand-up comic turned serious actor Robin Williams the perfect showcase for his talents, allowing him to demonstrate his excellent range for playing heavy situations while at the same time letting him display his virtuoso gifts at improvisation, resulting in his most satisfying screen exposure to date.

GOOD MORNING, VIETNAM: Robin Williams as real-life disc jockey Adrian Cronauer, who was never quite so irreverent, outrageous or ingenious as Williams made him out to be: This was less an example of docudrama than a case of myth-making.

It wasn't surprising to learn that screenwriter Mitch Markowitz tailored (at Williams's specific request) the project's central character especially for him. In the film, Adrian Cronauer arrives in Saigon, circa 1965, to assume his role as morning announcer on the local armed forces radio station. Previous jocks played pleasant Percy Faith recordings, read the heavily edited news verbatim, passed on innocuous hygiene tips (a favorite was reminding servicemen to rinse their razors with cold water to avoid heat rash), and maintained an unshakably upbeat tone (jokes were taken from *Reader's Digest*). Stunned by this facade of forced optimism, Cronauer reacts to the squalor and suffering around him by making it the subject of his show. Shortly, his distinctive opening shriek of "Good Morning, Vietnam!" is followed by rock 'n' roll, rowdy humor, undeleted expletives, even attempts to slip some of the darker news stories past censors like strict Lt. Hauk (Bruno Kirby). Though the servicemen immediately take to Cronauer, the brass believes he is out of control and plot devious ways to muzzle his flow of "radical" words and music.

The film's Cronauer transforms the radio medium into a manic, makeshift art form, letting loose with guerrilla theatre of the airwaves. Disguised as anecdotes and jokes, his sharp, savage opinions capture the absurdity of war in general and of the Vietnam experience in particu-

GOOD MORNING, VIETNAM: The film's Cronauer finds himself a hero of the G.I.'s who have just begun to realize the war they are fighting is absurd.

GOOD MORNING, VIETNAM: Amidst the chaos and violence of the escalating war, Cronauer finds his infatuation with Trinh (Chintara Sukapatana), a beautiful local woman, allows him a greater awareness and understanding of the Vietnamese people.

lar. Shortly after the release of *Good Morning, Vietnam*, though, the real Cronauer admitted he was never as inspired or outrageous as Williams made him appear in the film, neither as quick-witted nor as ingenious; while he did indeed run afoul of his superiors, and censors, the situation never became so pointed as in the film. Simply, this was Cronauer's story folded craftily into an entertaining movie myth, with Cronauer liberally recreated as an ideal vehicle for Robin Williams.

Screenwriter Markowtiz and director Barry Levinson were less interested in creating a docudrama of Cronauer's actual experience, sticking as close to the facts as possible, but rather in making a service comedy with serious undertones (a tradition ranging from *What Price, Glory?* to *Mister Roberts* to *M*A*S*H*) that ultimately plays as a metaphor for Vietnam. The film takes place during 1965, that pivotal year when President Johnson (having recently been elected on a promise that American boys would not die doing the job Vietnamese boys were supposed to be doing) escalated the American commitment in men from the tens to the hundreds of thousands. In the course of one year, what had been a minor conflict which mainstream America chose to overlook forced itself into the center of the national consciousness. Against this backdrop, we view a variety of interesting characters, including a jovial fellow disc

200

GOOD MORNING, VIETNAM: Accompanied by Trinh's younger brother Tuan (Tung Thanh Tran, right), Cronauer meets one of his youngest listeners; the film allowed Williams to do his wild improvisational stunts but also to play heartwarming scenes like this one.

jockey (Forest Whitaker) who quickly comes to idolize Cronauer, and the pretty young Vietnamese woman (Chintara Sukapatana) Cronauer initially wants only to seduce, then comes to love and respect. With the development of his feelings for her (and his warmth for her young brother, played by Tung Thanh Tran), we see Cronauer's moral growth and eventual ability to appreciate the Vietnamese as people. Most of this was fictional, created to make the story fit into the pattern of a traditional redemption saga. But what a powerhouse of a performance it allowed Williams: more even than his excellent work in *The World According to Garp, Moscow on the Hudson* and the later *Dead Poets Society,* this rates as his finest film work during the Eighties, perhaps because it's a role that never would have been written the way it was were it not for his enthusiastic intention to play it.

Wall Street

A 20TH CENTURY-FOX RELEASE OF AN EDWARD R. PRESSMAN PRODUCTION 1987

CREDITS:

Produced by Edward R. Pressman and A. Kitman Ho; directed by Oliver Stone; written by Stanley Weiser and Oliver Stone; photography, Robert Richardson; editor, Claire Simpson; Running time, 124 min.; Rating: R.

CAST:

Gordon Gekko (Michael Douglas); *Bud Fox* (Charlie Sheen); *Carl Fox* (Martin Sheen); *Darien Taylor* (Daryl Hannah); *Sir Larry Wildman* (Terence Stamp); *Kate Gekko* (Sean Young); *Realtor* (Sylvia Miles); *Roger* (James Spader); *Marvin* (John McGinley); *Lou* (Hal Holbrook).

The timing of *Wall Street*'s release was the most inadvertently brilliant since *The China Syndrome* opened in 1979 even as the Three Mile Island meltdown, predicted in that film, occurred. Both films starred Michael Douglas, who, by innate intelligence or sheer good fortune, ferreted out projects in which he and his collaborators foresaw disasters in the making and turned out cinematic versions which arrived on-screen even as the reality made headlines. Douglas eventually won a Best Actor Oscar for playing Gordon Gekko, *Wall Street*'s modern Midas and a fictional counterpart of real-life high roller Ivan Boesky. Despite the aura of a white-collar wheeler-dealer, Gekko's success derives from an abiding corruption. He tantalizes boyish brokers who are eager to win his approval by engaging in "insider trading." Living beyond their means, these impressionable, ambitious yuppies are easy marks. The latest is a Michael Milken-ish Bud Fox (Charlie Sheen), whose father, Carl (Martin Sheen), is a decent blue-collar airline engineer. Bud becomes privvy to information Gekko—for whom greed is not only a byword but also his philosophy—industriously translates into stock market ploys.

Wall Street's knowledgeable vision of contemporary amorality helped its audience better understand the

201

WALL STREET: Charlie Sheen as Bud Fox: a young trader eager to succeed, lacking any strong moral convictions, despite the influence of his old fashioned father.

WALL STREET: Gordon Gekko (Michael Douglas, in his Oscar-winning performance) reminded many viewers of Ivan Boesky: King of the Greed Decade, though about to tumble.

WALL STREET: Bud (Charlie Sheen) likewise reminded viewers of Michael Milken, junk bond salesman also headed for a fall.

WALL STREET: "Greed is good!" snarls Gekko, the modern devil in Oliver Stone's latest morality play.

203

October 1987 Black Friday stock market disaster, occurring virtually on the eve of the film's release. Dramatically, this was an old-fashioned morality play. At the end, Gekko and Bud faced hefty price tags they couldn't pay up with plastic; Bud at last grasps the superficiality of his upscale sleaze existence and, for a shorter jail term, helps the government get Gekko. As always, the clear intent of filmmaker Stone was to galvanize an audience with a heartfelt if highly schematized treatise, ending with a speech from the film's man of values, Carl. As a peek behind the closed-door world of big bucks manipulation, *Wall Street* offered a vivid and accurate portrayal. However, the chief problem with the script by Stone and Stanley Weiser (*Project X* the same year) was its creation of two-dimensional figures who served as mouthpieces for positions, stating ideas outright, rather than creating believable three-dimensional human beings.

Douglas here created one of those slick, superficial weaklings his dad had played in early films like *Out of the Past* and *The Strange Love of Martha Ivers*. In real life, though, even sinister, manipulative types like Gekko have other sides; the richest and most complex drama offers rounded, multidimensional villains, given the kinds of interesting edges Stone does not care to explore. The scenes depicting Gekko at home were too conventional to serve such a purpose. Sean Young, as Gekko's wife, was glimpsed too briefly to add further

WALL STREET: Daryl Hannah's character seemed contrived, inserted into the story to create an overly familiar romantic triangle and allow her to splash about a bit in a bathing suit during a beach scene.

WALL STREET: The good angel opposing devilish Gekko for Bud's soul is his decent, moral father (played by Martin Sheen, Charlie's real-life Dad).

204

WALL STREET: Bud wheels and deals with (clockwise, from top left) by-the-book broker Lou Mannheim (Hal Holbrook); colleague Marvin (John McGinley); company boss Lynch (James Karen); and fellow yuppie Roger (James Spader).

coloring or dimension to his character. Any depth to Bud's personality came from what the younger Sheen brought to the role rather than deriving from the script. The real clunker: a trite romantic triangle in which the two men battled over a beautiful blonde cipher (Daryl Hannah), with a beachside scene included for no better purpose than to briefly get her into a wetsuit. This love interest was as maudlin and melodramatic as anything in a prime-time soap, the only saving grace being that it was here contained within the context of a thematically ambitious project.

Stone's great gifts as a filmmaker are his seriousness of intent and total sincerity. At his best—*Salvador, Born on the Fourth of July*— he transcends his limitations and capitalizes on his qualities, creating a balance between ideas and drama. More often—*Wall Street, Talk Radio*—he's hampered by a superficial understanding of psychology and an awful ear for dialogue. Nobody anywhere, even on Wall Street, talks the way these people do.

Gekko and Fox shout ideas at each other (overtly verbalizing what a more sophisticated filmmaker would have implied) so no viewer will fail to get Stone's drift. "Greed is good," Gekko snarls, but if the moment was unsubtle, it was unquestionably effective. If the Black Friday market crash was the event which shook middle Americans into an awareness of their faulty values during this decade, *Wall Street* was undeniably the first film to make everyone reconsider their decade-long attitudes about money and morality.

Essentially, Stone stands as the 1980s recreation of a noble if naïve artist: the sociologically conscious man angrily attempting to correct some social ill through paint-by-the-number portraits of victimized people. Like those turn-of-the-century muckraking novels illustrating such social ills as corruption in railroads (*The Octopus*) and meat-packing (*The Jungle*), Stone's work is searing in immediate impact, then of historical (rather than artistic) value once the particular problem has passed.

Moonstruck

A METRO-GOLDWYN-MAYER
PRESENTATION   1987

CREDITS:

Produced by Patrick Palmer and Norman Jewison; directed
by Norman Jewison; written by John Patrick Shanley;
photography, David Watkin; editor, Lou Lombardo; Running
time, 102 min.; Rating: PG.

CAST:

Loretta (Cher); *Ronny Cammareri* (Nicolas Cage); *Cosmo
Castorini* (Vincent Gardenia); *Rose* (Olympia Dukakis);
Johnny (Danny Aiello); *Rita Cappomaggi* (Julie Bovasso);
Perry (John Mahoney); *Raymond* (Louis Guss); *Old Man*
(Feodor Chaliapin); *Mona* (Anita Gillette).

In 1983, Cher failed to receive a Best Supporting
Actress Oscar nomination for her scene-stealing role in
Silkwood; in 1985, she again was slighted, despite her
worthy performance in *Mask*. But Cher was deservedly
nominated for *Moonstruck* and, when the awards were
handed out several months later, she danced onstage—in
her notorious negligee-type outfit—as the winning Best
Actress. The transition is less interesting in terms of
what it tells us about Cher—she maintained her off-
center image, never compromising to win over Hollywood's elite—than for what it tells us about the Establishment of the contemporary movie capital. In the early
Eighties, her personal style and off-camera antics may
have been too much to accept, despite the star's box-
office allure and the quality of her work. But by decade's
end, the old guard had passed, and the hip new Hollywood perceived in Cher—see-through, bare-nearly-all
outfits, frizzed hair, frankly stated and unbleeped opinions—a person quite appropriate to represent them.

In a way, awarding her the statuette was something of
a throwback to earlier days, when a performer received
the Academy Award not necessarily for some single role
but for an especially impressive output during one
particularly strong year. There was a certain sense that
Cher actually won for the diversity of roles, and depth
with which she'd invested in each, in a relatively short
period of time: the quirky artist in *The Witches of
Eastwick*, the intense lawyer in *Suspect*, finally the quiet

Italian-American princess in *Moonstruck*. No question,
though, Loretta Castorini was her most appealing and
demanding part, if only because it showed such a
different side of Cher, in striking contrast to her funky
popular image as a biker's dream of leather-bedecked
beauty, acting talent notwithstanding. Demure and responsible, Loretta was a role that all but jumped from
the script pages, screaming: "Get me Anjelica Huston!"
but from the moment Cher appeared as Loretta (Maerose
Prizzi without the "connections") she made the part her
own; when she subsequently took the dowdy Loretta's
convincing transformation to glamour, the magic in
Cher's eyes made *Moonstruck* click as a fairy tale for
adults.

The members of an Italian Brooklyn clan discover the
truth about themselves and each other on one of those
magical nights when the moon, as Shakespeare put it,
comes too close to the earth and makes men mad. While
that line derives from a tragedy, *Moonstruck* boasts the
quality of one of those enchanting comedies like *A
Midsummer Night's Dream*, with diverse people slipping
in and out of entangling romantic relationships. Just
engaged to the lumpy, likable Johnny Cammareri (Danny
Aiello), Loretta sees him jet off to Sicily to pay respects
to his dying mother. His parting request: that she call his
younger brother, Ronny (Nicolas Cage), mending the bad
blood between the two. Loretta ultimate gets up the
gumption to visit Ronny, a baker who turns out to be a
cross between Stanley Kowalski from *A Streetcar Named
Desire* and Tony Manero from *Saturday Night Fever*:
inarticulate, brutish, yet sensitive and lonely.

She can't help but fall madly in love, though her
mother has sternly warned Loretta romance is the worst
thing for a woman planning a practical marriage. Mother
is played by Olympia Dukakis. Not well known to movie
audiences but a respected stage veteran, she walked off
with the Best Supporting Actress Oscar. Her sensible
Italo-American housewife, while rarely leaving the confines of her kitchen, has somehow managed to amass the
wisdom of the ages; that was the essence of her appeal.
Her husband Cosmo (Vincent Gardenia) may be cheating on her, but she accepts this, sensing it's because men
fear death, believing both of them are cheating it by
living double lives. The pseudo-macho one-handed
Ronny (he lost the other in an accident he wrongly
blames on his brother) shouts out the film's comic
message, telling Loretta their passion wells up not in
spite of the fact it's forbidden but because of it: "We are
here to ruin ourselves and break our hearts and love the
wrong people and then die," he wails in the manner of a
lovestruck Woody Allen hero.

Ronny is a big fan of opera, so no wonder he lives his
life with the exaggerated grand passions he regularly
witnesses at Lincoln Center. Yet despite the fine en-

MOONSTRUCK: Plain, drab Loretta Castorini (Cher) graciously accepts a proposal of marriage from her decent, unexciting suitor, Mr. Johnny (Danny Aiello) . . .

. . . only to fall head over heels in love with her prospective brother-in-law, the outrageous but passionate Ronny (Nicolas Cage); overnight, she experiences a fairy-tale changeover from frump to beautiful lady.

MOONSTRUCK: Loretta's serious-minded mother Rose (Olympia Dukakis, Best Supporting Actress Oscar-winner) warns her daughter against a marriage based on passion and romance.

207

MOONSTRUCK: Rose Castorini arranges for a heart-to-heart conversation with her daughter's timid fiancé, Mr. Johnny, hoping to discover why men in general (and her own husband in particular) chase other women.

MOONSTRUCK Nicolas Cage, as the hot-headed baker who loves opera—and adds some grand operatic passion to his own life when he falls in love with his brother's fiancée.

208

MOONSTRUCK: The superb ensemble cast brought together by director Norman Jewison for his warm, whimsical contemporary fairy-tale: (seated, from left) Nicolas Cage, Cher, Feodor Chaliapin; (standing, from left) Julie Bovasso, Olympia Dukakis, Louis Guss, Vincent Gardenia and Danny Aiello.

semble approach, there was never any doubt this was Cher's show. Bringing the John Patrick Shanley script to the screen was Norman Jewison, adept at comedies like *The Thrill of it All*, with Doris Day, and *The Russians Are Coming! The Russians Are Coming!* and musicals such as *Fiddler on the Roof*, as well as solid, serious works (*In the Heat of the Night* and *A Soldier's Story*). He brought to the film the required wry, dry wit with remarkable dexterity. *Moonstruck* featured ethnic humor that never became abusive; the film is as charming and kookie as the lady who assayed the leading role.

Three Men and a Baby

A TOUCHSTONE PICTURES RELEASE IN ASSOCIATION WITH SILVER SCREEN PARTNERS III   1987

CREDITS:

Executive producer, Jean Francois Leptit; produced by Ted Field and Howard Teets; directed by Leonard Nimoy; written by James Orr and Jim Cruickshank, based on the French film *Trois Hommes et un coffin*; photography, Adam Greenberg; editor, Michael A. Stevenson; Running time, 102 min.; Rating: PG.

CAST:

Peter (Tom Selleck); *Michael* (Steve Guttenberg); *Jack* (Ted Danson); *Sylvia* (Nancy Travis); *Rebecca* (Margaret Colin); *Detective Melkowitz* (Philip Bosco); *Baby Mary* (Lisa Blair, Michelle Blair).

The surprising success of the 1987 Christmas holiday season was *Three Men and a Baby*, soaring to the top of the box-office charts, remaining there for months. The rapid shifting of moral attitudes in the post-AIDS era had brought about a return to family values, and *Three Men*, more than any of the other "baby" movies (*Baby Boom, Look Who's Talking*), captured the spirit of the times in which single guys were gradually won over to the joys of child rearing.

Grudging admiration is the phrase most critics used when discussing the film: admiration as, on the whole, *Three Men* disarmingly mixed warmth and humor; grudging, as everything about it seemed a tad over-calculated. *Three Men* was nothing if not commercial, featuring a trio of popular male stars, allowing them to

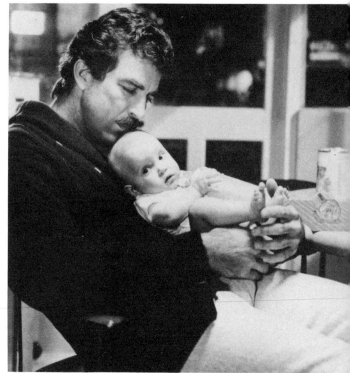

THREE MEN AND A BABY: Bachelor Peter Mitchell (Tom Selleck) finds his maternal side tapped when he cares for a baby found abandoned on his doorstep.

reveal sides of themselves they'd not previously exposed, particularly the fascinating vulnerability macho men are capable of when suddenly stuck in the position of playing mother. Too bad no one involved with the project was willing to take that theme very far. Director Leonard Nimoy and his team instead settled for the expected and obvious gags, including a man changing a diaper for the first time. Still, it was to Nimoy's credit as a director that he coaxed his cast into playing out those gags effectively, sometimes even enchantingly.

A radiant sweetness was in evidence, resulting in enough rewarding moments that anyone approaching this with modest expectations—desiring only to be passingly entertained—did not come away disappointed. The plot was High Concept: three agreeable guys share a nifty bachelor apartment. Peter (Tom Selleck) is athletic, Michael (Steve Guttenberg) is artistic, and Jack (Ted Danson) is romantic, a womanizing hack actor about to leave for an on-location shoot. Before departing, he mentions that a package for a mutual friend will shortly arrive, asking them to hold it. What shows up on their doorstep is a baby the two awkwardly attempt to care for. Then some menacing men show up, claiming the "package" is theirs. Our amiable heroes don't realize there are two packages: the baby's been deposited by the actor's former girlfriend, who became pregnant by him and

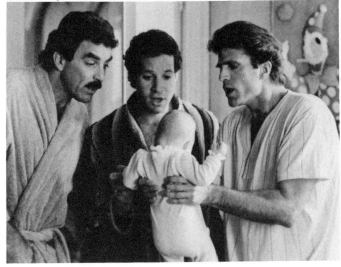

THREE MEN AND A BABY: Peter (Tom Selleck), Michael (Steve Guttenberg), and Jack (Ted Danson) care for the baby: "Goodnight, sweetheart, goodnight!"

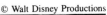

THREE MEN AND A BABY: The joys of diapering.

can't handle both a child and a career. The other package is drugs, which those menacing hit men want—so badly they're willing to kidnap the former "package" and exchange it for the latter.

This causes problems for Selleck and Guttenberg (as well as Danson, when he returns), for after the expected awkward period, they grow to love the child and want to keep her. There are moments of Hitchcockian suspense (normal characters menaced by villains from a dark shadow world of corruption they did not previously acknowledge, a double McGuffin) as well as dollops of warm humor (as the boys care for the baby, this occasionally seemed like the pilot for a TV sitcom). Though based on a French film (*Three Men and a Cradle*), hugely popular *Baby* stood as the exception to the rule: the rare Hollywood remake that was better than its foreign predecessor, here a charming realization of an idea that had in its original gallic version been presented in a lukewarm, lackluster manner. More often, French comedy classics (*The Toy, A Pain in the A, The Tall Blonde Man With One Black Shoe, Pardon Mon Affaire*) were turned into duds when Americanized. Though hardly a great comic film, this American version clearly rated as an improvement.

THREE MEN AND A BABY: Peter and Michael put their usual concerns aside to feed the baby.

So long as the film stuck with suspense and sitcom, it worked as a highly watchable confection. Toward the end, the heroes face a more formidable adversary than the drug dealers—the mother of the tot, who has a change of heart and returns for her baby. For a moment, something impressive appeared ready to happen: the movie would transform, before our eyes, into a more dramatic work on the order of *Kramer vs. Kramer*. Instead, there was a less-than-believable fantasy-resolution, in which all five characters—mother, baby and the three guys—decide to live together happily ever after. Also dimming the film was the fact that for budgetary reasons this Manhattan-set movie was shot in Toronto (a regular if depressing filmmaking trend throughout the Eighties); instead of making the city's unique personality a vivid element in the movie, director Nimoy was constantly forced to avoid allowing us a view of the city. None of New York's unique rhythms—such an important part of great Manhattan movies by Woody Allen, Martin Scorsese and Sidney Lumet—was present. But by coming up with a tale in touch with the tenor of his times, Nimoy created a crowd-pleaser, if one that sacrificed true poignancy to the sentimentally endearing.

Broadcast News

A 20TH CENTURY-FOX RELEASE   1987

CREDITS:

Executive producer, Polly Platt; produced, written and directed by James L. Brooks; coproducer, Penney Finkleman Cox; photography, Michael Balhaus; editor, Richard Marks; Running time, 131 min.; Rating: R.

CAST:

Tom Grunick (William Hurt); *Jane Craig* (Holly Hunter); *Aaron Altman* (Albert Brooks); *Ernie Merriman* (Robert Prosky); *Jennifer Mack* (Lois Chiles); *Blair Litton* (Joan Cusack); *Paul Moore* (Peter Hackes); *Bobby* (Christian Clemenson); *The Anchorman* (Jack Nicholson).

With *Broadcast News*, writer-director James L. Brooks returned to a comedy milieu he knows well. Warmly remembered as the man who elevated TV sitcom to the level of an art form with *The Mary Tyler Moore Show*, he there proved that a weekly show about an ever-smiling career woman could generate sur-

prisingly on-target insights about television journalism. His first feature in the four years since *Terms of Endearment* mercilessly savaged network-level reporting. The film concerned a trio of broadcasters at an unidentified network, locked in a romantic triangle. Tom Grunick (William Hurt) is a younger, upscale, more successful Ted Baxter, an ambitious if somewhat vapid anchorman whose considerable impact on the public is based on the way his skin tones photograph for color TV. No matter that Tom does not have an original idea in his pretty head, or that his knowledge of current events barely extends beyond the identity of the current President. Tom is the slightly exaggerated but frightfully

BROADCAST NEWS: Holly Hunter leaped from obscurity to stardom as Jane Craig, the intense news producer.

BROADCAST NEWS: Tom Grunick (William Hurt) is partially a realistic characterization, partially a satire on news anchors chosen more for flesh tones and pleasing voices than any grasp of national or international affairs.

BROADCAST NEWS: If Tom represents style, Aaron Altman (Albert Brooks) is substance: A knowledgeable reporter stuck in a low-paying behind-the-scenes job because he doesn't come off well on television.

BROADCAST NEWS: Jane finds herself torn between the two men, physically attracted to the suave Tom . . .

accurate extension of what the ratings wars have given us as our real-life national source of information, confidently speaking into the camera while unseen wires pump facts and figures into his hidden earphone. To paraphrase a slogan from the socially activist 1960s: in 1987, bland is beautiful.

Less bland but also less beautiful is Aaron Altman (Albert Brooks, no relation to James L.), a whiz-kid reporter who knows more about history than the *Encyclopedia Britannica*, more about today's important events than this morning's edition of *The New York Times*. He's the person we'd get the news from, if life only worked the way it ought to and substance mattered more than style. It doesn't, and on camera, Aaron looks too New York ethnic for the folks in Peoria, is cursed with facial features that photograph awkwardly. Worse still, Aaron visibly sweats when under the glare of studio lights. So while the well-mannered but mindless Tom can ask for and get a multi-million dollar yearly salary, whereas the smart but schlumpy Aaron must take a cut in pay to keep his behind-the-scenes job.

Torn between them is Jane Craig (Holly Hunter), gutsy, clever, up-and-coming producer of the news. The choice should be easy: Holly realizes the difference

between personality and performance, ingratiation and intelligence. But she is, after all, only human; so like everyone else in the country, Jane is swept off her feet by Tom's irresistible charm. The only difference between Jane and the public is that she, of all people, should know better.

At a key moment, Aaron refers to Tom as the devil, walking the earth and smiling pleasantly as he gradually lowers standards. Clearly, filmmaker Brooks shares that sentiment. What made his film so remarkable is that Brooks refused to do what Oliver Stone did in *Wall Street*; there the devil (Michael Douglas) all but sprouted horns and hissed. Brooks's vision of morality is more complex. Rather than oversimplifying, providing good guys and villains, Brooks creates characters who are well-rounded people first, representations of ideas second. If Stone's greatest flaw as a filmmaker is his lack of convincing dialogue, that is Brooks's forte. Every line, however funny, rings incredibly true; we never doubt this is the way TV journalists speak, in and out of the newsroom. The supporting actors do not simply embody types (as they do in *Wall Street*) but stand as perfectly realized cameos, three-dimensional people glimpsed briefly but fully and thoroughly understood at once. At the top of the list was unbilled Jack Nicholson as the network's aging Chancellor-Brinkley-Cronkite anchor.

. . . while emotionally drawn to the intelligent Aaron.

214

But the focus remained on Hunter (attaining long-predicted stardom and an Oscar nomination as Best Actress), an absolute stunner in a role clearly written with Debra Winger in mind and: surprising the viewer at every turn, always rising to the level of Brooks's unschematized script.

There are no true heroes or villains in *Broadcast News*, only victims of the way things are. Which is why the film doesn't tie up in a nice neat knot at the end, simply stopping after a while, the relationships petering out rather than climaxing, just as in real life. Viewers waiting to see which man would finally be chosen by Hunter were taken aback when she walked out on both, remaining friends with each. Brooks made clear his anger over the breakdown of a line between the networks' entertainment and news divisions. Moviegoers who recalled Democratic presidential candidate Walter Mondale's 1984 post-election speech, in which he insisted the viewers had not so much rejected his political agenda as his lack of presence and charisma on TV, saw that theme powerfully realized here.

215

The Last Emperor

A COLUMBIA PICTURES RELEASE OF A JEREMY THOMAS PRODUCTION 1987

CREDITS:

Produced by Jeremy Thomas; directed by Bernardo
Bertolucci; written by Mark Peploe with Bernardo
Bertolucci; photography, Vittorio Storaro; editor, Gabriella
Cristiani; Running time, 160 min.; Rating: R.

CAST:

Pu Yi (John Lone); *Wan Jung* (Joan Chan); *R.J.* (Peter
O'Toole); *The Governor* (Ying Ruocheng); *Big Li* (Dennis
Dun); *Amakasu* (Ryuichi Sakamoto); *Eastern Jewel* (Maggie
Han); *Interrogator* (Ric Yung); *Pu Yi, Age 3* (Richard Yuu);
Pu Yi, 8 (Tijger Tsou); *Pu Yi, 15* (Wu Tao).

Once in every decade a film reminds us of the
grandeur that cinema, at its most ambitious, can
achieve. Francis Coppola's *The Godfather, Part II* was
the 1970s example, brimming with well-wrought characters, vivid period ambience, striking sights and sounds,
a feast for the eyes, providing food for thought, epic in
scope though intimate in detail. In 1987 came Bernardo
Bertolucci's *The Last Emperor*, an equally impressive
example of moviemaking at its most spectacular, standing alongside not only Coppola's contemporary classic
but also Abel Gance's *Napoleon* and D. W. Griffith's
Intolerance as a mammoth masterpiece, powerfully
recreating the past while also revitalizing a true story for
the present.

The title refers to Pu Yi, who at age two was literally
yanked from his mother's side when the elderly, dying
Dowager Empress of China chose this distant relative to
succeed her. Overnight, the life of the uncomprehending
child was radically transformed as, seated on the Dragon
Throne of Beijing's Forbidden City, he wielded power
beyond the wildest imaginings. Like other children, he
became frustrated when painting with pen and ink;
unlike others, he could relieve his boredom by casually
suggesting his servants drink the ink, then curiously wait
to see if the substance would kill them. Whether or not
Pu Yi would eventually grow into a responsible adult or
remain a spoiled, whimsical creature will never be
known, for the changing political situation saw his power
stripped away. At six, Pu Yi literally became the
proverbial bird in a gilded cage, still treated as a prince
but now a virtual prisoner in his elegant surroundings.

THE LAST EMPEROR: Richard Vuu portrayed the infant Pu Yi, last
emperor of China, in the film's early moments.

THE LAST EMPEROR: The adult emperor (John Lone) finds his life changing drastically as China undergoes drastic political movements; director Bernardo Bertolucci managed to balance epic sweep with political insight.

THE LAST EMPEROR: Pu Yi (John Lone) yearns to become Emperor once again and emerges as Japan's puppet head of the new state of Manchukuo, despite contrary advice from his Empress Wan Jung (Joan Chen).

That was only the beginning of a life marked by endless ups and downs. Civil war caused him to be exiled in 1924, and for a while he and his wives adopted Western attitudes, imitating the jazz-era lifestyle they had perceived in American films, confusing real with reel and thus perfect candidates to become cinema characters in the Eighties. In time, Pu Yi would again briefly know a semblance of power, when his country's archenemy, Japan, allowed him to serve as a puppet ruler of conquered Manchuria. But when Japan was crushed in 1945, Pu Yi found himself accused of collaboration with China's hated foe.

If there was a flaw to the film, it's that Bertolucci and coscreenwriter Mark Paploe were unnecessarily ambiguous. Was Pu Yi a traitor, or was he truly convinced that Manchuria would fare better with him in command rather than if lorded over by a Japanese? Historians can argue that man's motivations, but as a work of drama, this would be more comprehensible had the filmmakers committed themselves to an interpretation. Otherwise, the remarkable film deserved its Oscar as Best Picture, packaging artistry and history into its sprawling three-hour running time. Essential to the impact was Bertolucci's successful negotiation to film inside the Forbidden City. He stages the scenes there—the three-year-old Pu Yi (Richard Yuu) darting through dazzlingly costumed armies of servants and soldiers, guards and eunuchs—as though they were grand paintings blessed with movement, while Oscar-winning cinematographer

Vittorio Storaro (*Apocalypse Now*) captured not only the grandeur but also the sharp irony of such an immense reaction to so minuscule a ruler. Peter O'Toole was quirkily effective as the young emperor's Scottish tutor (the scene in which they rig up a tennis court in the center of a China engulfed by revolution is unforgettable), Joan Chen quietly impressive as the emperor's first and favorite wife. John Lone won audience emotion for a man whose entire life appeared characterized by an inability to grasp what was happening to him or why.

At heart, though, Bertolucci has always been a political filmmaker, as his masterful *The Conformist* (1971) makes clear. It was easy to grasp, then, why he was drawn to this material. How could he resist the resolution, in which Pu Yi is finally as happy as could be hoped for when allowed to work as a gardener, in ironic proximity to the very throne he briefly occupied? Pu Yi was essentially a common man who had greatness thrust upon him; in Bertolucci's version of the story, he ends his days with a satisfied smile when at last allowed to return to the humble origins in which he would have gladly lived. As China came to dominate America's interest during the late Eighties, *The Last Emperor* provided (as Woodrow Wilson once said while describing D. W. Griffith's *Birth of a Nation*) "a lesson in history, written in lightning."

Hope and Glory

A COLUMBIA PICTURES RELEASE IN ASSOCIATION WITH NELSON ENTERTAINMENT AND GOLDCREST   1987

CREDITS:

Produced, written and directed by John Boorman; co-producer, Michael Dryhurst; photography, Philippe Rousselot; editor, Ian Crafford; Running time, 113 min.; Rating: PG-13.

CAST:

Bill Rohan (Sebastian Rice-Edwards); *Grace Rohan* (Sarah Miles); *Clive Rohan* (David Hayman); *Dawn Rohan* (Sammi Davis); *Mac* (Derrick O'Connor); *Molly* (Susan Wooldridge); *Bruce* (Jean-Marc Barr); *Grandfather George* (Ian Bannen); *Grandma* (Annie Leon) *Sue Rohan* (Geraldine Muir); *Faith* (Jill Baker); *Hope* (Amelda Brown); *Charity* (Katrine Boorman); *Luftwaffe Pilot* (Charley Boorman).

Forties nostalgia reached the level of high art in *Hope and Glory*, which began in suburban London during the Blitz. A child, Bill Rohan (Sebastian Rice-Edwards), is less fearful he'll be killed (like all children, he's certain he'll live forever) than delighted at the prospect that a well-placed parcel from the Luftwaffe may close down school. "Thank you, Hitler!" he sighs. His mum, Grace (Sarah Miles), cares for her brood of three, maintaining the proper patriotic facade while searching her soul as to why she's inexplicably, undeniably happier since her husband left for the front. In time, she discovers strengths and weaknesses about herself that might never have surfaced in the mundane marriage she previously had little cause to question. When their house is bombed, the Rohan family treks to a riverside village to live with Gramps (Ian Bannen). Neither a lovable curmudgeon nor an impossible tyrant, he's a unique combination of the two, utterly unpredictable and all the more human for it.

That was true about everybody and everything in this brilliant, sometimes rambling memory-piece, nominated for Best Picture of the Year. The agreed-on view about the past—the Brits remained grim but quietly courageous through it all—was sharply undercut by writer-director John Boorman, who revealed tense humor as well as human frailty, a full tapestry of life's emotions heightened by living under the constant threat of immediate oblivion. Like Steven Spielberg's simultaneous release, the expansive *Empire of the Sun*, the compact *Hope and Glory* was about an English child growing to adolescence during World War II. Spielberg's film, intended to win him respect as an adult filmmaker, only solidified his reputation as a master creator of family-oriented films. What was best about *Empire* were the fabulous visual technique and the Disney-esque sweetness. Boorman is a striking stylist, too: his finest films (*Point Blank, Deliverance, The Emerald Forest*) and his worst (*Exorcist II: the Heretic, Zardoz*) all attest to that. Significantly, though, he is also a mature moviemaker with a profound, disturbing, complicated vision. Whereas Spielberg really had only one character in his film—the child, with everyone else emerging as a cipher in cameo—Boorman brought all the many characters, adults and children alike, to vivid and complex life, including those glimpsed but briefly. Boorman scripted from his own wartime experiences, whereas Spielberg was interpreting another person's recollections, causing his film to seem slightly secondhand, his intention uncertain as to whether he wanted to put together a fairy-tale adventure or a dramatic recreation of reality.

HOPE AND GLORY: Bill (Sebastian Rice-Edwards) and Sue Rohan (Geraldine Muir) grow up amid the excitement and destruction of World War II Britain: John Boorman drew on his own wartime experiences to create striking images of childhood innocence set against the evil of the Blitz.

HOPE AND GLORY: Unable to find any Nazis to shoot, Grandfather instead turns his shotgun on a river rat who invades the family's tranquility; Sarah Miles, Sebastian Rice-Edwards, Annie Leon, Sammi Davis and Geraldine Muir brace themselves.

HOPE AND GLORY: To escape the Blitz, Bill and his family take refuge at the riverside home of Grandfather (Ian Bannen) and Grandmother (Annie Leon).

HOPE AND GLORY: Teenager Dawn Rohan (Sammi Davis) grows up fast during the war as she comforts a Canadian soldier (Jean-Marc Barr) and learns about love.

HOPE AND GLORY: Dear friend Mac (Derrick O'Connor) helps make the loneliness of war more bearable for Grace (Sarah Miles), while causing her to question her loyalty to her husband, away in combat.

223

HOPE AND GLORY: Clive Rohan (David Hayman) passes the family secrets for playing cricket on to his son Bill just before leaving for the war.

Boorman is to be admired for never sentimentalizing or savaging members of his own family. Does he admire or admonish his well-intentioned but often weak and ambivalent mother? A bit of both, which is the way it should be. That's also true for grandfather and the other characters: Boorman clearly comprehends but forgives them their foibles; he admires but never aggrandizes their virtues. Importantly, he is toughest on, yet fairest to himself, recalling his own weaknesses while maintaining a positive sense of self-worth. So many autobiographical works—Bob Fosse's *All That Jazz*, Woody Allen's *Stardust Memories*, Richard Pryor's *Jo Jo Dancer, Your Life Is Calling*—seem smug, shallow, either overly self-serving or unnecessarily self-despising.

Still, great art certainly can be produced from one's own life: the novels of Thomas Wolfe, the plays of

HOPE AND GLORY: The cast of Hope and Glory.

Eugene O'Neill, and the films of Federico Fellini find universal implications in the artist's unique experiences; more than mere personal considerations of one man's past, they communicate something important to us in the viewing public. *Hope and Glory* was the film that raised Boorman to their plateau. This was a breathtakingly orchestrated film: the stunning photography, striking editing effects, and superb performances all attest to a master craftsman at work. What elevated it beyond admirable craftsmanship to serious art of the first order was the filmmaker's depth of understanding, complexity of sensibility, and maturity of his worldview.

Hairspray

A NEW LINE CINEMA RELEASE IN
ASSOCIATION WITH STANLEY F.
BUCHTHAL   1988

CREDITS:

Executive producers, Robert Shaye and Sara Risher; produced by Rachel Talasy; written and directed by John Waters; photography, David Insley; editor, Janice Hampton; Running time, 90 min.; Rating: PG.

CAST:

Franklin Von Tussle (Sonny Bono); *Motormouth Maybell* (Ruth Brown); *Edna Turnblad/Arvin Hodgepile* (Divine); *Amber Von Tussle* (Colleen Fitzpatrick); *Link Larkin* (Michael St. Gerard); *Velma Von Tussle* (Deborah Harry); *Tracy Turnblad* (Ricki Lake); *Tammy* (Mink Stole); *Wilbur Turnblad* (Jerry Stiller); *Penny Pingleton* (Leslie Ann Power); *Beatnik* (Pia Zadora); *Corny Collins* (Shawn Thompson).

John Waters, king of the cult movies and hip-nerd idol of the outrageous-alternative set, went Establishment for the first time in this campy, quirky send-up of the early Sixties nostalgia other filmmakers approached in a far more serious and reverent vein. The mid-Eighties acceptance of the New Wave fashions into the American mainstream suggested that the Underground had caught up with the commercialized center of American pop culture; it made sense then that Waters, who predated punk and perhaps helped create it, would at this point make a film that could play at suburban-mall movie houses, even receiving a mild PG rating—a real surprise from the avant-garde auteur who once shocked the nation

with *Pink Flamingos* but here turned out a film that seemed closer in mood and method to John Hughes's *Pretty in Pink*.

The year is 1962, a year and a half before The Beatles first appearance on the Ed Sullivan show, and rock 'n' roll is at an awkward stage. The energetic era of early Elvis, Chuck Berry and Bo Diddley had come and gone, after five years, no longer provoking immediate anger on the part of parents and teachers, who have accepted clean-cut TV discjockeys like Dick Clark as acceptable purveyors of a middle-of-the-road pop-rock mainstream. That period of mediocrity and complacency would shortly, abruptly end as radicalized teens turned their back on Leslie Gore and Frankie Avalon after discovering Bob Dylan and the Rolling Stones. For the moment, though, every American city has its own imitation *American Bandstand* show, including Baltimore, favorite setting of filmmaker Waters. It's *The Corny Collins Show*, where kids dress neatly and dance within acceptable limits established by adults.

Waters's heroine is Tracy Turnblad, a chubby girl with a grotesquely incongruous bouffant hairdo. At his best, Waters as always confronts us with the essential absurdity of outrageous trends in hairstyles, clothing, dance steps and the like, forcing us to consider their ridiculousness by presenting them on society's outcasts as they absurdly imitate the perfect-looking role models on TV. Newcomer Ricki Lake looks like a teen version of Waters's favorite performer, Divine, the cult female impersonator not surprisingly cast as Tracy's mom, in his/her last performance before an untimely death. When the more conventionally attractive and socially acceptable teens are finished mocking Tracy, even they have to admit that she's the best dancer on the floor. That doesn't sit well with Amber Von Tussle (Colleen Fitzpatrick), an American WASP princess who desperately wants to regain her position as the queen of the televised hop.

The struggle between the two—Tracy representing every overweight, disparaged outsider in America who ever dreamed of challenging the captain of cheerleaders for the Miss Popularity title—was developed in the broad, cartoonish strokes expected from this king of high camp. Waters portrayed Tracy with a sensibility-bashing blend of savage satire and sensitive concern, causing the film to veer madly from nasty to nice as the eclectic cast (including Pia Zadora as a beatnik) conveyed the pop-culture tackiness Waters so adores. But there was more going on here than that. The contrast between Tracy's mom and Amber's (played by aging rock-performer Deborah Harry) was both clever and cruel, deftly delineating the difference between a woman comfortable with her own tackiness and one sadly (and unsuccessfully) struggling to rise above it,

HAIRSPRAY: John Waters made his personal attitudes clear in his visual approach to the film's two families: the unpretentious and lovable if ultra-tacky Turnblads (Jerry Stiller, Ricki Lake, and Divine), as opposed to the obnoxiously pseudo-sophisticated Von Tussles (Colleen Fitzpatrick, Deborah Harry, and Sonny Bono).

HAIRSPRAY: In his/her last role, Divine played Edna Turnblad, whose days of ironing for the neighbors come to a happy end when daughter Tracy becomes a local TV star.

HAIRSPRAY: Franklin (Sonny Bono) plants a bomb in Velma's (Deborah Harry) sky-high hairdo as part of a devious plot that backfires in a big way.

226

HAIRSPRAY: Pia Zadora as the groovy beatnik chick who introduces the teenagers to a "hep" new world: The decade long wallow in nostalgia took a decidedly different turn in the hands of John Waters.

making pretensions (despised by Waters) to haute couture.

When Waters moved into social commentary—attempts to racially integrate the bandstand show—it was difficult to tell whether he was serious or kidding, offering a heartfelt message or poking fun at movies that try to layer serious themes onto flimsy teen-exploitation flicks. Still, it all more or less worked, as Waters chronicled that key moment in our culture when the white-bread bandstand shows finally broke the color barrier. Like music in the early Sixties, the movies of the late Eighties co-opted a once outrageous and controversial style, now matter-of-factly accepted. As this left-of-center filmmaker moved toward the middle, the wary mainstream audience proved willing to meet him halfway.

Who Framed Roger Rabbit

A BUENA VISTA RELEASE OF A
TOUCHSTONE PICTURES/AMBLIN FILM
PRODUCTION   1988

CREDITS:

Executive producers, Steven Spielberg and Kathleen
Kennedy; produced by Robert Watts and Frank Marshall;
directed by Robert Zemeckis; written by Jeffrey Price and
Peter S. Seaman, from the book *Who Censored Roger
Rabbit?* by Gary K. Wolf; photography, Dean Cundey;
editor, Arthur Schmidt; Running time, 103 min.; Rating:
PG.

CAST:

Eddie Valiant (Bob Hoskins); *Judge Doom* (Christopher
Lloyd); *Dolores* (Joanna Cassidy); *Marvin Acme* (Stubby
Kaye); *R. K. Maroon* (Alan Tilvern); *Raoul* (Joel Silver);
Voice of Roger (Charles Fleischer); *Jessica, speaking*
(Kathleen Turner)/*singing* (Amy Irving); *voice of Baby
Herman* (Lou Hirsch); *voice of Daffy Duck* (Mel Blanc).

The Disney company had diminished their output of
animated films during the Seventies, owing to rising
costs, changing attitudes and a blasé public reaction;
with Touchstone films, they created R-rated entertain-
ments like *Down and Out in Beverly Hills* and *Ruthless
People*, a far cry from the traditional Disney family film.
But with the brilliant *Who Framed Roger Rabbit*, Dis-
ney/Touchstone found a remarkable middleway between
two approaches, coming up with an entertainment that
was as enjoyable for adults as for kids. It not only revived
the art of animation, (only Ralph Bakski, of *Fritz the
Cat* fame, and ex-Disney artist Don Bluth, with his *The
Secret of Nimh*, were continuing the tradition), but
stretched it light years ahead on technical levels—a film
that was to the animated cartoon what *Citizen Kane* had
been to live action. In the process, director Robert
Zemeckis created a typical movie of the Eighties, ripe
with nostalgia for the Forties and based on the theme
that real and reel are inseparable.

The premise was brilliant in its simplicity: What if,
the film asked, those fabulous animated characters of
the past had been actual people, going to work at various

WHO FRAMED ROGER RABBIT: Eddie Valiant (Bob Hoskins) saws through the cuffs
that link him with Roger; the integration of real people and cartoons was never so
perfectly achieved as in this Disney/Spielberg collaboration.

228

WHO FRAMED ROGER RABBIT: Breathtaking, breathless Jessica sings a torch song to Eddie and Marvin Acme (Stubby Kaye); whereas in previous films the people and toons appeared to exist on different planes, here they were totally enmeshed in one another's world.

studios much as other "live" actors did, then returning at night to a place called Toontown where they all lived? It was altogether possible, then, that Disney's top-billed duck Donald might meet his arch rival and web-footed Warner Bros. counterpart Daffy in a nightclub, and slip into an impromptu musical competition before an audience of "toons" and real people. Practically every movie cartoon character put in at least a cameo appearance, as the plot—halfway between a spoof of Raymond Chandler's detective tales and a serious example of one—followed hard-boiled detective Eddie Valiant (Bob Hoskins), hired to spy on Jessica, the beautiful and apparently adulterous wife of distraught Toon star Roger Rabbit. Eddie takes the incriminating pictures, and Roger, upon seeing them, goes off the wall—in his case, literally. Shortly thereafter, Jessica's "companion" turns up dead and Roger is accused of murder. Desperate, he hides out in the only place the police would never suspect: Eddie's home. Once the private eye becomes convinced of the Toon star's innocence, the two set out to discover who framed Roger Rabbit.

An almost indescribable film, *Roger* broke new ground in the combination of live action and animation.

Ordinarily, cartoon characters and actors exist on two different planes, with minimal interaction: Even such Disney classics as *Song of the South* and *Mary Poppins* suffered from this "painted on" effect. Here, they clearly existed in the same dimension. There is a startling three-dimensional quality to the Toons that made them appear every bit as rounded as the actors. In fact, the cartoon characters continually turn as they walk and talk, the way humans always do and cartoon characters rarely do, simply because of the difficulty (and expense) of animating them that way. The legendary Disney craftsmanship and care was here revived overlaid with an Eighties sense of nostalgic irony; the effect was seamless and completely convincing.

The murder mystery plot, about a scheme by Judge Doom (Christopher Lloyd) to exploit the changing industrial terrain and transportation system of Los Angeles, was not unlike Roman Polanski's *Chinatown*. But even with a strong story line, the danger here was that this would eventually wear down to a one-joke film and prove unable to sustain a feature-length telling. That never happened, as director Zemeckis, animator Richard Williams, and a virtual army of artists and technicians

229

WHO FRAMED ROGER RABBIT: Baby Herman wants to know why Eddie can't find the real killer.

WHO FRAMED ROGER RABBIT: Evil Judge Doom (Christopher Lloyd) threatens Roger; the victim may be reel, but the violence was real.

WHO FRAMED ROGER RABBIT: Eddie attempts to rescue Jessica and Roger when they are all trapped in Toontown.

kept topping themselves, always managing to come up with some virtuoso sequence that outdid everything that went before it. The effect of Eddie Valiant driving the cartoon car is so dazzling that it's hard to believe the filmmakers can come up with anything better, until their surreal Toontown sequence takes the viewer's breath away.

Zemeckis's idea was to combine the best of the best into a single film: the vivid and realistic backdrops of Disney animation, the marvelous characterizations of Chuck Jones, and the wild Grouchoesque gags of Tex Avery, all so delightful in their separate guises, here coming together for the first time. Steven Spielberg, tagged as the visionary Disney of the Eighties, finally got to do a film at Disney. Sophisticated enough for grown-ups to enjoy but simple enough for kids to understand, *Who Framed Roger Rabbit* proved a happy meeting of Disney's past and future.

231

The Last Temptation of Christ

A UNIVERSAL/CINEPLEX ODEON FILMS
PRESENTATION   1988

CREDITS:

Executive producer, Harry Ulfand; produced by Barbara De
Fina; directed by Martin Scorsese; written by Paul Schrader,
from the novel by Nikos Kazantzakis; photography, Michael
Ballhaus, editor, Thelma Schoonmaker; Running time, 164
min.; Rating: R.

CAST:

Jesus (Willem Dafoe); *Judas* (Harvey Keitel); *Mary
Magdalene* (Barbara Hershey); *Saul/Paul* (Harry Dean
Stanton); *Pontius Pilate* (David Bowie); *Mary Mother of
Jesus* (Verna Bloom); *John the Baptist* (Andre Gregory); *Girl
Angel* (Juliette Caton); *Aged Master* (Roberts Blossom);
Zebedee (Irvin Kershner); *Andrew* (Gary Basraba); *Lazarus*
(Thomas Arana).

In retrospect, *Temptation* is more notable for the furor
it elicited in the summer of 1988 than anything in the
movie itself. Most of the protest against the film as anti-
Christian came from people who hadn't seen it. From
the first moment to the last, this was clearly fashioned by
people who believed in the divinity of Jesus Christ, but
were fascinated by the dramatic possibilities of one
conceit in the Scriptures—the duality of Jesus, as both
man and God. Not surprisingly, then, when *Last Temptation* finally reached Golgotha and the "last temptation,"
audiences witnessed something original, though safely
within the traditional and reverent interpretation of the
Crucifixion. Up until that point, the film dragged.
Familiar episodes from the New Testament (the turning
of water into wine, etc.) were retold in distressingly low-
key fashion. Since everyone already knows them, and
since they have been depicted in far more exciting films
over the years (*King of Kings, The Greatest Story Ever
Told*), the Martin Scorsese interpretation unimpressively
covered familiar ground. The irony is, the only audience
for such tepid treatment would seem to be the very
Fundamentalists who howled with horror at the film's
existence.

Occasionally, director Scorsese did create images that
reminded us of his capacity to dazzle. When viewers
saw Jesus (Willem Dafoe, though Robert De Niro was
Scorsese's first choice) curled in a near-fetal position,
attempting to grasp why He's different from His friends,
film buffs recalled most Scorsese heroes (like Travis
Bickle on *Taxi Driver* and Rupert Pupkin in *King of
Comedy*) on a similar search for self-understanding and
spiritual redemption. Unfortunately, Scorsese was here
undermined by Paul Schrader's obtuse adaptation of the
Nikos Kazantzakis novel, which had been around for
years without ever eliciting the intense reaction that met
the movie on its release. Attempting to avoid the purple
prose that frequently plagued Hollywood versions of the
Bible, Schrader erred in the other direction. His characters speak a kind of guttural contemporary slang,
intended as unpretentious but too often prosaic. Worse,
Schrader had Jesus and Judas (Harvey Keitel) discuss
theology on a level that might be likened to Religion 101.

The most intriguing element of the film's first half is
the depiction of Jesus' relationship to Mary Magdalene
(Barbara Hershey). Here, she's become a whore owing to
the inability of her childhood boyfriend to consummate
their relationship. That Christ sits for hours outside a
brothel led to the rumor Scorsese portrayed Jesus as
obsessively lustful; the opposite is true, as Christ only
goes to the brothel after learning Mary works inside,
then sits outside suffering (not fantasizing) as he experiences a "passion" (in the Catholic, not the sexual,
sense), troubled that he may be responsible, waiting for
her to finish "work" so they can talk about it. Both Jesus
and Mary gradually come to understand and accept that
his divinity stands in the way of their marrying and
enjoying a normal life together.

Still, the film fails to focus on this theme during the
uninspired first half. Dull if not lifeless, it wasted David
Bowie as Pilate in a brief throwaway confrontation with
Jesus. But as Christ ascended the cross, the film
miraculously performed a turnabout and moved into a
compelling, disquieting final hour. We know from Scrip-
ture that Christ was tempted by Satan during his last
moments; we also know He is perfect in goodness.
What, then, could possibly tempt Him? The Bible is
vague on this point, but the film's concept is brilliant:
perfection would not be tempted by "bad" things—
money, power, sensuality—but by something He had
preached was "good," though paradoxically for everyone but Himself: an honest hard-working life, including
loving sex within marriage for the purpose of procrea-
tion. An angelic child (Juliette Caton) sweetly shows
Jesus what His married life would be like with Magdalene; then Judas and the other disciples help Jesus
understand the child was in fact the devil. Realizing this,
Jesus rejects the gentle pleasures of a decent, simple life,

THE LAST TEMPTATION OF CHRIST: Willem Dafoe as Jesus; despite the controversy, this was essentially a tame and reverential relating of Old Testament tales.

THE LAST TEMPTATION OF CHRIST: The sermon on the mount.

willingly passing back through time to the Crucifixion, understanding Himself and his place in God's scheme at last. The final sequence is a reaffirmation of both his faith and his divinity. While Fundamentalists were busily picketing a totally reverent film they had not seen, fearful their children might attend it and have their faith shaken, the latest Freddie Krueger movie was playing—unpicketed—in nearby multiplexes, where it had teenagers applauding and cheering its satanic hero.

Big

A 20TH CENTURY-FOX FILM RELEASE   1988

CREDITS:

Produced by James L. Brooks and Robert Greenhut; co-producers, Anne Spielberg and Gary Ross; directed by Penny Marshall; written by Gary Ross and Anne Spielberg; photography, Barry Sonnenfeld; editor, Barry Malkin; Running time, 102 min.; Rating: PG.

CAST:

Josh Baskin (Tom Hanks); *Susan* (Elizabeth Perkins); *Paul* (John Heard); *Billy* (Jared Rushton); *MacMillan* (Robert Loggia); *Young Josh* (David Moscow).

By the time *Big* arrived on multiplex screens, audiences had already been deluged by movies about adults and children who change bodies, ranging from the dreadful (*18 Again!*) to the mediocre (*Like Father, Like Son*) to the passingly pleasant (*Vice Versa*). But *Big* was the best, thanks to the considerable charm of leading man Tom Hanks, along with the wit and warmth in this retelling of an already overfamiliar tale, with the formula finally being done to perfection.

Josh Baskin (David Moscow) is a normal kid harboring a huge crush on the prettiest blonde in the school (though she only dates guys "who drive") and generally feels an outcast, except when with his best pal, Billy (Jared Rushton). One evening at an amusement park, when Josh has been denied entrance to a thrill ride because he's not big enough, the frustrated youngster wanders over to an old gypsylike make-a-wish machine, drops in his quarter and wishes he was big. When he wakes up the next morning, he's just that: though Josh's personality remains unchanged, he now inhabits the body of a 35-year-old man (Hanks).

Penny Marshall, the actress (*Laverne and Shirley*) turned director, immediately created a distance between her movie and others of its ilk. There's a delightful sense of wonder in the carnival scene: the off-kilter lighting, the on-target acting, and every other element a filmmaker has to work with are effectively orchestrated to create a magical mood. This has less to do with what's said or done than with the stylish way the scene was shot. As absurd as the premise might seem, Marshall makes a viewer suspend disbelief. Working from a savvy script by Anne Spielberg (filmmaker Steve's sister) and Gary Ross, she surprisingly but effectively went for realism.

BIG: Tom Hanks as Josh Baskin, a brilliant performance of a 12-year-old boy inhabiting a 35-year-old body.

Once we accept the patently contrived idea, there's little fantasy to this film.

So the moment Josh becomes big, he has a terrifying confrontation with his mom, who finds a strange man in her child's room and believes, as any mother would, he's a kidnapper or killer. Later, when big Josh approaches old pal Billy for help, the youngster draws back, certain this unknown person who claims to be his friend is actually a child molester. The film focuses on the subjects others of its type avoided: how such a person will live and function in the real world. In an inspired plot development, Josh finds work at a toy company, where his natural instincts at what would or would not be fun to play with soon win him a promotion.

He wins the admiration of his progressive boss (Robert Loggia), the enmity of a success-driven yuppie (John Heard), and the attention—love, even—of the firm's sexiest career woman (Elizabeth Perkins). Happily, each of these characters is presented as a flesh-and-blood person presented with just the right edge of satire without slipping into a stereotype. A ball game between Hanks and Heard that transforms into an emotional power struggle was upsetting to watch; an impromptu dance on a giant piano in a toy store by Hanks and Loggia had audiences applauding; the bittersweet, doomed romance between Perkins and Hanks, in which his radical innocence allows her to transform from cynical pseudosophisticate to reborn spontaneity, was truly touching. Most memorable was her decision to sleep over at his apartment; when he insists he be on top,

BIG: Elizabeth Perkins and Tom Hanks.

236

she has to adjust to the fact he's talking about bunk beds. There's an ingratiating feeling as the two choose between a romantic attachment or close friendship.

Most of the credit goes to Hanks, who played this comically charming role with the craft and intelligence of a serious actor. Audiences watched admiringly as, without tricky actor's gambits or going for the big guffaw, he pulled off the near impossible: we honestly believe his adult's body is motivated by the mind and emotions of a child. If ever an actor was going to win the Oscar for a comic performance, this might have been the year—were it not for Dustin Hoffman appearing, at year's end, in *Rain Man*. One major disappointment: the relationship between Josh and the pretty blonde teenager was so carefully set up at the beginning that audiences assumed it would serve as a framing device, with Josh returning to her at the end, succeeding where he'd once failed, owing to all he's learned in the big people's world. That doesn't happen. And while there is a tender parting scene between Hanks and Perkins when—as we always knew he must—the boy in him heads home to "grow up" normally, there also needed to be a similar farewell (there wasn't) between Hanks and Loggia, since their relationship, in its own way, was just as special. The only small thing about *Big* was its letdown ending. Otherwise, this joyous little gem lived up to its title.

A Fish Called Wanda

AN MGM/UA FILM RELEASE   1988

CREDITS:

Executive producers, Steve Abbott and John Cleese; produced by Michael Shamberg; directed by Charles Crichton; written by John Cleese and Charles Crichton; photography, Alan Hume; editor, John Jympson; Running Time, 108 min.; Rating: R.

CAST:

Archie Leech (John Cleese); *Wanda* (Jamie Lee Curtis); *Otto* (Kevin Kline); *Ken* (Michael Palin); *Wendy* (Maria Aitken); *George* (Tom Georgeson); *Mrs. Coady* (Patricia Hayes).

During a summer season which saw moviegoers lining up for mindless spectacles and endless sequels, who would even notice this bizarre little British-made black comedy was in town? The happy surprise was that

Wanda became the box-office hit of the season, accompanied by critical acclaim, proving once again no one has any idea what will click with the public.

Wanda boasted a neat blending of the two grand traditions of English postwar humor. First came the era of Ealing Studios, that legendary film factory which in the late Forties and well into the Fifties turned out a number of tart, wry, understated comedy classics, such as Charles Crichton's *The Lavender Hill Mob* and *The Titfield Thunderbolt*. Later, in reaction to the unique elegance of Ealing, came the youthful Monty Python group of the Sixties and Seventies, with its off-the-wall approach. Ealing and Python seemed irreconcilable poles of Brit humor, though amazingly enough, *Wanda* resolved them. Written by former Python zany John Cleese but directed by Ealing alumnus Crichton (being brought out of retirement at age 77), this agreeable caper offered the best of both British comedy worlds.

Wanda begins as a revival of a lost genre, the sophisticated heist movie in the *Topkapi* mode, in which a small group of clever thieves plot an intricate robbery, pull off the "perfect" crime, then fall victim to their own petty jealousies and nasty betrayals. But the brilliant ploy of Cleese and Crichton's snappy screenplay was that these thieves are merely dolts who mistakenly believe themselves to be sophisticates. Among them are Ken (Python's Michael Palin), a low-key killer who can't stop stuttering; Wanda (a woman, not a fish), would-be femme fatale who drops her gun and rolls over in sexual writhing whenever a man speaks some foreign language, her big turn-on; and Otto (Kevin Kline), an incredible jerk who considers himself an intellectual because he reads Nietzsche, managing to miscomprehend every idea he encounters.

Unlike the premises for most contemporary movies, *Wanda*'s plot can't be simply summarized, and certainly no one could call this High Concept. The incongruous, uproarious story takes so many bizarre twists it eventually ceases to make much logical sense, though that's not a criticism. It simply exists as an excuse to develop character, allowing the oddballs to bounce off each other as if they were members of a non-animated, adults-only *Roger Rabbit* cast. The focus of attention shifts to a barrister with the power to either get an apprehended gang member off or blow the lid on everyone in the band of robbers. He's the target of the seductive Wanda's charms and the bullying Otto's cruelty.

This barrister, played to perfection by Cleese, is called Archie Leech. At first, the name seems nothing more than an in-joke for film fans, Cary Grant's real name. And Archie strikes us as anything but Cary Grant. He's a smug, self-important member of the English Establishment, able to make us like even the hysterical, often

A FISH CALLED WANDA: While Archie Leech (John Cleese) makes like Cary Grant by seducing the non-fish Wanda (Jamie Lee Curtis), Otto the idiot-existentialist (Kevin Kline) jealously peeks in.

A FISH CALLED WANDA: Wanda tries to soothe the ruffled feathers and rumpled ego of Otto, who can't find the jewelry he stole.

A FISH CALLED WANDA: Archie Leech, the straightlaced barrister who finds himself caught up in the lunatic escapades of an inept band of jewel thieves.

A FISH CALLED WANDA: Michael Palin (left) as Ken, the hit man who hates humans and loves animals but can't stop accidentally killing poodles, along with John Cleese, Kevin Kline (right), and Jamie Lee Curtis as Wanda—the woman, not the fish.

crude Otto by comparison. But something touching happens to Archie. As he's seduced by cold-blooded Wanda (never mind precisely why, since her motivation is unexplainably crazy), his corruption is employed for something more than the usual gags about a stuffy chap being caught with his pants down, though that convention does appear here. We learn, in good time, he's really a sweet, sad soul; when we sense that, we hope he won't be hurt too badly by dragon-lady Wanda manipulating him for personal profit. Then we realize even she's grown aware of that special quality about Archie: deep down inside him, there is a potential to truly be like Cary Grant, if anyone gave him the chance. This part of the plot effectively tugs at an audience's emotions. Around the story, such as it is, exists a madcap world, the wildest element being the desire of Palin, the stuttering hit man, to eliminate a little old lady (shadows of the Ealing classic *The Ladykillers*), though he manages to kill only her dogs (these unfortunate murders are pure Monty Python), an exasperating experience since he's an animal lover.

The doggie deaths could easily have been crude, but register as clever. Best of all, the film alternates its romantic moments with its more bizarre ones; somehow, the oddly shaped pieces of this crazy jigsaw puzzle manage to fit. The pleasant surprise was Kline, a first-rate stage actor and musical comedy star whose previous film work (*Cry Freedom*, and *Violets Are Blue*)) seemed uninspired, though his potential talents were clearly demonstrated in *Sophie's Choice* and *The Big Chill*. His Otto rated as an absolute gem, deservedly winning him a Best Supporting Actor Oscar. Cleese and Palin were as delightfully droll as ever, proving Britain's angry young funnymen of a decade earlier had mellowed to the point where they could comfortably rejoin the comedy establishment they had once rebelled against.

Die Hard

A 20TH CENTURY-FOX RELEASE OF A GORDON CO./SILVER PICTURES PRODUCTION   1988

CREDITS:

Executive producer, Charles Gordon; produced by Lawrence Gordon and Joel Silver; directed by John McTiernan; written by Jeb Stuart and Steven E. de Souza, from the novel *Nothing Lasts Forever* by Roderick Thorpe; photography, Jan DeBont; editors, Frank J. Urisote and John F. Link; Running time, 131 min.; Rating: R.

CAST:

John McClane (Bruce Willis); *Hans Gruber* (Alan Rickman); *Holly Gennaro McClane* (Bonnie Bedelia); *Karl* (Alexander Godunov); *Sgt. Al Powell* (Reginald Veljohnson); *Dwayne T. Robinson* (Paul Gleason); *Argyle* (De'voreaux White); *Thornburg* (William Atherton); *Ellis* (Hart Bochner); *Takagi* (James Shigeta); *Big Johnson* (Robert Davi); *Little Johnson* (Grand L. Bush).

This nonstop action film's story takes place on Christmas Eve in Los Angeles, as New York City police detective John McClane (Bruce Willis) arrives in town with but one thought in mind: to visit his estranged wife (Bonnie Bedelia) and two children in hopes of winning them back. He stops by the high-rise building where his

DIE HARD: Bruce Willis as John McClane, an ordinary man rising to heroic stature under extraordinary circumstances; his vulnerability made him far more interesting than the Stallone/Schwarzenegger invincible superheroes.

wife's company holds its annual office party; while the festivities are in progress, a group of 12 terrorists appears, taking hostage the partygoers while attempting to unlock a safe containing $600 million in negotiable bearer bonds. In response to the crisis, McClane (whose presence is at first unknown to the terrorists) is transformed into a one-man army. But if that sounds like yet another variation on the Stallone/Schwarzenegger plots, there was a key difference. McClane was not an invulnerable macho man, an urban Rambo coldly and calculatedly terminating those massed against him.

What early Eighties audiences had found most enjoyable about their ruggedly individualistic Reagan-era heroes was that these guys could not lose. In *Die Hard*, the filmmakers instead created a likable, threatened hero who, we believed, might go under at any moment. McClane cried in terror and screamed in anger, made serious mistakes in judgment, sweated profusely. He was, clearly, a man with limits. So audiences rooted for McClane, but also watched with awe as this ordinary guy reluctantly rose to heroic proportions under extraordinary circumstances. *Die Hard* was the brainchild of coproducer Joel Silver, the decade's prime purveyor of action-adventure—*Predator* and *Lethal Weapon* were among his hits. John McTiernan, who previously helmed *Predator*, directed this slickly packaged and emotionally appealing item, insisting his inspiration was Shake-

DIE HARD: John and Holly McClane are reunited under fire.

DIE HARD: McClane readies for action.

DIE HARD: McClane desperately crashes through a high rise window to try and save the hostages inside; Willis based his characterization on such Fifties heroes as William Holden in *Bridge on the River Kwaii*.

speare's *A Midsummer Night's Dream*, in which the ghosts and goblins come out after dark, wreak havoc throughout the long night, then subside at sunrise. That may be stretching the point, but certainly *Die Hard* boasted, despite its extreme violence, a fairy-tale quality, rather than another stark presentation of a one-man killing machine. Willis, popular star of TV's *Moonlighting*, proved a marvelous choice for McClane, making him a variation of that vulnerable Everyman-as-hero from 1950s films: William Holden in *The Bridge on the River Kwai*, Cary Grant in *North by Northwest*, Gary Cooper in *High Noon*.

The supporting cast was equally impressive. Though glimpsed but briefly, Bonnie Bedelia made Holly Mc-Clane a unique and believable woman rather than a generic silent-sufferer. Instead of casting typical movie heavies as the villains, Silver wisely created new kinds

of menace by going for something out of the ordinary. Hans Gruber, brains of the terrorist operation, was played by Alan Rickman, a respected British actor from the Royal Shakespeare Company and Broadway's *Les Liaisons Dangereuses*, in an unconventionally low-key (and chillingly effective) manner. His chief henchman, Karl (Russian ballet star-turned-actor Alexander Godunov) emerged as a creature of nearly choreographed movements, transforming the final fight between Karl and McClane into a brutal but beautiful ballet.

The production design by Jack DeGovia (*Roxanne*) stunned moviegoers as wave after wave of explosion rocked the besieged building. The editing by Frank J. Urioste (*RoboCop*) kept this rather lengthy film moving along at breakneck pace. Impressive too was the screenplay by Jeb Stuart and Stephen E. de Souza, which paid the audience off again and again: just when we thought the story (adapted from a novel by Roderick Thorpe) was about to run out of steam, some unexpected twist was created which, on consideration, we realized had been neatly set up in the early, highly economic exposition. Likewise, the tension was effectively undercut by sharp humor. One of the most satisfying elements was the buddy-buddy police team, the unique twist being that here, for the first time, the buddies didn't know each other or even meet until the final scene. The beleaguered McClane must rely on an L.A. cop, Al Powell (Reginald Veljohnson), as his radio contact and sole source of help outside the captive building. A junk-food addict and quiet chap whose main concern is his pregnant wife, Powell was—an everyday person—a convincing cop-on-patrol, just doing his duty, only to be stuck in a bizarre, extreme situation. As violent action-adventure, *Die Hard* boasted enough blood and guts to satisfy fans of the genre. The key to its wide popularity and immense success was that it also featured involving characters and a clever story, bringing in the vast mainstream audience as well, while suggesting that the common man might just once more supplant the Superman as a populist hero.

Dangerous Liaisons

A WARNER BROS. RELEASE OF A NFH LIMITED/LORIMAR FILM PRODUCTION   1988

CREDITS:

Produced by Norma Heyman and Hank Moonjean; co-producer, Christopher Hampton; directed by Stephen Frears; written by Christopher Hampton, from his play and the novel *Les Liaisons Dangereuses* by Choderlos de Laclos; photography, Philippe Rousselot; editor, Mick Audsley; Running time, 120 min.; Rating: R.

CAST:

Marquise de Merteuil (Glenn Close); *Vicomte de Valmont* (John Malkovich); *Madame de Tourvel* (Michelle Pfeiffer); *Madame de Volanges* (Swoosie Kurtz); *Chevalier Danceny* (Keanu Reeves); *Madame de Rosemonde* (Mildred Natwick); *Cecile de Volanges* (Uma Thurman).

A period piece is only as dated as the filmmakers' sensibilities. Fortunately, the people who fashioned *Dangerous Liaisons* were nothing if not modern. They

DANGEROUS LIAISONS: Glenn Close as the scheming Marquise de Merteuil and John Malkovich as the aristocratic rogue Valmont plot the seduction of a virtuous married woman.

wisely chose Glenn Close—after *Fatal Attraction*, the cinematic symbol of the contemporary woman, confused to the point of trauma by her hard-earned, unsatisfying liberation—and John Malkovich, that quirky actor with less-than-memorable looks but an unmistakable, unforgettable voice, as her partner in crime. Michelle Pfeiffer—whose radiant, drop-dead beauty too often clouded consideration of an impressive acting range—played the young innocent caught in a wicked game of wills. In the capable hands of British director Stephen Fears (*My Beautiful Laundrette*), the saucy, seductive French romanticism of earlier historical items gave way to an abiding cynicism which seemed perfectly appropriate for the Eighties.

Fittingly, then, no attempt was made to disguise the fact (through such devices as affected accents) that these were American actors. True, they wore costumes deliciously designed by James Acheson which were true to the silken spirit of an earlier age, if colored by interpretation and exaggeration, playfully recreating the past for purposes of parody. Out of this effective meeting of then and now grew the film's implied statement: the amorality depicted here was not presented simply as history lesson but as an objective correlative for our own age. Like the moviemakers, filmgoers experienced the joy of having it both ways, seeing a work which richly re-created the bygone look of brocades while always suggesting the human drama we witnessed on screen was relevant.

Screenwriter Christopher Hampton, who effectively brought to the London and Broadway stages the 1782 novel by Choderlos de Laclos (it previously had been filmed against a contemporary setting in 1959 with Jeanne Moreau and Gerard Philippe), here neatly retained the literate répartée of his stage work while providing director Frears with a streamlined script that allowed for a less theatrical, more cinematic creation. The smirking lizard Vicomte de Valmont (Malkovich) stands as a case study in divine decadence, bedding every woman he meets, not for the sensual kick of sexual dominance, but for the mental rush of conquest. He's uneasy when the equally icy Marquise de Merteuil (Close) spurns him, though certainly not for any moral reasons. They are equals—in intelligence, pride, cruelty, debauchery, affectation—and have been lovers in the past. So why shouldn't they be such again now? Since their lives consist of complicated game playing rather than spontaneous actions, the marquise insists he complete a pair of conquests she desires: despoil a pretty virgin (radiant newcomer Uma Thurman), then seduce a sincere, pious young wife, Madame de Tourvel (Pfeiffer). Thereafter, the Vicomte may return to the Marquise's boudoir.

The first task is easily accomplished; the teenager turns out to be anything but a naïve, rather a maturing kitten in first heat. The second emerges as a more complicated matter, in which the Vicomte must slowly, laboriously persuade the deeply religious woman of the depth of his sincerity: she'll succumb only if she thinks him a sweet, lovestruck swain. A master actor, the Vicomte plays that part to perfection. Then something fascinating happens to him, and to the movie. For as he continues his ridiculous line of sentimental overture, Valmont suddenly realizes he means every word he says. He really has fallen madly in love. That irony takes a deliciously naughty tale and turns it into something far grander: a film that at first studiously considers amorality, then brilliantly closes with a moral vision. As

DANGEROUS LIAISONS: Valmont converses with the elusive Madame de Tourvel (Michelle Pfeiffer), pretending to love her in order to lure her into an affair and thereby win his wager, though somewhere along the line his pretense of love transforms into the real thing.

DANGEROUS LIAISONS: Listening intently to a singer in concert, the guests at this elegant evening affair include (left to right) Cecile de Volanges (Uma Thurman), Madame de Rosemonde (Mildred Natwick), and Madame de Volanges (Swoosie Kurtz); seated directly behind them are the scheming ex-lovers Marquise de Merteuil and Vicomte de Valmont.

DANGEROUS LIAISONS: Between two women: Glenn Close, John Malkovich and Michelle Pfeiffer.

246

such, it served in 1988 as a precise objective correlative for the social experience of its audience: having survived the casual experimentation of the Seventies sexual revolution, retreating to more traditional values in the AIDS-conscious Eighties.

For a brief moment at the beginning of screenings, the decidedly American speech patterns are a surprise to audiences that have come to accept the convention that French men and women from the distant past ought to speak like contemporary Brits. But only for a moment; quickly, they adjust to Frears' tone. Laclos may have originally intended his novel as a portrait of the kinds of aristocrats whose debauchery demanded a revolution be waged against them, but the book happily contained meaning when far removed from the social context of its original purpose and publication. Interpreted again and again during the next two centuries (indeed, it was made once more by Milos Forman as *Valmont* less than a year later), *Dangerous Liaisons* demonstrated its durability as a story for all times; this version perfectly told it as a story for our time.

Mississippi Burning

AN ORION PICTURES RELEASE   1988

CREDITS:

Produced by Frederick Zollo and Robert F. Colesberry; directed by Alan Parker; written by Chris Gerolmo; photography, Peter Biziou; editor, Gerry Hambling; Running time, 125 min.; Rating: R.

CAST:

Anderson (Gene Hackman); *Ward* (Willem Dafoe); *Mrs. Pell* (Frances McDormand); *Deputy Pell* (Brad Dourif); *Mayor Tilman* (R. Lee Emery); *Sheriff Stuckley* (Gallard Sartain); *Townley* (Stephen Tobolowsky); *Bailey* (Michael Rooker); *Lester Cowens* (Pruitt Taylor Vince).

When, in mid-December 1988, *Mississippi Burning* opened in limited release to qualify for the Oscars, there was a confidence among its producers about this socially conscious if fictionalized movie, which tapped into the emerging rebirth of interest in the 1960s as an era, while providing a thoughtful antiracist treatise. Some early reviews were raves, and *Time* featured a cover story on the return of the message movie. The Academy Award

for Best Picture of the Year did not seem unlikely. Then, week by week, the film's stature diminished, as it came under ever harsher consideration. By the time Oscar night finally rolled around, it was obvious to all that *Mississippi* would be passed over, for Academy members heard and considered the objections of black leaders, who felt the film underplayed the role of their people in the civil rights movement; of historians, who noted serious tampering with the facts, though this fictionalized account was presented as absolute truth; of moralists, who noted that in the film FBI agents become Dirty Harry clones, there being no notable complexity in the movie's point of view on their morally dubious, illegal approach; of white Southerners, who complained of prejudice toward them, since the film shows only rednecks; of drama critics, who pointed out storytelling flaws and unconvincing character arcs.

As these revelations appeared in rapid succession, the intelligentsia gradually turned against a movie that, ironically, had been custom-made for them. British filmmaker Alan Parker frequently has run into such problems. His works—*Bugsy Malone, Midnight Express, Fame, Birdy, Shoot the Moon, Angel Heart*—initially strike a serious-minded moviegoers as instant classics; by the last scene, we sense we've been had by a slickly packaged but facile film. Here, Parker focused on the FBI search for the bodies of three activists—a black Southerner and two white Northerners—murdered during the protest summer of 1964, basing his film on the real-life Mickey Schwerner, James Chaney and Andrew Goodman case. The script Parker concocted with Chris Gerolmo paired two radically dissimilar federal agents, Anderson (Gene Hackman), a Southern liberal with a witty cracker-barrel philosophy, and Ward (Willem Dafoe), a Kennedy-era intellectual-idealist and by-the-book G-man, eager to make the world a better place. Neither is based on agents who actually investigated the case. A bigger problem: would such men ever have joined the Bureau? Anderson likely would have spent his life as a small-town sheriff, while Ward probably would have been in the Peace Corps.

The opening, depicting the killing of the civil rights workers, was stunning, as were other sequences: the terrorization of a black church congregation by the Klan; a distraught, neglected wife's determination to do the right thing even if it means turning her own guilty husband over to the federal authorities. Gene Hackman's fully fleshed-out characterization, and Frances McDermond's touching portrait of the simple, confused, decent southern wife won accolades. The sequence in which an increasingly terrified McDermond gives Hackman the information he needs, unsure whether she's doing so because of moral commitment to justice or romantic yearning for this man, is undeniably marvelous. A pity,

MISSISSIPPI BURNING: Gene Hackman and Willem Dafoe as F.B.I. agents Rupert Anderson and Alan Ward; though the case was factual, the characters were fictional. While such blending of historical reality and movie myth had gone on throughout the decade, this was the film that caused the public to finally balk at "poetic license."

MISSISSIPPI BURNING: Anderson and Ward visit the home of black witnesses to Klan harassment, speaking with Aaron (Darius McCrary) and Willy (Ralnardo Davis).

MISSISSIPPI BURNING: Rupert Anderson seduces the truth out of the vulnerable and quite terrified Mrs. Pell (Frances McDormand).

then, the film finally rings false, a well-intentioned but overwrought British outsider's misconception of what the 1960s civil rights movement was all about. Parker's great gifts—his striking technique with cinematographic effects, crackerjack control of sound and music for

MISSISISPPI BURNING: The Choctaw Man (Barry Davis Jim, Sr.) leads the agents on a search through the swamps as they look for the three missing civil rights workers.

heightened impact, expert work with actors—are in ample evidence. But the clunking plot turns a potentially great film into a mess. It's impossible to believe that Anderson, having seduced this woman into telling the truth, would then obliviously leave her alone where her vicious husband (Brad Dourif) would shortly return. Anderson isn't insensitive or stupid enough to make such a blunder; he operates not out of character but because such an action suited the purpose of the scriptwriters.

Throughout, Dafoe's pompous, preachy quality is deflated by Hackman, deprecating Agent Ward's self-righteousness. Yet at the end, when Ward delivers one last secular sermon, it's presented at face value, as if we're now expected to take him as the author's spokesman. Before Parker became a feature film director, he designed highly effective TV commercials. *Mississippi* made clear his sensibility had not expanded, boasting all the technical flourish of a state-of-the-art electronic age advertisement while suffering the same lack of in-depth insight. Which explains why a film that, in its opening moments, dazzled an audience, ultimately left it disappointed.

MISSISSIPPI BURNING: A Klansman (Michael Rooker) terrorizes a black church and attacks Aaron.

The Accused

A PARAMOUNT PICTURES RELEASE OF A JAFFE/LANSING PRODUCTION   1988

CREDITS:

Produced by Stanley R. Jaffe and Sherry Lansing; directed by Jonathan Kaplan; written by Tom Topor; photography, Ralf Bode; editors, Jerry Greenberg and O. Nicholas Brown; Running time, 110 min.; Rating: R.

CAST:

Kathryn Murphy (Kelly McGillis); *Sarah Tobias* (Jodie Foster); *Ken Joyce* (Bernice Coulson); *Cliff "Scorpion" Albrecht* (Leo Rossi); *Sally Fraser* (Ann Hearn); *Paul Rudolph* (Carmen Argenziano); *Bob Joiner* (Steve Antin); *Larry* (Tom O'Brien); *Attorney Paulson* (Peter Van Norden); *Danny Rudkin* (Woody Brown); *Asst. D.A.* (Allan Lysell).

THE ACCUSED: Jodie Foster as rape-victim Sarah Tobias, her Academy Award-winning Best Actress performance.

The growing consciousness of rape as a postfeminist nightmare, along with the blurring of distinctions between fact and fiction, combined to make *The Accused* a controversial and brutal as well as memorable movie. The story line sounded all too familiar: A provocatively-dressed woman walks into a bar, is sexually assaulted there, afterwards running hysterically into the street; but when law enforcement officials finally arrive, hours later, the perpetrators have not even bothered to flee, so unaware are they that what transpired might constitute a crime. An incident such as this occurred in 1983 in Massachusetts, though *The Accused* was not a docudrama recreation of the factual case (though many viewers assumed it was) but rather a fictional film. In docudrama, filmmakers often can't see the forest for the trees, so mired are they in getting specific details precisely right (and so entangled in the legalities of what they can or cannot portray without invading privacy) that in many cases, the essential meaning of a case becomes lost in recreating its surface.

Instead, *The Accused* had it both ways, exploring the kind of incident which had happened in Massachusetts without being limited to or by the specific details, while also fleshing out some fascinating psychological characterizations. Sarah Tobias (Jodie Foster) screams out for justice after being assaulted by three men in a north Washington State bar, but no one listens, owing to her lower-class background. Since she dresses in a sexy-tacky style, has had previous brushes with the law, and is not known for telling the truth, she wouldn't make an effective witness; the local D.A.'s office has little

THE ACCUSED: Before being assaulted, Sarah plays pinball with Danny Rudkin (Woody Brown, center) and Bob Joiner (Steve Antin).

THE ACCUSED: Accompanied by Assistant D.A. Kathryn Murphy (Kelly McGillis, right) and Detective Duncan (Terry David Mulligan, left), Sarah returns to the scene of the assault.

interest in prosecuting a case they most likely won't win. Instead, lawyer Kathryn Murphy (Kelly McGillis) settles for a plea bargain that puts each of the rapists behind bars for several months on a charge of reckless endangerment. Kathryn feels proud, knowing the young men

THE ACCUSED: Kathryn cross-examines Kenneth Joyce (Bernie Coulson), witness to the act of sexual violence perpetrated by his best friends.

A rapport slowly develops between the lowerclass Sarah and the uppercrust Kathryn.

might otherwise have been back on the street. But instead of gratitude from her client, Kathryn is shocked to receive a visit from the infuriated Sarah who feels the slap-on-the-hand sentences are worse than no jail time at all. She pursues Kathryn, browbeats her, insisting on being heard. At first, she strikes Kathryn as a nuisance and an ingrate. Gradually, though, Kathryn comes to see that letting the men off that easily is wrong.

The most remarkable thing about the script by Tom Topor (*Nuts*) was the decision to quickly dispense with the rape case. Though they may be behind bars on a lesser charge, the rapists are nonetheless swiftly locked up. Instead, the film takes an unexpected but powerful alternative approach, as Kathryn goes after other men who were in the bar watching, some obscenely cheering on the act of rape, all doing nothing to prevent it. Her D.A. boss tells her she's throwing away her career, but Kathryn has a courtroom tactic in mind that will force the legal system to focus on a fascinating issue, raising the question of whether someone can be held accountable for not acting to stop a crime, a sin of omission.

As Sarah, Foster delivered the best performance to date of her adult career, winning a much deserved Oscar for her portrayal. Though at first her character seems a stock, vulgar, obscenity-spouting figure, Foster revealed all sorts of fascinating and unexpected shadings: vulnerability hidden beneath the surface sheen of toughness, intelligence beyond her limited education. McGillis's role remained more conventional, played as

THE ACCUSED: Sarah and Kathryn find the rape case being turned into a media circus.

an easily identifiable type, the upscale career woman of the Eighties. Still, there was an effective dramatic arc for Kathryn, forced to reevaluate her glib, pseudosophisticated approach to her job by committing to a case that has real meaning for her.

Finally, though, what was most effective about the film was the intense relationship that developed between these radically different women as their mutual dedication to a cause literally changes their lives. Director Kaplan (*Heart Like a Wheel*) achieved this without the kind of oversimplification that might have, in less skillful hands, reduced *The Accused* to an antimale diatribe created for feminist propaganda purposes. Neither of the women is a perfect heroine, and each can be quite unpleasant. Likewise, the young men are not portrayed as snarling, nasty bullies, easy to hate and condemn, but as happy-go-lucky guys out for a night of fun, convinced they haven't done anything but give a woman what, in their estimation, she made clear she wanted. *The Accused* drove home its important theme with the power that the great Hollywood socially oriented films have always, at their best, displayed.

Working Girl

A 20TH CENTURY-FOX FILM
RELEASE   1988

CREDITS:

Executive producer, Robert Greenhut and Lawrence Mark; produced by Douglas Wick; directed by Mike Nichols; written by Kevin Wade; photography, Michael Ballhaus; editor, Sam O'Steen; Running time, 113 min.; Rating: R.

CAST:

Tess McGill (Melanie Griffith); *Jack Trainer* (Harrison Ford); *Katharine Parker* (Sigourney Weaver); *Cyn* (Joan Cusack); *Mick Dugan* (Alec Baldwin); *The Office Men* (Philip Bosco, Oliver Platt, James Lally, Kevin Spacey, Robert Easton); *Intense Woman* (Nora Dunn); *Older Woman* (Olympia Dukakis); *Heavy Woman* (Ricki Lake).

Screwball comedies that delight audiences can often have something significant to say, while appearing to be nothing but light entertainment. At the decade's beginning, *9 to 5* was a feminist comedy which caught the spirit of its times, as three working women, mistreated by their male boss, banded together in solid community to wreak vengeance on him. Just as typical of its time was *Working Girl*, arriving in the late Eighties and representing the postfeminist sensibility. Once again, a young working woman is mistreated in the office; the difference is, the boss is now another woman, a feminist herself (feigning solidarity with the newcomer), but in fact using her position of importance to exploit her underlings, female as well as male. No longer are women portrayed as natural allies, and men the enemy, as was the case at the decade's beginning; now women are natural enemies, fighting over the same man and same job.

Melanie Griffith had already headlined a number of films, including Brian DePalma's *Body Double* and Jonathan Demme's *Something Wild*, without attracting a great deal of attention other than as the daughter of Hitchcock's one-time "bird" woman, Tippy Hedren. But this was her star-making (and Oscar-nominated) performance, playing Tess McGill, a humble stenographer in a New York brokerage firm. Young male executives frequently promise Tess a more important job as private secretary only to pass her around to their friends. But things are no better at home in Staten Island, where her urban redneck boyfriend (Alec Baldwin) buys Tess the same birthday present every year, slinky lingerie she can later wear to bed for him. Then Tess, who has been diligently attending night school in order to better herself, gets a glimmer of hope. Her new boss, the chic Katharine Parker (Sigourney Weaver), is everything Tess has come to admire: brash, ambitious, no-nonsense, assertive. Katharine makes it clear that despite the obvious difference in office rank and social class, she and Tess will be a team, two women standing together against the hostile male world.

Would that it were so. No sooner does the bright if unsophisticated Tess confide a breakthrough business idea than Katharine steals the concept, selling it as her own. Tess would never know this were it not for a convenient skiing accident that temporarily sends Katharine to a hospital, from which she phones in her instructions. Tess is rudely, suddenly educated as to the lack of true sisterhood in the cutthroat business world. At that point, Tess undertakes one of those plausibility-stretching plans that were the basis for so many 1930s screwball comedies. She upscales her hairdo, borrows the boss's clothes and office with the help of a co-conspirator office pal (Joan Cusack) and elevates her speech patterns. Then, passing herself off as Katharine, Tess sets out to make the deal before Katharine returns. To do that, she needs the help of Jack Trainer (Harrison Ford), a handsome broker from a competitive firm who gradually realizes he's smitten with Tess, deciding to break up with the lady he's been dating: Katharine.

WORKING GIRL: Working girl Tess McGill (Melanie Griffith) labors for low wages all day in fashionable Manhattan, then takes the ferry back to her simpler home in Staten Island every evening.

254

WORKING GIRL: Whereas feminist comedies of the early Eighties, like *9 to 5*, portrayed disparate women uniting as comrades to stand against men (all of whom were evil), post-feminist films late in the decade took a more complex approach; Melanie's "sophisticated" boss Katherine Parker (Sigourney Weaver) is a back-stabber . . .

. . . but the man in both their lives, Jack Trainer (Harrison Ford), proves to be a decent enough sort, only too eager to leave the pretentious Katherine for the smart, gutsy Tess.

This was one more example of how effectively nostalgia-encrusted movie genres of the past could be updated to play for a modern sensibility. The aura of romantic screwball was deftly refurbished by director Mike Nichols, while the implied social comment could be slipped in without interfering with the entertainment values. As up to date as the vivid depiction of modern big-city life was, and as contemporary as Kevin Wade's ear for the current idiom proved to be, there was still something about the tone that evoked the classics. It wouldn't be difficult to imagine Jean Harlow or Carole Lombard as Tess, Clark Gable or Cary Grant as Jack, Rosalind Russell or Katharine Hepburn as Katharine, though in fact even they couldn't have done much better by the material than this cast did.

Getting the role of Jack was important to Harrison Ford, who (like William Hurt) wisely chose to take supporting roles that would educate the audience as to his ability to play ordinary men as well as superheroes like Han Solo and Indiana Jones, ensuring his career did not become limited in scope. Oscar-nominated Weaver was suitably bitchy as Katharine, while Griffith effectively portrayed Tess's transformation from frenetic office worker to ladylike fashion plate. This was a perfect comedy for the retro-Eighties, making clear that the feminist attitudes of the Seventies were over, and that working conditions for women had reverted to a Thirties situation.

WORKING GIRL: Alec Baldwin as Mick, the untrustworthy boyfriend of Tess.

WORKING GIRL: Cornered after her scheme to steal Tess's idea fails, Katharine (hampered by a ski accident) becomes vitriolic and near hysterical; Weaver was nominated for a Best Supporting Actress Oscar, as well as Best Actress for *Gorillas in the Mist*, but failed to pick up the statuette for either.

The Thin Blue Line

AN AMERICAN PLAYHOUSE
PRESENTATION OF A THIRD FLOOR
PRODUCTION   1988

CREDITS:

Executive producer, Lindsay Law; produced by Mark Lipson; written and directed by Errol Morris; photography, Stefan Czapsky and Robert Chappell; editor, Paul Barnes; Running time, 106 min.; Rating: Not rated by MPAA on initial release.

Quite possibly no commercially distributed film of 1988 had a smaller audience than *The Thin Blue Line*, which received spotty theatrical booking before its video release and PBS telecasting. It's also possible that no American film made during the decade was as significant in terms of blurring the boundaries between real and reel while also proving the remarkable impact a movie—even an all-but-unseen movie—can have.

The Thin Blue Line would probably have won an Oscar as Best Documentary if it had been nominated in that category. It wasn't, primarily because it contained staged sequences in which a brutal real-life crime and its aftermath were recreated to make the film's subject vivid and immediate for the audience. This caused many purists to complain that filmmaker Errol Morris had violated the sanctity of the documentary form by augmenting reality with such theatrics. In fact, England's BBC had for years featured "dramatized documentaries" in which events that filmmakers wanted to deal with were necessarily recreated, since no one had been around with a camera when they occurred; the complaint was that the public did not always discern when they were watching the documentary material as opposed to dramatized elements. ABC News soon was criticized harshly when it dramatized a news event (and unaccountably not labeling it as such), but by late 1989, important and prestigious pseudonews shows like *Saturday Night With Connie Chung* were regularly featuring re-creations of events for added impact.

The Thin Blue Line stood at the very center of this storm, the study of a murder and the trial and conviction of a suspect from 12 years earlier. Filmmaker Morris previously had made more conventional documentary films, including *Gates of Heaven*, about a pet cemetery. Here, though, he absolutely insisted on breaking all the rules. Not only did he mix and match recent interviews with surviving participants with re-creations of the brutal event, but he appears to have purposely attempted

THE THIN BLUE LINE The re-creation of Officer Robert Wood's roadside murder, with unknown actors standing in for the actual participants, further clouded the distinction between real and reel.

THE THIN BLUE LINE Filmmaker Errol Morris, who became fascinated with the question of condemned man Randall Adams' possible innocence while visiting prisons to do a more inclusive documentary.

257

THE THIN BLUE LINE: Randall Adams, convicted of the murder of Officer Robert Wood and originally sentenced to death, spent 11 years in prison before this film finally caused his case to be reopened—at last setting Adams free.

to keep the viewer from grasping where one begins and the other ends. The case involved Randall Dale Adams, who at the time of the film's release continued to serve a life sentence after his initial one—death—was commuted. Adams, who was 27 at the time of the murder, had been convicted of killing a Dallas policeman named Robert Wood one fall evening in 1976. Adams was convicted on the evidence of David Harris, a then 16-year-old who had picked up hitchhiker Adams earlier that evening, later insisting to the police that it was Adams who did the killing. Yet the police questioned Harris (who even then had a lengthy criminal record) after picking him up, when they learned he was bragging in bars it was he who had killed the officer. Why the authorities would accept the word of an unsavory character like Harris is difficult to determine, especially considering the fact that Adams had no criminal record.

At the time of filmmaking, Morris interviewed Harris on death row, where he awaited execution for yet another murder. The comments offered by Harris (who by that time had nothing to lose by lying) certainly suggested that when he fingered Adams, he was willing to say anything to save his own skin. However, the authorities who railroaded Adams into jail did not want to reopen the case and risk another trial. Perhaps they would have rather seen a man who might be innocent go on paying for a crime he did not commit than deal with the embarrassment (and proof of incompetence or, worse still, corruption) that would surface at a new hearing of the case. At any rate, Adams continued to watch his life waste away, even as the evidence that put him there became flimsier.

Morris initially became intrigued with the case when he met Adams while visiting the prison to research a far broader film about lifers; listening to the man's impassioned plea of innocence, Morris was moved to narrow his focus to this one case, making a crusading film that had, as its immediate goal, the reopening of Adams's case. There were some who believed Adams had conned Morris into making a movie that would set him free, insisting Adams was guilty as charged. Certainly, Morris's film is highly subjective, making no attempt to show both sides of the case but angrily, emphatically taking the position that Adams was absolutely innocent. No viewer will doubt his innocence after seeing the remarkable restaging—and, doubtless, accepting it as the gospel truth it's effectively presented as. Following the initial screening of the film, the case was finally, begrudgingly, reopened; shortly thereafter Adams left jail a free man. By implication, then (though certainly not by direct statement), the film could be considered an anticapital punishment movie, making the viewer painfully aware that if Adams's death sentence had not been commuted, the apparently innocent man would have been long dead when Morris arrived to make a movie about prison life.

Rain Man

A UNITED ARTISTS RELEASE OF A GUBER-PETERS CO. PRODUCTION   1988

CREDITS:

Executive producers, Peter Guber and Jon Peters; produced by Mark Johnson; coproducer, Gerald R. Molen; directed by Barry Levinson; written by Ronald Bass and Barry Morrow; photography, John Seale; editor, Stu Linder; Running time, 140 min.; Rating: R.

CAST:

Raymond Babbitt (Dustin Hoffman); *Charles Babbitt* (Tom Cruise); *Susanna* (Valeria Golino); *Dr. Bruner* (Jerry Molen); *John Mooney* (Jack Murdock); *Vern* (Michael D. Roberts); *Lanny* (Ralph Seymour); *Iris* (Lucinda Jenney).

A road movie, a buddy-buddy film, a disease-of-the-week flick. By 1988, moviegoers had seen enough of each to last a lifetime. But *Rain Man* offered a fascinating combination of all three. In this quietly powerful motion picture, Barry Levinson drew such original performances from his stars, while telling his tale in such an edgy, off-center way, that *Rain Man* broke genre boundaries as a one-of-a-kind movie, eventually winning the Academy Award as Best Picture of the Year; its success at the box office offered proof that despite a

RAIN MAN: Dustin Hoffman in his Academy Award-winning role as Raymond Babbitt, takes to the road with his brother Charlie (Tom Cruise).

RAIN MAN: Susanna (Valeria Golino) is the girlfriend of slick but sleazy Charlie...

plethora of high-tech diversions, the public would still flock to an intimate human drama.

In an Oscar-winning performance, Dustin Hoffman brought Raymond Babbitt to unforgettable life on screen, vividly creating an autistic unable to deal with everyday reality. Instead, Raymond relies heavily on a series of carefully defined habits, daily routines that have become precise rituals. This might seem the basis for an educational melodrama on the order of TV's *Bill* (written by Barry Morrow, who provided the first draft of *Rain Man*), but *Rain Man*'s bigger, broader scope offered stylish entertainment. Raymond's father dies, leaving his $3 million fortune to the mental institution housing his son. This doesn't sit well with Raymond's brother Charlie (Tom Cruise), a smug, self-centered L.A. car salesman. Charlie, in fact, was unaware he even had a brother, let alone one in an institution.

In the screenplay Ronald Bass fashioned from Morrow's original, Charlie abducts Raymond in hopes he'll be able to gain control of the inheritance. But as they travel across America, a stop in Las Vegas makes clear there's another element to Raymond. He's a savant: appearing retarded to casual observers, Raymond demonstrates near-genius in certain narrow, specific areas. His memory is photographic, his abilities at math surpassing those of a computer bank. Standing amid the

... though she finds herself deeply touched by the autistic savant Raymond.

RAIN MAN: Charlie, originally interested only in the money that Raymond means to him, gradually grows as a person owing to their developing relationship; one way to interpret *Rain Man* was as an allegory for the era of greed, and the need for Americans to move beyond such thinking.

slot machines, Charlie suddenly realizes this side of Raymond may be exploited to make a fortune at gambling.

Charlie will go through another change; in addition to finding a meal ticket, he gains a brother and friend. The young man who initially cared for nothing but Number One finds himself deeply loving Raymond as a person, wants to keep Raymond by his side not only for his unexpected abilities but for his companionship as well. Just when we stop hoping the proper authorities will whisk Raymond away from his nasty sibling, Charlie changes into a brother in the best sense of the term; just when we begin hoping the two will stay together always, we realize the authorities will shortly tear them apart. Which made *Rain Man* a male bonding fable in the same league as *Midnight Cowboy* and *The Last Detail*.

Hoffman's flawless performance was completely normal and without affectation; this was like nothing he'd ever done before. Sadly, though, the praise heaped on Hoffman left little room for proper recognition of Cruise's contribution. Eager to be accepted as a serious actor as well as a star, he here tried a risky role, daring to initially appear unsympathetic, making his character's arc completely believable. It's worth noting, too, that, despite the title and Hoffman's Best Actor award, the focus of *Rain Man* is really on Charlie, the character who changes. Levinson beautifully captured their bittersweet cross-country odyssey from Cincinnati to Los Angeles in a '49 Buick Roadmaster, making it not only a

fascinating, singular story but also a parable about brother-love in the extreme. Valeria Golino, whose only previous credit was opposite Paul Reubens in *Big Top Pee-wee*, provided an effective counterpart to the film's preoccupation with male bonding, her character something of a contrivance to lend the script some sorely needed female texture. But Levinson effectively employed her for something beyond the obligatory love interest. Early on, she voices the morality and conscience Charlie lacks; later, she provides the outlet for Raymond's first sweet sexual encounter, a gentle kiss in an elevator. *Rain Man* might easily have become sentimental tripe, but Levinson's sure-hand as a filmmaker kept that from happening. He was not the first choice for director: among others, Sydney Pollack came on board, then departed in a huff after he and Hoffman fought more often than they had on *Tootsie*. Once again, though, "difficult Dustin" achieved what he wanted: fighting with producers, firing writers, infuriating directors, ultimately arriving at a movie masterpiece. Since that sort of artistic combat produced *Kramer vs. Kramer* as well as *Tootsie* and *Rain Man*—and was notably absent from *Ishtar*, in which Hoffman had no interest other than acting—it seems safe to conclude the legendary perfectionism which makes him so irritating to fellow moviemakers is basic in providing quality pictures for us to view.

Field of Dreams

A UNIVERSAL PICTURES RELEASE OF A
GORDON CO. PRODUCTION   1989

CREDITS:

Executive producer, Brian Frankish; produced by Lawrence and Charles Gordon; written and directed by Phil Alden Robinson, from the book *Shoeless Joe* by W. P. Kinsella; photography, John Lindley; editor, Ian Crafford; Running time, 106 min.; Rating: PG.

CAST:

Ray Kinsella (Kevin Costner); *Annie Kinsella* (Amy Madigan); *Karin Kinsella* (Gaby Hoffman); *Shoeless Joe Jackson* (Ray Liotta); *Mark* (Timothy Busfield); *Terence Mann* (James Earl Jones); *Dr. "Moonlight" Graham* (Burt Lancaster); *John Kinsella* (Dwier Brown).

For the better part of half a century, conventional wisdom in Hollywood held that Americans love movies and baseball but incongruously hate baseball movies. The box-office returns over several decades left little doubt that, aside from *The Pride of the Yankees*, the baseball diamond did not click as a movie setting—until the 1980s. First came *The Natural*, an overblown version of the arguably greatest baseball novel of them all. Its commercial success was no fluke, as a half-dozen baseball films followed later in the decade, all about the same time: *Major League*, the most popular with the public, *Eight Men Out* (about the Black Sox scandal of 1919), the most critically acclaimed. *Bull Durham* established Kevin Costner as the leading late-Eighties star, a happy combination of modern enlightened male and traditional understated-macho. Costner returned to baseball with *Field of Dreams*, though all similarity to *Bull Durham* ended with star and subject. Stylistically, this was not another realistic mood piece but a surprisingly satisfying updating of yet another bygone movie staple, boasting the charm and corn which were the hallmarks of filmmaker Frank Capra. In two dozen films, including the Christmas classic *It's a Wonderful Life*, Capra glorified the common man while shamelessly stating his belief that miracles could really happen. Often referred to as a Walt Disney for adults, Capra made movies about grown-ups who wish upon a star and, after much adversity, see their dreams come true.

As played by Costner in *Field of Dreams*, Ray Kinsella is an updated Capra hero. He is not, like Jimmy Stewart's Mr. Smith or Gary Cooper's Mr. Deeds, some small-town naif, but a contemporary man who has been to the barricades and the barrios. In the late Sixties, Ray was a student activist at Berkeley; in the Eighties, he's gone back to the basics, living on an Iowa farm with wife (Amy Madigan) and daughter: Their existence falls somewhere between *The Big Chill* and *The Egg and I*. Then, suddenly, it turns into *It's a Wonderful Life* with baseball substituted for Christmas. While Ray stands in his cornfield, he hears a voice from on high: "If you build it, he will come." This is followed by an incandescent image of what Ray is expected to build in that cornfield: a baseball diamond.

At that point, cynics wanted to abandon ship, because what followed was a journey of faith. In writer-director Phil Alden Robinson's version of W. P. Kinsella's 1982 novel, the savior is none other than Shoeless Joe Jackson, the legendary Chicago White Sox left fielder suspended from the game after being convicted of throwing the 1919 World Series. Before long, there's a baseball diamond amid the cornstalks, and Jackson (Ray Liotta) is walking alongside Kinsella. A sweet but unsentimental whimsy is what Robinson went after, and pulled off. In large part, that's because *Field of Dreams* was not really a baseball movie, any more than, say, *High Noon* was a western in anything but the most obvious sense. There, the Old West was employed as a metaphor for a fearful Hollywood during the period of McCarthy anti-Communist witch-hunting; here, baseball is used as a symbol of American innocence and healthy competitiveness, forever corrupted when Jackson threw that game seventy years ago, tarnishing the cherished concept of the American Dream.

If Jackson needs to be redeemed, so, too, does Kinsella. His life on the farm has been a form of hiding away from the big dreams of making the world a better place that he and his generation briefly lived, then turned their backs on. *Field of Dreams*, like so many great American tales (from *Huckleberry Finn* to *Rain Man*), is a picaresque story, following the fascinating (and, for thirtysomething American audiences of the late Eighties, an idealized representation of themselves) central character as he journeys across the American landscape, ultimately arriving at a sea of self-knowledge. On his personal odyssey, Kinsella meets a literary activist (James Earl Jones) patterned on the ultraprivate J. D. Salinger, and a small-town doctor (Burt Lancaster) who had given up the joys of the baseball diamond for the less spectacular but more significant job of caring for the sick. Both actors delivered delightful cameo performances. Ultimately, though, the movie belonged to Costner, heir apparent to those soft-spoken but masculine movie heroes of several generations earlier. Like

FIELD OF DREAMS: The ghost of World Series past: Ray (Kevin Costner), Annie (Amy Madigan), and Karin (Gaby Hoffman) Kinsella face the spirit of misunderstood baseballer Shoeless Joe Jackson (Ray Liotta).

FIELD OF DREAMS: Shoeless Joe returns to earth and convinces Ray Kinsella to build a baseball diamond in the middle of his Kansas wheatfield.

FIELD OF DREAMS: The reclusive author Terence Mann (James Earl Jones) is enlisted to help Ray on his quest for truth; Capra-corn of the Thirties variety proved far more palatable to today's "sophisticated" moviegoers than anyone would have guessed.

Costner himself, this film was at once contemporary and classic, an up-to-the-moment interpretation of old beliefs about the stubborn faith of rugged individualists, and the potential for positive action in a disparaging world, that is ingrained in the American self-image. *Field of Dreams* proved that, like movie popcorn, Capra-corn still could be popped to please.

Do the Right Thing

A UNIVERSAL PICTURES RELEASE OF A
40 ACRES AND A MULE FILMWORKS
PRODUCTION   1989

CREDITS:

Produced, written and directed by Spike Lee; coproducer, Marty Ross; photography, Ernest Dickerson; editor Barry Alexander Brown; Running time, 120 min.; Rating: R.

CAST:

Sal (Danny Aiello); *Da Mayor* (Ossie Davis); *Mother Sister* (Ruby Dee); *Vito* (Richard Edson); *Buggin' Out* (Giancarlo Esposito); *Mookie* (Spike Lee); *Radio Raheem* (Bill Nunn); *Pino* (John Turturro); *Tina* (Rosie Perez); *ML* (Paul Benjamin); *Coconut Sid* (Frankie Faison); *Sweet Dick* (Robin Harris); *Jade* (Joie Lee); *Clifton* (John Savage).

Independent writer-director Spike Lee's fourth film (following the little seen *Joe's Barbershop—We Cut Heads*, striking, funky *She's Gotta Have It*, and the energetic but sophomoric *School Daze*) elicited strong if varied responses. No one questioned the moviemaking skills with which Lee built his ideas into a briskly paced, well-acted work, deftly balancing comedy and drama. Many, however, did question whether the youthfully angry New York filmmaker understood the impact his latest creation might have, or comprehended the responsibility of the artist for the audience actions afterwards. The controversy simmered because, in the film's climactic scene, Mookie (Lee)—initially a mellow youth employed by the white pizza-store owner in a black neighborhood—has been transformed, by embittering experience, from an apologist for the whites to an inciter of violence. Worse, this violence was directed not against the white policeman who killed Mookie's friend, but against his compassionate boss, Sal the Pizza Man (Danny Aiello, in an Oscar-nominated performance).

DO THE RIGHT THING: Mookie (Spike Lee) tries to seduce Tina (Rosie Perez), mother of his son, though he has no intention of marrying her and spends little time with the child; it was a measure of writer-director Lee's integrity that he cast himself in one of the film's least likeable roles.

264

DO THE RIGHT THING: Sympathetic and fair-minded pizzeria owner Sal (Danny Aiello), flanked by his sons Vito (Richard Edson) and Pino (John Turturro), continues to do business in the otherwise black Brooklyn neighborhood; likewise, it was a tribute to Lee's talent that he refused to simplify the white characters, making Sal the most complicated and fascinating person onscreen.

Because Lee was the auteur, as well as the actor playing this key character, many observers misinterpreted the film, assuming Lee must necessarily approve of everything Mookie does, thereby hoping to inspire riots in the streets. Lee was not necessarily saying that when Mookie turned violent, he was doing the right thing. The point Lee was making: Mookie did the only thing he could, right or wrong. Which also explains why the film ended with two quotes, one from Dr. Martin Luther King (insisting violence is always counterproductive), another from Malcolm X (endorsing violence when all else fails). Some observers insisted the double quote served as Lee's unintentional admission that he hadn't decided for himself. Lee had in fact made up his mind, realizing he was ambiguous about violence. An artist has a right to such a complex, rather than simple, vision.

As in a Greek tragedy, *Do the Right Thing* takes place in one setting on one day, the hottest of the summer. The street looked bizarre, like a real Brooklyn neighborhood spruced up and made over by the MGM set designers of a half-century ago. Lee's tone: the illusion of slice-of-life naturalism, undercut by a visual poet's sense of purpose. Which explains why Lee could get away with a ghetto street devoid of crack dealers. This was an artist's personal rendering of a post-Howard Beach incident, not a docudrama recreation; Lee captured the mood of the black community as, at decade's end, it struck out against the retro-attitudes of the Eighties. So there was a Greek chorus, three elderly men (Frankie Faison, Robin Harris and Paul Benjamin) commenting wryly on every action. As Greek myth's Tiresias with sight as well as insight, Ossie Davis played the wise old "Mayor" who

DO THE RIGHT THING: Radio Raheem (Bill Nunn) and Buggin' Out (Giancarlo Esposito) proudly display Raheem's prized boom box, which will shortly cause escalating tension and eventual violence; filmmaker Lee's fascinating vision of the area looked like a semi-surreal combination of an actual Howard Beach neighborhood and an old-fashioned Hollywood sound stage recreation of a street scene.

265

offers the title advice to Mookie, although Lee's character hardly listens: an amoral (though black) Reagan-era youth, he's too busy making fast money by delivering pies, then sneaking off for a quick hop in the sack with his woman and a moment or two with the illegitimate child he barely acknowledges.

Tempers begin to boil when a customer in Sal's asks why all the pictures on the wall are of Italian stars: Sinatra, Pacino, etc. "Why no brothers?" Sal is stunned. Isn't he the one white who chose to remain in the neighborhood after all the others fled to the suburbs? Wisely and fairly, filmmaker Lee (Oscar-nominated for his screenplay) makes Sal the real focus of the film, a man who can't comprehend there might be a legitimate claim of racism to what Sal believes is nothing more than his legitimate Italian pride. One of Sal's sons (John Turturro) claims to hate blacks, but rather than reduce him to a living cartoon of negative behavior, Lee allowed him moments of compassion a lesser filmmaker would not have included.

Lee did not allow black viewers the luxury of hooting at every white character on view. No one elicited less audience sympathy than Mookie, a smug, self-serving, superficial youth from his first gesture to (with time out only for his existential act of violence) his last, when he grabs his week's pay from Sal after feeling honor bound to return the money. Conversely, no one won the emotions of a viewer (white or black) more than the multidimensional Sal. In the end, though, no one character dominated; the story, theme and raw emotions were what the audience took from this bruising film. Lee did not condone violence any more than he condemned it. Rather, his movie graphically illustrated the why and wherefore of social/political violence, the unavoidability of it even when such violence proves misdirected and counterproductive. Unlike his alter ego Mookie, Spike Lee clearly did the right thing.

Batman

A WARNER BROS. RELEASE OF A GUBER-PETERS CO. PRODUCTION 1989

CREDITS:

Executive producers; Benjamin Melniker and Michael Uslan; produced by Jon Peters and Peter Guber; coproducer, Chris Kenny; directed by Tim Burton; written by Sam Hamm and Warren Skaaren, based on characters created by Bob Kane; photography, Roger Pratt; editor, Ray Lovejoy; Running time, 126 min.; Rating: PG-13.

CAST:

Batman/Bruce Wayne (Michael Keaton); *Jack Napier/The Joker* (Jack Nicholson); *Vicki Vale* (Kim Basinger); *Alexander* (Robert Wuhl); *Commissioner Gordon* (Pat Hingle); *Harvey Dent* (Billy Dee Williams); *Alfred* (Michael Gough); *Grissom* (Jack Palance); *Alicia* (Jerry Hall); *Mayor* (Lee Wallace); *Bob the Goon* (Tracey Walter).

If the decade began brightly with *Superman II*, featuring a patriotic image of the red, white and blue bedecked hero flying high while carrying an American flag as he soared upward, the decade ended with another nostalgic comic-book hero, this one as dark as the night and fittingly glum for an end-of-era audience that had survived Iran-Contra, the sleaze factor, the Wall Street crash, the Alaskan oil spill that seemed to symbolize the lack of care we had lately paid our environment, and cities which were likewise rotting with crime and dirt from benign neglect. Though shot entirely on a London sound stage to give it the stylized look of a German film from the Twenties, *Batman* symbolized our grim mood at decade's end as perfectly as *Superman* had the sense of optimism with which it began.

Michael Keaton's crimefighter bore scant resemblance to Adam West's clean-cut and campy send-up from the mid-Sixties. In keeping with Tim Burton's brilliant if

BATMAN: Batman (Michael Keaton) protects photojournalist Vicki Vale (Kim Basinger) as he fights off The Joker's goons in a Gotham city back street; the movie was shot entirely on a vast soundstage in England, giving it the heightened visual sensibility of a German Golden Age expressionistic classic like *Metropolis*.

BATMAN: The Joker (Jack Nicholson) appears in a TV commercial for his own highly toxic "Smylex" line of toiletries; some critics felt Nicholson so dominated the movie that it ought to have been called "The Joker."

267

Intriguing as Keaton was, the film belonged to Jack Nicholson as the Joker. Nicholson barely needed makeup: The glassed-over eyes and seductive yet sinister grin projected in earlier movies (*The Shining, Witches of Eastwick*) seemed straight out of a D.C. comic. Nicholson played The Joker with such relish and reckless abandon that he threatened to go completely over the top, effectively counterpointed by Keaton's subdued approach. In the film's most memorable moment, Joker and Batman face each other high atop an ancient building, as Evil in a clown's white face battles Good in a black cape and mask. The complex confrontation allowed each to discover he has created the other out of his own worst fears and fantasies. Obviously, this was no comic-book (in the pejorative sense) battle blown up into an expensive but simplistic cinematic diversion. At its

BATMAN: In the final confrontation high up in the belltower of Gotham's cathedral, Batman confronts The Joker as each realizes he is the product of the other; if the patriotic Eighties began with a flag-waving red, white, and blue Superman, it ended with this morally complicated vision.

erratic (and occasionally all but incoherent) vision, Keaton offered a flawed, confused little man, achieving stature only after slipping into the kinkiest costume ever employed for a mainstream movie. No red, white and blue for him, no open face shown to the world: if Christopher Reeve's Superman was American pride personified, Keaton's Batman was his doppelgänger, our deep, dark fear that crime could not be faced squarely but had to be ferreted out by a masked avenger who struck at night.

BATMAN: Vicki Vale and Batman (deep in the shot) rush to the Batmobile.

conclusion, Batman borrowed from biblical allegory and ancient myth.

If this was in many respects a superior film, it was also an imperfect one. In the middle, *Batman*'s story line began to sag, the movie threatening to sour. Joker's complicated but never convincing scheme to seize power by poisoning the world's cosmetics was briefly funny, then grew tiresome; the plot by Vicki Vale (Kim Basinger) to make her reputation as a photographer by snapping a shot of Batman's true identity was exhaustively established but never developed, much less resolved. Still, this Batman seemed less concerned with narrative sense than visual flamboyance.

Director Tim Burton, a former Disney animator, collaborated with set designer Anton Furst to create a living-cartoon world of Gotham as a nightmare image of

New York, marvelously conceived as past, present, and future all at once. In the striking opening, characters dressed as if for a 1940s film walk through a dangerous present-day street and find themselves in front of an awesome building of tomorrow. The tone was bleak and bitter, with Prince's streetwise soundtrack songs effectively underscoring *Batman*'s subversive, apocalyptic rock-'n'-roll sensibility. Perhaps the scene that most typifies Burton's vision was also the most threatening moment for middlebrow audiences, as Jack the Joker gleefully runs through an elegant art museum, destroying one after another of the world's great paintings.

Producers Peter Guber and Jon Peters were courageous in allowing the relatively untried Burton (whose only previous films were *Pee-wee's Big Adventure* and the surprise Keaton hit *Beetlejuice*) full freedom, despite the fact that more than $35 million was riding on this movie, along with a high-profile production schedule that led to massive public expectations and an immense network of merchandising tie-ins. With all those commercial considerations, *Batman* might have easily degenerated into a compromised and commercialized bomb. That was not the case: though surrounded by an unprecedented amount of hype, the film that finally emerged on screen lived up to any film fan's wildest hopes for it, a somber and unsettling work that is as emblematic of the late Eighties as the bright, upbeat flag-waving *Superman II* was of the decade's hopeful beginning.

sex, lies, and videotape

A MIRAMAX FILMS RELEASE OF AN OUTLAW PRODUCTION   1989)

CREDITS:

Executive producers, Nancy Tenenbaum, Nick Wechsler and Morgan Mason; produced by Robert Newmyer and John Hardy; written, directed and edited by Steven Soderbergh; photography, Cliff Martinez; Running time, 100 min.; Rating: R.

CAST:

Graham Dalton (James Spader); *Ann Millaney* (Andie MacDowell); *John Millaney* (Peter Gallagher); *Cynthia Bishop* (Laura San Giacomo); *Therapist* (Ron Vawter); *Barfly* (Steven Brill); *Girl on Videotape* (Alexandra Root); *Landlord* (Earl T. Taylor).

sex, lies, and videotape proved the big hit at the Cannes Film Festival in the spring of 1989, where it was much appreciated by audiences weary of big, expensive, oftentimes empty movies. Here was an obvious gem, a remarkable first film, a movie made on a shoestring budget (less than $1.25 million) boasting scads more style and substance than the more pretentious items. In awarding it the highest honor, the grand jury was not only acknowledging the talents of writer-director Steven Soderbergh or the unique film he'd made, but also making clear the decade of overstuffed turkeys was at an end. Here was an intimate ensemble piece about a quartet of upscale people, who, in their intricately dishonest relationships, create miserable lives ironically set against the picturesque places where they live. As the ending proves, not all exist in a "No Exit" situation. Some escape their morass, others do not. Still, a paraphrase of Sartre seems apt. The theme: Hell is other yuppies.

In Baton Rouge, Louisiana, Ann (Andie MacDowell) confides to her psychiatrist that she can't stand having her husband touch her. Other than that, she insists, the marriage is fine. Her smug spouse, John (Peter Gallagher), a fast-track lawyer, would agree: his relationship with Ann is all facade, maintained for his corporate upward mobility. As for the sex thing, John is pinning Ann's sister Cynthia (Laura San Giacomo) to her living room floor on his afternoons away from the office. Cynthia may be involved in the tryst partly because she finds John attractive, but her offhand words reveal there's a deeper motive. Back in high school, Ann was always the more popular, the sister from whom everyone expected great things. Seducing John provides Cynthia with emotional vengeance. The three-way stretch appears likely to go on indefinitely, until an unexpected catalyst is dropped into the strange brew.

This occurs with the arrival of Graham (James Spader, named Best Actor at Cannes), one of John's college frat brothers. Graham seems a sensitive male, soft-spoken yet somehow quietly, creepily menacing. There's no threat of sexual aggressiveness toward either sister, for Graham quickly makes clear he's not interested in (or even capable of) sex. A state-of-the-art Eighties guy, Graham would rather videotape women than hit on

SEX, LIES, AND VIDEOTAPE: Andie MacDowell as Ann, the Eighties yuppie who would rather talk about sex than have it.

SEX, LIES, AND VIDEOTAPE: James Spader as Graham, the strange, non-sexual man who enters the lives of several complacent yuppies and soon has the women revealing all their secrets to him.

them. With seductive vulnerability, Graham manages to talk first one, then the other of these radically different women into revealing her secret thoughts about sex before his videotape camera. The experience provides a wild, weird sexual kick for the participants: the women can strip, strut, stretch out naked on a couch and tell the truth or lie like mad, whatever turns them (and Graham) on.

sex, lies, and videotape was the talkiest film of the year, since nothing "happened." Whenever John and Cynthia were about to have at it on her floor, the camera discreetly cut away. Sex was not, despite the title, the subject of this film in the usual sense, for there was less sexual activity on view than in the romantic moments of a family film like *Indiana Jones and the Last Crusade.* Sex was not the visual subject but the verbal theme: what sex means to people like John and Cynthia, what the absence of sex means to people like Ann and Graham; what they obsess about, lie about, seek after or desperately avoid. Sex is less something to do than something to talk about.

The ensemble work by the young actors was remarkable. MacDowell, a former fashion model whose performances were generally considered the weakest elements in *Greystoke: The Legend of Tarzan, Lord of the Apes*

SEX, LIES, AND VIDEOTAPE: John (Peter Gallagher) no longer makes love to his wife, though he likes to spend his free afternoons away from the office with his wife's sister, Cynthia (Laura San Giacomo); filmmaker Steven Soderbergh wowed the crowd at Cannes, proving even in the age of *Batman*, there was still room for inventive independent shoestring budget sleeper hits.

271

and in *St. Elmo's Fire*, here proved as natural, believable and complex as Diane Keaton in a Woody Allen film. Gallagher was able to neatly convey his character's volatile sex appeal while simultaneously making a viewer's skin crawl. San Giacomo's desperation brought sympathy to a woman whose every action was vulgar, every word nasty. Spader continued to make clear, in the shadings he gave his psychologically unbalanced character here (as in *Pretty in Pink* and *Jack's Back*), that he had the potential to be his generation's Anthony Perkins.

Soderbergh's striking self-assurance reached far beyond his control of the cast. His camera always appeared to be in the right place at the right time; his editing, understated but on target, kept viewers constantly involved with a film in which the characters never shut up long enough to do anything. Best of all, Soderbergh suggested that by peering into these troubled people's lives, he revealed something important about sexual relations in the late Eighties. Though the charac-

SEX, LIES, AND VIDEOTAPE: While Ann and Graham talk, Cynthia and John make love.

ters constantly lied, audiences were at the end left with the sensation of having just witnessed the truth.

Parenthood

A UNIVERSAL PICTURES RELEASE OF AN IMAGINE ENTERTAINMENT PRODUCTION   1989

CREDITS:

Executive producer, Joseph M. Caracciolo; produced by Brian Grazer; directed by Ron Howard; written by Lowell Ganz and Babaloo Mandel, from a story by Ganz, Mandel and Howard; photography, Donald McAlpine; editors, Michael Hill and Daniel Hanley; Running time, 124 min.; Rating: PG-13.

SEX, LIES, AND VIDEOTAPE: Graham (James Spader) seduces Ann (Andie MacDowell) into telling him everything; though the relationship is fraught with erotic undercurrents, the two never consummate it physically.

PARENTHOOD: Steve Martin as Gil Buckman, conscientious father who strives too hard for perfection as a Dad because of haunting memories of a father who never had time for him; allowing Martin to do occasional wild and crazy bits but also show empathy and strong emotion, *Parenthood* allowed him the long sought-after balance in his career.

CAST:

Gil (Steve Martin); *Karen* (Mary Steenburgen); *Helen* (Dianne Wiest); *Frank* (Jason Robards); *Nathan* (Rick Moranis); *Larry* (Tom Hulce); *Julie* (Martha Plimpton); *Tod* (Keanu Reeves); *Susan* (Harley Kozak); *David Brodsky* (Dennis Dugan); *Gary* (Leaf Phoenix); *Marilyn* (Eileen Ryan); *Grandma* (Helen Shaw); *Kevin* (Jasen Fisher).

Throughout the Eighties, there were films for the new youth of the era (*Fast Times at Ridgemont High, Risky Business*) which took the attitude that all adults were impossible to deal with. The great irony in that: the adults caricatured were the aging hippies of the late Sixties, that generation which had dedicated itself to youthful rebellion, tried to change the world for the better, and had always believed in time it would be the first set of parents able to easily relate to their kids, without the hang-ups of previous generations. It didn't turn out that way, as the *thirtysomething/Big Chill* set found themselves unable to deal with the values and attitudes of *The Outsiders/Breakfast Club* bunch.

At decade's end, Ron Howard fashioned a fine ensemble comedy which took this as its premise. Steve Martin headed the cast as Gil, forced into a yuppie lifestyle but still hanging on to some yippie convictions as he maintains a suburban home and corporate job. *Parenthood* was an important film for Martin, who made his first major impact early in the decade as *The Jerk*, an incredibly popular though mindless comedy which immediately established him as a name star but also locked him into a bind he rejected, as the Jerry Lewis of the Eighties. Martin's subsequent choices of films (*Pennies From Heaven, Dead Men Don't Wear Plaid, Roxanne*) revealed his firm dedication to become a "serious comedian," winning the kind of respect that

PARENTHOOD: Nathan (Rick Moranis) attempts to teach his youngest daughter Patty (Ivyann Schwan) the art of self-defense; Moranis neatly balanced realistic characterization with satire on an entire type of upscale yuppie.

PARENTHOOD: Gil attempts to put his difficulties at the office behind him whenever he's home with the kids.

regularly goes to a Woody Allen. His performance here was an effective balance between the two sides of his career. While standing in for Cowboy Bob after that children's performer fails to show at a birthday party, Martin displayed the gross physical humor that had initially won him an audience; while playing softer comedy scenes with Mary Steenburgen as his wife, Karen, Martin proved that he was not limited to being a wild and crazy guy.

As Gil, Martin was the first among equals in an impressive cast that included Rick Moranis, neatly playing a near-caricature (without ever going over the top and getting too arch) of the success-oriented yuppie pushing his three-year-old child to learn everything from karate to Kafka. Gil on the other hand only desperately hopes that his own eight-year-old son may overcome some emotional problems which have him acting ever more autistic. While Karen appears far more in control of that situation, Gil falls apart every time the child has an emotional breakdown over some seemingly minor thing.

Dianne Wiest, veteran of several Woody Allen movies, created a striking characterization as Helen, the divorcée-working mother who cannot cope with her arrogant, rebellious teenagers (Leaf Phoenix and Martha Plimpton). Then there's Larry (Tom Hulce), the lovable loser who charms everyone into forgetting that he messes up whatever in life he touches. In many ways, though, the central character of the story is Frank (Jason Robards), the family patriarch whose neglect in raising his own boys (taking Gil out to a ball game, but dumping him there alone while he ran off to attend to more "important" business) is at the source of all their problems. Part of why Gil is so arch a parent is that he's incredibly resentful of his father though forever in danger of becoming like him.

At moments, the screenplay by Lowell Ganz and Babaloo Mandel reminded one what Neil Simon might have done with just such material, an effective blend of serious issues handled with a light comic touch. Ron Howard's direction effectively brought the varied characters to life, though at times he did let the film slip into a TV sitcom style and often allowed it to grow sentimental. It's worth mentioning, too, that the movie brought into question the PG-13 rating, established after 1984's *Indiana Jones and the Temple of Doom* made clear there needed to be some category that reached beyond PG but not to the point of R. Numerous viewers complained about an oral sex act performed on Martin (driving a car) by dutiful wife Steenburgen (attempting to relax him); though the act took place just below camera range, numerous parents who had brought their own children to the film (assuming, from the title and cast, that it was an all-family comedy) were shocked—not so much by the act itself (completely unseen) but by the implication of such an act in the context of a PG-13 movie. On the more serious side, Plimpton and Keanu Reeves perfectly incarnated the attitude of rebellious youth. Little wonder that Universal used such a direct but effectively simple advertising campaign: "This could happen to you!"

PARENTHOOD: The cast of *Parenthood*, Ron Howard's slightly bent portrait of aging yuppies.

275

A Dry, White Season

A METRO-GOLDWYN-MAYER
PRESENTATION OF A PAULA WEINSTEIN
PRODUCTION   1989

CREDITS:

Executive producer, Tim Hampton; produced by Paula
Weinstein; directed by Euzhan Palcy; written by Colin
Welland and Euzhan Palcy, based on the novel by Andre
Brink; photography, Kevin Pike and Pierre-William Glenn;
editors, Sam O'Steen and Glenn Cunningham; Running
time, 101 min.; Rating: PG-13.

CAST:

Ben du Toit (Donald Sutherland); *Susan du Toit* (Janet
Suzman); *Stanley* (Zakes Mokae); *Captain Stolz* (Jurgen
Prochnow); *Melanie Bruwer* (Susan Sarandon); *Ian McKenzie*
(Marlon Brando); *Gordon Ngubene* (Winston Ntshona);
Emily Ngubene (Thoko Ntshinga); *Mr. Bruwer* (Leonard
Maguire); *Suzette du Toit* (Susannah Harker); *Julius* (John
Kani).

A DRY, WHITE SEASON: Stanley (Zakes Mokae) and Ben du Toit
(Donald Sutherland) find that the color of a man's skin
becomes irrelevant if he dares to stand up to the South African
government's apartheid policy; Ben is as endangered as Stanley.

A Dry, White Season was not the first major film on the
subject of South African apartheid, *Cry Freedom* and *A
World Apart* and TV's Mandela having preceded it. But
as the first major U.S. release directed by a black
woman, featuring the mercurial Marlon Brando in a

A DRY, WHITE SEASON: Marlon Brando
made a triumphant, Oscar-nominated return
to the screen (following a nine year absence)
as civil rights lawyer Ian MacKenzie; though
apartheid had barely been covered by serious
filmmakers in the early Eighties, this—and
other socially conscious subjects—were becoming popular again by decade's end.

A DRY, WHITE SEASON: Schoolteacher Ben gradually realizes even his own wife Susan (Janet Suzman) does not support his anti-apartheid crusade; admirable as the film was, like *Cry Freedom* and *A World Apart* before it, *A Dry, White Season* paradoxically was a film about the tragic situation for South African blacks that could not have been financed without a white character as its point of focus.

Season effectively played on two levels: at once an involving murder mystery and a serious study of contemporary racism. In the supporting role of Ian McKenzie, a white South African lawyer who stands with the blacks against their oppressors, Brando (in his first movie since 1980) made the show "his" for the 20-minute courtroom sequence, delivering a dream performance: Brando played the part as if he was Sydney Greenstreet doing Clarence Darrow. McKenzie is a sly, sharp-witted attorney who employs irony as the ultimate weapon to challenge a system stacked against him. But Brando never threw the movie off balance by turning it into a tour de force, admirably commanding the screen without confounding the meaning of the larger drama around him.

The drama is the story of a family divided—and destroyed—by racism. With quiet efficiency neatly complementing Brando's cagey bombast, Donald Sutherland played Benjamin du Toit, a white schoolteacher living with his wife (Janet Suzman) and two children in a serene suburb of Johannesburg. He enjoys a quiet life, teaching history and attending to his family, until his gardener, Gordon Ngubene (Winston Ntshona), tells du Toit that his (Gordon's) son was taken when the government police fired at nonviolent demonstrators against apartheid, shooting and clubbing women and children. When Ngubene insists on recovering his son, he, too, is taken into police custody and, according to official

showy, Academy Award-nominated role, *Season* attracted more attention than its worthy predecessors. And while many American moviegoers may have bought a ticket just to see how overweight the erstwhile *Wild One* star had become, they shared the intense experiences of apartheid. As a result, moviegoers were reminded that there was more to life—and to movies—than *Ghostbusters* and *E.T.*, as *Season* helped reestablish the socially conscious message movie, in virtual hibernation during the Eighties, as possible harbinger of film themes for the next decade.

Though a fictional film, *Season* employed the actual 1976 Soweto uprising for its dramatic pivot. The second film by Martinique-born Euzhan Palcy, here working in conjunction with American producer Paula Weinstein,

A DRY, WHITE SEASON: Stanley (Zakes Mokae), Margaret (Sophis MgCina), Ben (Donald Sutherland), Julius (John Kani) and Emily (Thoko Ntshinga) discuss the investigation into the death of Emily's husband and young son while in police custody.

A DRY, WHITE SEASON: Stanley, a local taxi driver, becomes a friend and confidant to Ben, a schoolteacher who at first does not believe his government could be as deeply involved in evil, repressive acts as his black friends tell him; Ben will learn differently.

report, commits suicide while in jail. The impact on du Toit is devastating. Formerly, he believed the government was sincerely trying to solve the problems as best as possible. Now he sets out on a quest for truth, trying by any means to learn precisely what happened to Ngubene. Although his own son stands by him, his wife and daughter do not. So far as they're concerned, the problem has nothing to do with them: du Toit is becoming a nuisance by sticking his nose where it doesn't belong. Du Toit sees things differently. For him, a racist crime perpetrated against the gardener he liked and respected is a crime against all men of good conscience.

Joining him on the search for the truth is journalist Melanie Bruwer (Susan Sarandon), who writes for a white newspaper but takes a liberal approach in her stories, willing to make the news as well as report it. Standing against them is Capt. Stolz (Jurgen Prochnow), head of the special services, which tortures social activists in an effort to maintain the status quo. Happily, Prochnow played Stolz not as a conventional villain, but as a man who firmly believes he is right, even idealistic.

The power and conviction of the film were enhanced by a docudrama look, and most moviegoers believed that everything they saw was a recreation of some actual event. Although the Soweto massacre was real enough, the key characters seen here—and the events that happen to them after the slaughter—were derived from a novel by Andre Brink. *A Dry White Season* was "historical fiction," the truth portrayed here an emotional rather than a literal one. Zakes Mokae, Thoko Ntshinga and John Kani were all effective as African blacks caught up in the periphery of the plot. The film had but one flaw: like both *Cry Freedom* and *A World Apart*, it attempted to portray the horrors of apartheid by focusing on white characters, the bitter irony being that such a film could not be financed otherwise. That compromise understood and accepted, however reluctantly, *A Dry, White Season* rated as a powerful indicator that the era of escapist entertainment might at last be over. Movies that attempted to correct some social injustice were returning now that the "L" word might not be considered dirty anymore.

Crimes and Misdemeanors

AN ORION PICTURES RELEASE OF A JOFFE/ROLLINS PRODUCTION   1989

CREDITS:

Executive producers, Jack Rollins and Charles H. Joffe; produced by Robert Greenhut; written and directed by Woody Allen; photography, Sven Nygvist; editor, Susan E. Morse; Running time, 91 min.; Rating: R.

CAST:

Barbara (Caroline Aaron); *Lester* (Alan Alda) (Woody Allen); *Miriam Rosenthal* (Claire Bloom); *Halley Reed* (Mia Farrow); *Wendy Stern* (Joanna Gleason); *Starlet* (Daryl Hannah); *Dolores Paley* (Anjelica Huston); *Judah Rosenthal* (Martin Landau); *Jerry Rosenthal* (Jerry Orbach); *Blind Ben* (Sam Waterston).

By the late Eighties, there was no longer any debate about Woody Allen's stature. He had produced enough enduring masterpieces (*Manhattan, The Purple Rose of Cairo, Annie Hall, Hannah and Her Sisters*) and fascinating failures (*Stardust Memories, Another Woman, September*) to establish him as the most important, ambitious and uncompromising of contemporary filmmakers, an American equivalent to his longtime idol, Sweden's Ingmar Bergman, combining that writer-director's deep, existential themes with a New York idiom and Jewish sense of humor that characterizes Allen films at their best. With *Crimes and Misdeameanors*, his last film of the Eighties, Allen created one of the decade's most important works, a movie which in its peculiar story encapsulated the era's characteristic greed-based amorality, and received another Academy Award nomination as Best Director.

Once again, Allen orchestrated a large ensemble cast, made up of first-rate actors willing to forego their usual star salaries to work on Allen's limited budget, so basic to making films without studio interference. Ophthalmologist Judah Rosenthal (Martin Landau, nominated for an Oscar for his performance) is first seen at a testimonial dinner honoring him as one of New York's great citizens, a man beyond reproach. Shortly after, Rosenthal calculatedly arranges to have his tough-guy brother (Jerry Orbach) murder his longtime mistress, a stewardess (Anjelica Huston) who threatens to ruin him if he doesn't leave his wife for her. Periodically, the film returns to Judah and the sorrow he suffers over what he believes a necessary act of evil, while also wallowing in the horrible guilt over what he's done. Just as often, though, the story focuses on a seemingly unrelated figure, Cliff Stern (Allen), an unsuccessful documentary filmmaker forced by financial need to shoot a laudatory tribute to a man he does not respect: his brother-in-law, Lester (Alan Alda). Lester has won public approval, critical accolades, and financial rewards by turning out silly, mindless sitcoms, while Cliff has forsaken his chance at such niceties to create serious art on important subjects. What a terrible irony, then, that Cliff can pay his bills only by adding to the reputation of a man he considers beneath contempt. How awful, too, that the woman he loves (Mia Farrow) is clearly succumbing to Lester's superficial charms, and not just because she's impressed by his money, fame and charisma. She

CRIMES AND MISDEMEANORS: Woody Allen as the independent documentary filmmaker who attempts to discern the truth in every subject; Mia Farrow as the woman who eventually leaves him for a creator of silly, escapist TV sitcoms.

CRIMES AND MISDEMEANORS: Alan Alda won rave reviews and new-found admiration for his biting, incisive portrait of the commercial film and TV producer whose junk makes him rich and famous, while more honest, deserving moviemakers go without money or notoriety; Joanna Gleason as his sister and wife of the documentarian (Allen) forced out of financial necessity to fashion a tribute to this man he despises—and envies.

actually believes Lester is more a man than Cliff. Is there no justice in life? Certainly not if Judah and Lester can, one in the literal and the other in the symbolic sense, get away with murder.

Getting away with murder was only part of what this remarkable film—not quite a comedy, not quite a drama, but very funny and very dramatic in odd, alternate moments—was all about. One of its many other subjects was the very idea of seeing. Judah is haunted by a childhood memory of a rabbi telling him about the eye of God, and how no one ever escapes it. He even jokes early on that it may be the reason why he chose to become an eye doctor. Cliff's life is based, correspondingly, on the camera eye, and his own desperate attempt to capture reality with some degree of objectivity. The business of seeing was ultimately symbolized by one character who indirectly caused Judah and Cliff to be thrown together finally at a party with Ben (Sam Waterston), a decent, sensitive rabbi who is progressively growing ever more blind. Ben stands as that ultimate irony, the man whose physically impaired eyes cannot diminish his true insight into the nature of the universe, a second-cousin to Tiresias in the Theban plays of Sophocles.

Ultimately, *Crimes and Misdemeanors* is about people who cannot decide if they should surrender to the nihilism and moral decay around them, or maintain their innate belief that the universe may operate out of a conscious plan they cannot comprehend. Allen managed to spotlight all his own continuing themes, including one particularly apt for the Eighties: though his character is an ultrarealistic documentarian, he loves to escape into the world of old black-and-white movies, wistfully wishing that life were more like them. The key to the film, though, is that Judah has his girlfriend killed less because she is about to blow the whistle on their affair to his wife than that she plans on going public with her information about his financial double-dealings. In the end, greed is not (as *Wall Street*'s villainous Gordon Gekko announced) good but (as *Wall Street*'s director Oliver Stone had tried to tell us) evil; greed kills. In this single and singular story, Allen encapsulated (and attacked) the moral attitude that had prevailed throughout the Eighties.

Born on the Fourth of July

A UNIVERSAL PICTURES RELEASE OF AN A. KITMAN HO AND IXTLAN PRODUCTION   1989

CREDITS:

Produced by A. Kitman Ho and Oliver Stone; directed by Oliver Stone; written by Stone and Ron Kovic, based on the book by Kovic; photography, Robert Richardson; editor, David Brenner; Running time, 151 min.; Rating: R.

CAST:

Ron Kovic (Tom Cruise); *Donna* (Kyra Sedgwick); *Charlie* (Willem Dafoe); *Marine Recruiter* (Tom Berenger); *Mr. Kovic* (Raymond J. Barry); *Mrs. Kovic* (Caroline Kava); *Steve Boyer* (Jerry Levine); *Timmy* (Frank Whaley); *Jimmy Kovic* (Jamie Talisman); *Young Ron* (Bryan Larkin); *Tommy Finnelli* (Rob Camilletti); *Marine Major* (John Getz); *Student Activist* (Abbie Hoffman).

Throughout the decade, films of various quality dealt with the residue anguish of Vietnam; even as these films were being made, a frustrated Oliver Stone labored to bring to the screen Ron Kovic's book, the most perfect distillation of that anguish into a single story. Though it often appeared this major movie might never got made, even as minor films on the subject came and went, Stone

BORN ON THE FOURTH OF JULY: In the movie that Oliver Stone could not get financed during the escapist era of the early Eighties but which proved both the last major hit of the passing decade and the first critical/box-office success of what promised to be the socially conscious Nineties, Tom Cruise brilliantly carried the real-life character of Ron Kovic through his early innocent involvement with a high school sweetheart (Kyra Sedgwick) . . .

and Kovic persevered and, in the end, created a work which derived part of its power by providing quite possibly the final work on the subject.

Cruise continued to establish himself as the Paul Newman of his generation—a star who balanced his sex symbol appeal with serious acting ambitions and a desire to become involved with thematically weighty material—playing Kovic quite convincingly at every stage in his life: rah-rah, straight-arrow, small town Long Island teen in the early '60s, blandly accepting patriotic hyperbole spouted by a Marine recruiter (Tom Berenger); hardened combat sergeant in Southeast Asia; terrified paraplegic stuck in a rat-infested hospital; semi-adjusted but growingly embittered war hero, trying to live a normal life with his parents while confined to a wheelchair; confused and wavering observer, watching college anti-war protests and gradually changing from defender of his country's policies to outspoken leader of veterans against the war. Cruise powerfully, touchingly took his

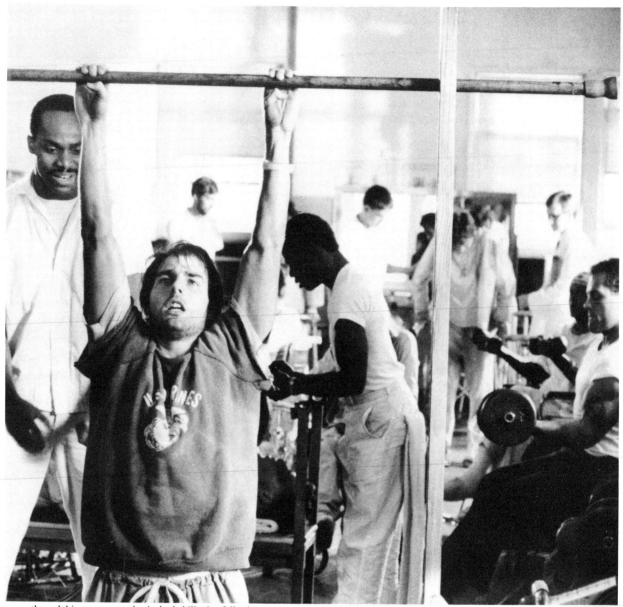

... through his attempts at physical rehabilitation following a severe wound incurred in Vietnam ...

character through every stage of development, as believable when playing the boyish, simpleminded Kovic (several years younger than himself) as when portraying the long-haired, early middle-aged Kovic (several years older than himself).

But Cruise's performance was only one element of this impressive, important, imperfect film. Stone, as always, was never subtle, and often guilty of overkill. When Kovic and another wheelchair bound vet (marvelously played by Willem Dafoe) get into an angry wrestling match while stranded in the Mexican desert, the sequence begins as brilliant black humor but ends

way too portentously, with Cruise's Kovic mouthing the movie's message too clearly, articulating outright what was better left implicit about the country's confusion after Vietnam. Dramatically, the film was often confusing. Early on, we're introduced to Kovic's high school girlfriend (Kyra Sedgwick) but when he doesn't refer to her while in combat or, later, the hospital, it is impossible for an audience to grasp whether they had broken up or if they were continuing to write. We didn't get a sense of the relationship, even though it was one of the most significant in the film.

The film was also characteristic of those 1980s movies

... to adjustment back into life with his family (Jamie Talisman, Josh Evans, Kevin Harvey Morse, Raymond J. Barry and Samantha Larkin)...

... to a growing awareness, in the company of other disgruntled vets like Charlie (Willem Dafoe), of how he was drawn into fighting for a cause he can no longer justify ...

... and finally, to a position as a leading Veterans Against the War activist.

that played fast and loose with the facts, presenting dramatic truths as if they were absolute actuality. At one point, Kovic is present at an anti-war demonstration on the Syracuse University campus, ending with police bashing in the heads of protesting students. In fact, there was no violence on the campus that day; there were, though, just such violent incidents on other campuses. Stone telescoped various real life incidents into a single

parts. This was a great film in terms of forcefulness, energy, sincerity and immediate impact, one of those films that devastate viewers—sending them out of the theater upset, angry, unable to get what they have seen out of their minds. As always, Stone the muckracker and moralist prevailed, refusing to apologize for the fact that this was his (and Kovic's) subjective truth on screen, presented with such conviction that it appeared to an audience as the objective truth. Stone won the Academy Award as Best Director (as he did with *Platoon*), but the film itself, the star, and the screenplay adaptation he and Ron Kovic did from the latter's book—all nominated— failed to garner Oscars.

If, at mid-decade, *Top Gun* and *Rambo* represented Hollywood's portrait of the audience's self-image, it was Stone who managed to turn that around with *Platoon*, leading to the less romanticized, more realistic portraits of combat in movies of the decade's second half. At first, Stone still seemed a lone voice crying out against the jingoistic-reactionary thinking that prevailed in the early Eighties movies; by 1989, Cruise had abandoned *Top Gun* to work for Stone, while Stallone's *Rambo* epics were faltering at the box office. *Born on the Fourth of July* was the last great film of the decade's second half, marked by an audience willingness to approach movies that dealt with complex themes of a social nature, and the corresponding Hollywood renaissance of films courageous enough to challenge that audience with such themes.

Sadly, the need to trim this epic film down to manageable length caused Stone to eliminate a key scene he had scripted and shot. As a child (played by Bryan Larkin), little Ron watches an old rah-rah John Wayne war film, *The Sands of Iwo Jima*. The implication was clear and simple: Ron Kovic was a victim of the old Hollywood movies, so meticulously crafted that they were wholeheartedly believed by a naive audience, so romanticized in their portrayal of events that any attempt on the part of a viewer to actually imitate the behavior shown on screen could lead only to tragedy. In that, the Ron Kovic of the film appeared not only a movie character based on a real person, but as the ultimate representative figure for the moviegoing public in a decade even then passing into history, while *Born on the Fourth of July* emerged as not only a film about the Vietnam experience but also about the business of existing in the Eighties.

real incident, creating a symbolic rather than literal truth.

In the end, though, *Born* overcame its weaknesses and flaws; simply, the whole was more than the sum of its

285

DOUGLAS BRODE (above, with Tom Cruise) divides his time between working as a film critic, college professor, radio announcer, TV talk-show host, free-lance writer, and regional theater actor. Mr. Brode has had a play, *Heartbreaker*, professionally produced, and is an aspiring screenwriter with several scripts currently under option at various studios. His previous books for Citadel Press include *Films of the Fifties, Films of the Sixties, The Films of Jack Nicholson,* and *Lost Films of the Fifties.* Mr. Brode resides in upstate New York with his wife, three sons, two schnauzers, one cat, and an ever-enlarging number of gerbils.

Photo by Paul Schumach

The author visits
Michael Douglas on the set.

Photo by Paul Schumach

The author interviews Danny DeVito on a late-night cable talk show.

FREE!

Citadel Film Series Catalog

From James Stewart to Moe Howard and The Three Stooges, Woody Allen to John Wayne, The Citadel Film Series is America's largest film book library.

Now with more than 125 titles in print, books in the series make perfect gifts—for a loved one, a friend, or yourself!

We'd like to send you, free of charge, our latest full-color catalog describing the Citadel Film Series in depth. To receive the catalog, call 1-800-447-BOOK or send your name and address to:

**Citadel Film Series/Carol Publishing Group
Distribution Center B
120 Enterprise Avenue
Secaucus, New Jersey 07094**

The titles you'll find in the catalog include:
The Films Of...

Alan Ladd
Alfred Hitchcock
All Talking! All Singing!
   All Dancing!
Anthony Quinn
The Bad Guys
Barbara Stanwyck
Barbra Streisand:
   The First Decade
Barbra Streisand:
   The Second Decade
Bela Lugosi
Bette Davis
Bing Crosby
Black Hollywood
Boris Karloff
Bowery Boys
Brigitte Bardot
Burt Reynolds
Carole Lombard
Cary Grant
Cecil B. DeMille
Character People
Charles Bronson
Charlie Chaplin
Charlton Heston
Chevalier
Clark Gable
Classics of the Gangster
   Film
Classics of the Horror Film
Classics of the Silent Screen
Cliffhanger
Clint Eastwood
Curly: Biography of a
   Superstooge
Detective in Film
Dick Tracy
Dustin Hoffman
Early Classics of the
   Foreign Film

Elizabeth Taylor
Elvis Presley
Errol Flynn
Federico Fellini
The Fifties
The Forties
Forgotten Films
   to Remember
Frank Sinatra
Fredric March
Gary Cooper
Gene Kelly
Gina Lollobrigida
Ginger Rogers
Gloria Swanson
Great Adventure Films
Great British Films
Great French Films
Great German Films
Great Romantic Films
Great Science Fiction Films
Great Spy Films
Gregory Peck
Greta Garbo
Harry Warren and the
   Hollywood Musical
Hedy Lamarr
Hello! My Real Name Is
Henry Fonda
Hollywood Cheesecake:
   60 Years of Leg Art
Hollywood's Hollywood
Howard Hughes in Hollywood
Humphrey Bogart
Ingrid Bergman
Jack Lemmon
Jack Nicholson
James Cagney
James Stewart
Jane Fonda
Jayne Mansfield

Jeanette MacDonald and
   Nelson Eddy
Jewish Image in American
   Films
Joan Crawford
John Garfield
John Huston
John Wayne
John Wayne Reference
   Book
John Wayne Scrapbook
Judy Garland
Katharine Hepburn
Kirk Douglas
Lana Turner
Laurel and Hardy
Lauren Bacall
Laurence Olivier
Lost Films of the
   Fifties
Love in the Film
Mae West
Marilyn Monroe
Marlon Brando
Moe Howard and The
   Three Stooges
Montgomery Clift
More Character People
More Classics of the
   Horror Film
More Films of the '30s
Myrna Loy
Non-Western Films of
   John Ford
Norma Shearer
Olivia de Havilland
Paul Newman
Paul Robeson
Peter Lorre
Pictorial History of Science
   Fiction Films

Pictorial History of Sex
   in Films
Pictorial History of War
   Films
Pictorial History of the
   Western Film
Rebels: The Rebel Hero
   in Films
Rita Hayworth
Robert Redford
Robert Taylor
Ronald Reagan
The Seventies
Sex in the Movies
Sci-Fi 2
Sherlock Holmes
Shirley MacLaine
Shirley Temple
The Sixties
Sophia Loren
Spencer Tracy
Steve McQueen
Susan Hayward
Tarzan of the Movies
They Had Faces Then
The Thirties
Those Glorious Glamour Years
Three Stooges Book of Scripts
Three Stooges Book of Scripts,
   Vol. 2
The Twenties
20th Century Fox
Warren Beatty
W. C. Fields
Western Films of John Ford
West That Never Was
William Holden
William Powell
Woody Allen
World War II